IN THEIR OWN RIGHT

IN THEIR OWN RIGHT

The Rise to Power of Joh's Nationals

Alan Metcalfe

University of Queensland Press

First published 1984 by University of Queensland Press
Box 42, St Lucia, Queensland, Australia

Typeset by University of Queensland Press
Designed by Paul Rendle
Printed in Australia by The Dominion Press-Hedges & Bell, Melbourne

Distributed in the UK, Europe, the Middle East, Africa, and the
Caribbean by Prentice Hall International, International Book
Distributors Ltd, 66 Wood Lane End, Hemel Hempstead, Herts.,
England

Distributed in the USA and Canada by Technical Impex
Corporation, 5 South Union Street, Lawrence, Mass. 01843 USA

Cataloguing in Publication Data

National Library of Australia

Metcalfe, Alan, 1946–
    In their own right: the rise to power of Joh's Nationals

    1. Queensland – Politics and government – 1976–   .
    I. Title.

320.9943

ISBN 0 7022 1719 0

Contents

Illustrations

Maps

Foreword

The power struggle between the forces of the political "left" and the "right" have predominated the modern history of Australian politics. In the past decade, quite dramatic changes have taken place. The success of the socialist left has been rapid, dramatic and far-reaching — threatening to engulf the entire nation and take us down the same road to economic destruction that we have seen pursued in our recent history in countries such as Britain, Sweden and France.

The escalation of deficit spending by governments and the consequential decreasing standard of living in Australia is evidence of this development. This book by Alan Metcalfe provides an insight into the struggle as it is affecting Queensland.

The mainland states of New South Wales, South Australia, Victoria and Western Australia, together with the Commonwealth, have all fallen under the control of socialist governments of the "left". Queensland now remains the last bastion of private, free-enterprise state government on the continent. With the island state of Tasmania (and the Northern Territory, to the degree that it has achieved statehood), we are the last frontiers of free enterprise in the Commonwealth.

Quite intentionally and unashamedly, the Queensland government, throughout the past twenty-six years, has sought to provide a lead to the anti-socialist forces of the "right", a lead based on the solid foundations of successful, reliable and honest government — the greatest strength of the free-enterprise anti-socialist argument. In this regard, the National

Party-led Queensland coalition government has been singularly successful.

Through soundly based organizational and parliamentary policies, Queensland has developed this strength and durability where others have failed.

The events of 4 August 1983, which are the climax of this book, were an attempt, intentionally or otherwise, to undermine the very foundations of Queensland's success. But there is a much wider picture and this is what I believe Alan Metcalfe has attempted to portray. Because of the current demise of the anti-socialist forces throughout Australia, the collapse of the Queensland coalition has considerably wider implications. In spelling out these implications, this book has a major contribution to make.

The unparalleled success of Queensland under free-enterprise government has been achieved through soundly based, time-honoured and proven principles, principles of encouraging the productive and creative elements of the community so that all can benefit from their talents. There is nothing radical or risky in that approach. People, not governments, are Australia's greatest natural resource. Only through private free-enterprise policies of low taxation and maximum government encouragement can people achieve their real potential. This is what Queensland has proven in the last twenty-six years. The Queensland government's widely criticized support of the state's mining industry over the years is the most outstanding irrefutable evidence of this. The massive benefits to the people of Queensland that are now being reaped are the envy of every other state in the Commonwealth.

In Queensland, the government has sought to provide the stability and the reliable foundations on which the state's enterprising people can achieve their every ambition. Good government can hope to achieve little more.

The dead hand of socialism offers a radically different picture for Australia. It seeks to perpetrate the myth that government and politicians can provide answers for every whim and ailment of the nation. Insidiously, it drags down the creative, productive strength of the nation, and progressively creates a totally dependent society, dependent on one source of hope, security and prosperity – government.

And this opinion cannot be lightly dismissed as pure party political diatribe. It is clearly demonstrated by the rapidly deteriorating economic positions of the socialist states and the Commonwealth compared with Queensland. While they regress into deeper and deeper debt and depression, Queensland, despite the constraints of living within a Commonwealth dominated by socialist thinking, continues to prosper.

As a result, creative, hard-working, successful people of Australia are flocking to Queensland at an unprecedented rate. An unprecedented, internal "brain drain" is taking place. The people with the proven capacity to create jobs, opportunities and wealth for Australia are moving to Queensland, away from the clutches of socialism. The writing is on the wall for all with the clearness of vision and desire to see. The long-term benefits for Queensland will be enormous. The problems ahead for the other states will be considerable.

Such mass exodus of studious, hard-working, productive people is of course not new in the history of the world — neither are the ultimate consequences that follow. Wherever the dead sisters socialism and communism extend their influence, they drive out the creative strength of the nation and economic stagnation and ultimate collapse become inevitable.

In the struggle against socialism, the defence of the free-enterprise way of life is not easy. The growing army of unproductive people now dependent on government hand-outs have a massive, vested interest in continuing the wasteful expansion of unproductive spending. They have time and public money at their disposal to disseminate their destructive propaganda, while the supporters of free-enterprising, self-reliant individualism are being restricted and squeezed from every direction.

And of course it is not always the "enemy" without that we must be concerned with. The "enemy" of impatience and misunderstanding within can be equally as dangerous and destructive.

In this struggle to protect this most basic of all freedoms (the ability to survive economically), things have to be done at times that are not popular. Decisions have to be made that are not always readily understood. There are always "softer" political options that can be taken for short-tem expediency. It is easy to criticize.

The Queensland government is continually advised to accept such alternatives. Fortunately, to date, it has had the strength of leadership, character and conviction not to sacrifice long-term stability and strength for such short-term political expediency. And the task is even further hampered by the national "sport" that has been fostered for many years by the socialists of "knocking" success. The nationally destructive socialist ALP-inspired campaign which seeks to suggest that there is something "evil" in encouraging successful people has been particularly damaging to the efforts of creative Australians to develop the long-term potential of our nation.

This is the message that the National Party in Queensland is seeking to give to all the people of Australia. This is the message for which we have sought support from our friends in the Liberal Party over the years, so that we could enter into coalition agreements to provide sound free-enterprise governments across the nation. It is the message that must transcend the short-term aggrandizement of individuals or groups. It is the message that I believe Alan Metcalfe has sought to convey in this book, where he seeks to provide an insight into the style and thinking of the Queensland National Party.

The increasing, socialist-encouraged centralization of Australia's population has naturally led the National Party to take an increasing interest in the politics and well-being of urban Australia. We are doing this because, as a truly national party, we are committed to the interests of all sections of the community, both urban and rural. Equally important, we have this concern because of our belief in balanced, decentralized development of industry and population.

Our increasing involvement in urban politics, especially in the Brisbane metropolitan area, has generated new pressures for the anti-socialist forces. Unfortunately, they are pressures that not all anti-socialist people have understood, or have been able to come to terms with. In consequence, the coalition relationship has suffered.

Understanding the conditions for harmonious cooperation and coexistence is now the foremost challenge that faces the anti-socialist forces of Queensland and Australia. Failure to come to terms with this situation will have far-reaching repercussions for the Australian community for many years to come.

Hence, the unification of the anti-socialist forces across the nation to protect our private-enterprise life-style must be our paramount concern.

Sir Robert Sparkes
President,
National Party of Australia (Q)

Preface

This book is about politics in the state of Queensland. More particularly, it is about the National Party of Australia (Queensland). Even more particularly, it is about the tumultuous decade of politics in Queensland between 1973 and 1983. It was during the premiership of Joh Bjelke-Petersen and the presidency of Sir Robert Sparkes that the National Party achieved its aim of governing Queensland in its own right.

Circumstances brought a troubled Premier Bjelke-Petersen and new president Robert Sparkes together in 1970. The premier's concern was his short-term personal political survival; Bob Sparkes' challenge was the long-term survival of the organization he had only recently been elected to lead — an organization that appeared destined for political oblivion. Yet the developments of their period of leadership changed the direction of state and federal politics in Australia. Their considerable political acumen and stature won them wide acclaim and recognition, and the organization they gathered about them revolutionized conservative politics in Australia.

In recent years, many newspaper column centimetres and several books have been written about the exploits of Premier Joh Bjelke-Petersen. Little, however, has been written about the contribution and vision of Sir Robert Sparkes and the importance of the National Party organization that has backed both men. This book is an attempt to redress this imbalance. It is also an attempt to put into context the historic collapse in 1983 of the National–Liberal coalition in Queensland, and to address the question of what lies in the future for the National Party, both federally and in Queensland.

In the months that have followed the 1983 Queensland state election, dramatic changes have taken place. A challenge has been mounted to the outcome of the poll in the seat of Maryborough, which threatens to whittle the Nationals' narrow majority. The socialist thrust throughout Australia has gained renewed momentum under the populist leadership of Labor Prime Minister Robert Hawke. The position of the federal Liberal Party has been greatly weakened by further retirements and the federal parliamentary leader of the National Party, Doug Anthony, resigned. A new federal National Party leader was elected amidst some of the most severe personal criticism ever inflicted on a federal leader of the party. The Queensland party has failed in its bid for the deputy leadership of the federal party, and the longstanding executive director of the Queensland organization, Michael Evans, resigned to pursue a future parliamentary career.

This book is not an official complete record of the National Party of Queensland, although it could not have been written without the close cooperation and encouragement of the State Management Committee of the party, the party's research staff, and Sir Robert Sparkes.

Thanks are also due to Mrs Barbara Campbell, widow of Alan J. Campbell, for access to her husband's *Memoirs of the Country Party in Queensland, 1920–1974* (unpublished), which assisted greatly in the writing of the first chapter of this book. Special thanks also to my wife, Mary, who encouraged me to write the book and who performed the duties of constructive critic throughout the months of its compilation.

Many of the photographs in this book were supplied by the Premier's Department, whose assistance was greatly appreciated. The owners of other illustrative material have been acknowledged in the respective captions.

1

The Foundations of Success

On 22 October 1983, Premier Joh Bjelke-Petersen and the Queensland National Party astounded Australia when they achieved a remarkable election result – one of the most remarkable in the history of politics in this country.

It was not that the National Party won with an overwhelming majority, but rather that it broke every "law" of modern politics and yet still managed to achieve the party's greatest-ever election result – majority government in its own right. The criticis were confounded, to say the least.

Now the enigmatic Premier Joh Bjelke-Petersen has vowed that his Queensland National Party will spearhead a national move to revolutionize conservative politics in Australia. As a result, the once popularly described "rural rump" of conservative politics in Australia, the National Party of Australia, is now being seen by many as the emerging force in Australia's somewhat uncertain political future.

There has never been an Australian political organization quite like Queensland's National Party. Emerging from the rural backblocks in the aftermath of the Great Depression that ravaged rural Australia, it has always been a party of deep emotions and equally deep commitment. In this respect it is comparable to the Australian Labor Party and different from the Liberal Party of Australia. Owing to the depth of its roots, it has defied its critics consistently over the years. As Dr J.F.S. Ross wrote in his book *Elections and Electors*: "Continuously down through the years since there first was a party system, men and women have struggled for the right to express their convictions and to have their views represented in Parliament, no matter what the odds against them. Never yet have those who seek to exclude all but two sets of opinions succeeded in their efforts to impose on us the tyranny of an exclusive two-party system, though they strain every nerve to do so." Students of politics in Australia who seek to assess the Country-cum-National Party will find much in Dr Ross' words.

The formative years

The taproot of the Queensland National Party, in fact, goes back to the very early days of the settlement of Queensland, to the days of the great debate between the exponents of free trade and protectionism. The Free Traders represented much of the thinking of conservative rural interests, as the Nationals do today. In Queensland, this ideology manifested itself in the formation of the Farmers' Union.

The equivalent of today's Liberal Party in those early days was the Protection Party. The Protectionists represented the conservative city interests of professional people and business folk predominantly engaged in, or dependent on, manufacturing.

The Australian Labor Party, born out of the Great Shearers' Strike of the 1890s, existed much as it does today, with the support of the major trade union organizations. The one difference is that, at the turn of the century, the Australian Labor Party had not yet committed itself to the socialist objective. That was to come in the 1920s.

As their name suggests, the Free Traders supported a laissez-faire economy free of tariff restrictions and protectionist fetters, while the Protectionists supported the use of government intervention to protect otherwise non-viable local industries. Protection versus free trade was the boiling political debate in Australia at the time of Federation, in many ways similar to the "wet" and "dry" factional debates that continue in Canberra today.

Politically, both the Free Traders and the Protectionists represented the vested interests of the nation. Neither had a strong affinity with the employee working class of the day. This was the fertile ground of the ALP. The Free Traders did,

however, have deep agrarian commitments which they
shared with farmers the world over. Their very existence
depended on rugged individualism, and free enterprise is the
only system of government that permits such a state. The
struggles of the farmers of Russia against communism, during
which millions died, exemplified this spirit.

At the turn of the century, in the wake of Federation,
Australia was struggling out of the collapsed gold-mining
boom and climbing cautiously on to the sheep's back. The
fabulously rich rivers of gold in north Queensland had been
worked out, and the deeper sinews of the underground lode
deposits of gold that inspired the establishment of "overnight
cities" at places like Charters Towers, Ravenswood, Croydon,
Gympie and Mount Morgan were either depleted or beyond
the reach of existing technology. The influx of migrant labour
resulting from the gold boom and the establishment of
Queensland's sugar industry led to employment problems and
the need for considerable social readjustment.

In this political climate support for the Australian Labor
Party increased rapidly. The Australian Workers' Union that
emerged from the Shearers' Strike and fostered the creation of
the ALP was quick to realize the potential of its new-found
political muscle in this era of economic and social uncertainty. Its stocks were also boosted by the continual bickering
within the ranks of the conservative opposition which was
divided over the trade issue.

Sacrificing the principles

The conservatives were left with no option but to put aside
their differences and unite to face Labor's challenge.

With the onset of World War I, there was pressure to accept
a partly planned economy to deal with the demands of war,
and this favoured both the forces of protectionism and
organized labour. The Free Traders were called on to sacrifice
their ideal of a free, competitive economy and, in the national
interest, to merge with the Protectionists against a greater
enemy: the socialists of the Australian Labor Party. In this
climate, Billy Hughes' Nationalist government emerged.

Protectionism flourished as a result. The Australian government propped up non-viable local industries to support the war effort, and reasoned debate on the benefits of free trade was impossible, if not considered downright unpatriotic.

With the end of war it was now a different story for the Australian economy, and inflation brought on by protectionist policies soared. Australia was now locked into high-cost production. The worst fears of the Free Traders had come to pass. The tariffs protecting city manufacturers had become entrenched and higher wages were enforced by the courts of arbitration and conciliation. Metropolitan conservatives and workers enjoyed security of investment and employment behind the high walls of their tariff system.

At the same time, however, the Protectionists and the city unionists vigorously resisted any realistic rises in the prices of food and raw materials. Rural producers were therefore seriously disadvantaged. It seemed to matter little that Australia's unsheltered rural and mining industries were almost totally responsible for earning the foreign exchange needed to balance the country's foreign trade accounts. From this injustice the Country Party was born.

The first candidates

The first successful candidates endorsed by rural organizations were in Western Australia in 1914, when two members of the Farmers' Union were elected to the Legislative Assembly. The first Queensland parliamentarians endorsed by the Farmers' Union appeared in 1915. Within five years the movement had spread across the nation.

In 1916 an interstate meeting of farmers' organizations from Western Australia, Queensland, Victoria and New South Wales met in Melbourne for the purpose of establishing an organization to "watch over and guard the interest of primary producers; to prevent duplication of taxation and the overlapping of State and Federal administrations; to obviate conflict between Commonwealth and State industrial laws and awards and to encourage scientific agricultural education and cooperative trading in the interests of primary producers". This led to the formation of the Australian Farmers' Federal Organisation.

The first meeting of the council of the AFFO was held on 17 April 1917, and in the 1919 elections fifteen of the organization's officially endorsed candidates were elected. All were members of existing political parties of the day but carried the additional endorsement of the AFFO. They operated in parliament under the unofficial leadership of W.J. McWilliams from Tasmania.

In 1920 the federal Country Party was formed comprising eleven members of the House of Representatives and one senator. At that time the indomitable Billy Hughes was prime minister and his Nationalist Party (no connection with the current National Party) was in power. Hughes vigorously opposed the formation of the Country Party and described the breakaway group as a "splinter group that should be promptly squashed". To many it seemed that Hughes fought the formation of the Country Party harder than he ever fought the ALP. The argument was bitter and divisive.

Billy Hughes' sacking

The Country Party survived Hughes' criticism and, following the 1922 elections at which the Nationalists failed to gain sufficient seats to form government in their own right, it exacted retribution. The Nationalists sacked Hughes and joined with the Country Party in the formation of the coalition government under the leadership of S.M. Bruce (later Lord Bruce) and Dr Earle Page (later Sir Earle Page). The Bruce–Page ministry comprised six Nationalist members and five Country Party members. The Country Party had arrived in Australian politics. Their first coalition was to survive until 1929 when they fell to the ALP.

Earle Page

Earle Page was the driving force of the Country Party in those formative years and is deserving of the title of father of the party's success. Under his leadership (he was federal president of the Australian Country Party until his death in 1961), a loosely knit but successful federal organization was developed.

Page was a young doctor from the Northern Rivers district of New South Wales when he won the seat of Cowper with the endorsement of the Australian Farmers' Federal Organisation in 1919. He died on 20 December 1961, only a few hours before the declaration of the poll held on 9 December in which he was defeated. Only Menzies led a parliamentary party for a longer period.

During his lengthy career, Page was a prolific innovator. Among his most notable achievements were the establishment of the Department of Markets (now the Department of Primary Industry), the establishment of the Agricultural Council with the states, the Rural Credits Department of the Commonwealth Bank, the Main Roads Act which led to the federal aid roads scheme and the reorganization of the Commonwealth Bank which made it a central reserve bank for the first time.

The federal Country Party, however, was never much more than a council of the various state bodies. Over the years, the party underwent many changes and never really acted in unison as, say, the ALP did. The state bodies had their own constitutions and controlled their parliamentarians.

The establishment of the party in Queensland in those formative years was particularly difficult. In reality it was never an easy road for any of the conservative parties, as former party president Alan Campbell recalls in his memoirs: "It is not easy in Queensland to develop one organisation and more particularly one political party, when large centres of population range up to and over one thousand miles from the capital city. Radical differences in climate and environmental conditions naturally occur. Similarly, differences develop in human outlook as well as economic factors. The remote regions are always suspicious of statewide organisations with their headquarters in Brisbane. They quickly accuse their head offices of being under Queen Street influence, implying disadvantages to and neglect of those remote districts. They are quick to suggest that too much public money is being spent in Brisbane at the cost of their own public works programmes and local development. This attitude of mind, held by important sectors of our population residing in districts remote from Brisbane, makes those people reluctant to accept political parties which hope to represent, in Parliament, the remote electorates along with the large number of Brisbane electorates." These prophetic words ring loud and clear even for the National Party of today.

Breaking Labor's domination

Queensland politics in the twenties was dominated by Labor, and the conservative forces had great difficulty getting their act together. Finally, in a last-ditch effort to break Labor's domination, the Nationalists succeeded in amalgamating the loosely knit Country Party forces in Queensland into the Country and Progressive National Party. The CPNP offered hope, but not much more.

In 1926 the ALP hit back at the formation of the CPNP with the introduction of the Primary Producers Organisation and Marketing Act which was aimed directly at undermining the influence of conservatives in rural Queensland. It was a move that captured the imagination of the rural heartland. The new act provided for the establishment of many of the producer boards and organizatons which still operate today. However, the ALP cunningly barred the rural organizations from political involvement. Fees and levies were collected, but they could not be used for political purposes. Primary producers were able to organize, but not to play politics the way the ALP could with the union movement.

Ironically, in 1929, the year the Bruce–Page coalition failed federally, the Queensland conservative amalgamation scored a surprising victory in the state elections. It was a backlash result against the ALP which was seen by many to be deserting the working class when the party moved against the unions to break a railway strike. In doing so the ALP alienated the powerful Queensland unions and the workers retaliated by turning to the conservatives.

The political fortunes of the Country and Progressive National Party government that came to power in 1929 under the leadership of A.V. Moore were, however, doomed from the start. This was the year of the Wall Street crash and the start of the Great Depression. By 1932, the Queensland government was being blamed by the ALP for the international disaster, and in the state elections that year the CPNP was swept from power.

The Depression entrenched socialism in Queensland. In the 1935 state elections the CPNP suffered yet another demoralizing defeat when only sixteen of its members were returned. In the year that followed the CPNP alliance slowly collapsed.

Formation of the Queensland Country Party

In March 1936, following encouragement from Earle Page, the Queensland Country Party was established. John Leahy, a Stanthorpe grazier, was elected president, and John Austin became the first secretary of the party. Federally, at this stage, the Queensland Country Party boasted only two parliamentary members – James Hunter (Maranoa) and Bernie Corser (Wide Bay), both of whom had held their seats against incredible odds since the early twenties.

Interestingly, the new Queensland Country Party was established along the lines of the successful New South Wales organization, the New South Wales constitution being adopted by the first branch at Roma when it was established. The formation of the Roma branch was organized by Alan J. Campbell, the president of the Roma Graziers Association. Campbell was to become a key figure in party affairs for the next fifteen years until his retirement for health reasons in 1951.

On 20 May 1936, delegates of the new Queensland Country Party met in Brisbane with representatives of the Country and Progressive National Party, and the two groups agreed to unite and form the Queensland Country Party. The following resolution was carried:

> That the Parliamentary members of the Country and Progressive National Party and branches join and assist in every way possible in the formation of one strong Country Party throughout Queensland, deeming unity in Country Party organisation as essential and indispensable.

Delegates to that meeting were John Leahy, J.A. Austin, J.J. McDonald and J. Sparkes representing the Country Party, and

J.A. Heading, A.J. Bryce, D. Gunn and J. Bird representing the
Country and Progressive National Party.

McDonald was the secretary of the successful Northern
Country and Progressive National Party that was based in
Townsville. This organization at the time was considered the
most successful conservative political organization in the
state, its success being attributed to its organization under the
chairmanship of north Queensland businessman Spencer
Hopkins and the financial support it received from the rural
industries of the north.

The Northern Country and Progressive National Party
agreed to join in the formation of the Queensland Country
Party and contributed considerably in finance and organizational experience to the establishment of the new organization.

Personalities and politicians

The first election that the new Queensland Country Party
faced was the 1936 by-election for the seat of Darling Downs.
The Country Party candidate was A.W. "Artie" (later Sir
Arthur) Fadden, and he won the seat with a clear margin.
Fadden's success started the ball rolling for the Country Party.
By 1937 it had amalgamated all other minor conservative
groups in rural Queensland under its banner.

Another new member of the Country Party in 1936 was
Francis Nicklin, then the member for Murrumba in the state
parliament. Nicklin had been elected as a Country and Progressive National Party member in 1932. He became leader of
the parliamentary Country National Party in 1941 and was
the first Country Party premier of Queensland in 1957.

By and large, however, the parliamentary members of the
now defunct CPNP who had joined the Queensland Country
Party were not happy with their new role, and problems
developed. The former CPNP members were used to political
freedom, but now they were part of a more demanding
political organization. Many resented this. The argument over
the value of party endorsement and support raged for many
years, some former CPNP members claiming that they didn't

need the party — that they won their seats not on party endorsement but on their own personal followings.

Alan J. Campbell, who deplored the disunity and disloyalty of these formative years, was highly critical of the attitude of some CPNP members. In his unpublished memoirs, Campbell made the following comment under the heading "Political Opportunists": "It is worth remembering that the tendency until the 1940s in conservative Queensland politics was for many candidates to project themselves for endorsement for whatever party was locally available, regardless of status or condition — any ticket would do! When elected, the average representative would gladly let his campaign committee disperse until the next election. It was then usual for him to work grudgingly for an effective rank and file organization (if one existed) in his electorate. He was content to sit in parliament and, if he had enough mates to gain control of government, well, that was just a bit of good luck! He might even be fortunate enough in securing a portfolio. Thus the reason for so many futile, ineffective, conservative political efforts." Campbell always believed that the petty membership fee charged by the party in those days contributed largely to the rank and file membership's toleration of this attitude by their parliamentarians.

Some members cared, however, and it was out of this dissension in the ranks of the QCP that the breakaway Western Division was established. Alan J. Campbell was elected inaugural president. The Western Division was particularly successful, introducing a number of innovations, such as a paid organizer, a greater emphasis on party loyalty and funding for political activities. At the height of their success, the Western Division had an income of some 4,000 pounds a year, an achievement previously unheard of in Queensland politics.

As the Depression passed and the nation looked forward to rebuilding its future, the conservatives under the banner of the United Australia Party gained control of the treasury benches in Canberra. The UAP, which emerged after the amalgamation of several minor conservative groups, was led by Joseph Lyons. Remarkably, Lyons had spent most of his political life within the ranks of the ALP — but the Depression brought about many unusual political developments. The emergence of Lyons on the other side of the political fence was but one of them.

During this time, the offer was made to the Country Party to accept amalgamation with the UAP, but Page and the Country Party elected to stay out. It was the first of a succession of differences which were to have a lasting influence on Country Party relations with the UAP and subsequently the Liberal Party throughout Australia.

Following the scandal involving federal Labor treasurer E.G. Theodore, the UAP was able to win enough seats in the 1931 election to govern in its own right until September 1934. In this election, however, they failed to gain sufficient seats to form government and were forced to take the Country Party into coalition.

Achieving this coalition agreement was not a simple matter, however, and it took desperate measures before Page was able to force Lyons to accept his terms. In fact, it reached the point where the UAP would have been defeated in the House on the unlikely matter of adjourning for the running of the Melbourne Cup before the UAP conceded.

Agreement was finally reached and the Lyons–Page coalition government was created. Earle Page became deputy prime minister, and R.G. Menzies was Lyons' deputy leader of the UAP.

The Lyons–Page coalition was not universally popular with country conservatives. Its trade diversion policies, which diverted Australian trade away from the profitable Australia–USA–Japan triangle to the new Ottowa agreement countries, created considerable tension at a time when many country people were struggling to get back on their feet after the crippling effects of the Depression. Trade policies again proved to be crucially important to rural interests.

Another issue of concern was the Earle Page-sponsored National Health and Pensions Insurance Act, which Page first attempted to introduce in 1928 and which he revived when back in power. This Bill, which was designed to bring state and federal insurance services and pensions under one umbrella, was the cause of bitter divisions in the Country Party. During its debate, several prominent CPA members voted with the Labor Party to emasculate the Bill before it was finally passed. Page was in Europe during this period. On his

Following in grandpa's footsteps? A young Earle Bailey (front centre) holds onto his grandmother's (Lady Earle Page) hand at the opening of Earle Page Park in Grafton. Next to Lady Page is Sir Earle Page. Earle Bailey won the former blue-ribbon Liberal seat of Toowong for the Nationals in the 1983 state election.

"L.B.J. . . . meet our member for Barambah . . . a promising young peanut farmer who flys his own aeroplane." Former National Party premier Sir Francis Nicklin introducing his deputy Joh Bjelke-Petersen to U.S. president Lyndon Johnson during his visit to Queensland.

return, he found his party bitterly divided. Prime Minister Lyons' failing health was also of concern. Page's adversary, Menzies, was also making a determined bid to follow Lyons into the leadership.

Finally, the National insurance scheme was abandoned, but not before Menzies resigned his portfolio.

Twenty-day government

The Lyons–Page coalition government survived until 1939 when Joe Lyons died after a difficult period of trying to arrange for his successor.

Former prime minister and Country Party critic Billy Hughes, who succeeded Menzies to the portfolio of Attorney-

General, recommended to the Governor-General that Page should be called to form a government. Page did so on the understanding that he would resign as soon as the UAP had selected a leader to replace Lyons.

Privately, Page hoped to entice former prime minister S.M. Bruce back to Australia to accept the position, and even offered to resign his seat of Cowper to allow Bruce to re-enter parliament. Bruce said he would return, but only as an independent, with the sole purpose of forming an all-party government to prepare for the war effort.

Page's government survived only twenty days. He resigned on 20 April 1939 following R.G. Menzies' election as leader of the UAP. Page had publicly declared that he would not serve in a government led by Menzies, and withdrew from the coalition.

Page's decision to resign his commission was marked by a vicious personal attack on Menzies in the House. Following the speech, two Queensland members, Artie Fadden and Bernie Corser, issued a statement dissociating themselves from the attack on Menzies and, despite party attempts, decided not to sit with the Country Party in parliament.

The tumultuous war years

This was the beginning of the end for Page's leadership and domination of the party in parliament. After a running battle with Menzies and estranged CPA members over efforts to form a coalition government, Page tendered his resignation on 13 September 1939. His position within the party had been eroded by the insistence of Fadden and Corser that they would not return until Page accepted Menzies' leadership.

In the subsequent ballot for the leadership, Archie G. Cameron narrowly defeated John (later Sir John) McEwen by seven votes to six with four dissidents (Badman, Collins, Corser and Fadden) staying away from the meeting. It was said at the time that had the four dissidents attended this meeting McEwen would have won. (One can only wonder at what might have happened had this been the case.)

Following Page's departure from the leadership, the CPA again entered into coalition with the UAP and five CPA members were appointed to the Menzies cabinet, including Cameron, McEwen and Fadden.

Archie Cameron led the party into the 1940 election and out of that poll the thirteen CP members of the House of Representatives and the three CP senators healed their differences. The election produced a tied parliament, however, with two independents holding the balance of power.

Following the 1940 election, Page and McEwen challenged for the leadership of the party. Cameron chose not to contest the ballot. The vote was tied 8-all, and Fadden was elected "acting" leader in a compromise decision. He was later confirmed as leader in March of the following year. As a result, however, Cameron resigned from the party and joined the UAP.

A meeting between Page and Menzies organized about this time saw a truce between the two, and Page returned to the ministry.

Artie Fadden returns

The departure of Cameron and the return of Artie Fadden and the breakaway faction did not end the squabbles and differences. The outbreak of World War II brought a new round of calls for an amalgamation of the UAP and the Country Party in the interests of national unity. On 28 August 1941, after the withdrawal of the Country Party from his government, Menzies agreed to stand down as prime minister and Artie Fadden was surprisingly elected prime minister – unopposed. Fadden was seen as the only conservative leader likely to unite the failing UAP and the Country Party in the national interest.

The state organizations of the Country Party opposed amalgamation. Nevertheless Fadden, in his capacity as federal leader, called a secret meeting in Brisbane to discuss the proposition. Out of this meeting the Country National Party was established and Frank Nicklin was elected leader of the Queensland opposition. Fergus (later Sir Fergus) McMaster was elected president of the CNP. (McMaster was later to become the first chairman of QANTAS.)

The formation of the Country National Party attracted

considerable resentment from the established Queensland Country Party and members of the estranged Western Division. A number of Queensland Country Party parliamentarians rejected the move, choosing to stay with the QLP.

If nothing else, however, the formation of the CNP proved to be the catalyst needed to heal the rift between the Queensland Country Party and the Western Division.

Despite Fadden's election as prime minister, nothing really changed for the government on the floor of the House. The federal parliament was still tied, with two independents holding the balance of power.

Fadden's government survived until the following October, when the two independents finally voted with the Labor Party to bring down the government. Labor leader John Curtin was then asked to form government.

In a series of amazing events, seventy-seven-year-old Billy Hughes was elected leader of the UAP and Fadden retained the position of leader of the joint opposition. In the 1943 election, the rift between Menzies and the UAP–CPA coalition widened, and Labor was consequently swept to power with a thirteen-seat majority. Following this election, Fadden remained leader of the CPA, but retired as leader of the opposition, and Menzies made a comeback to replace Hughes as leader of the UAP.

Springboard for the future

Finally, there arose from the ashes in 1944 Robert Menzies' Liberal Party of Australia. In Queensland the floundering Queensland Country Party was eventually taken over by the better-organized Western Division, and the Australian Country Party (Queensland) was established. Alan J. Campbell, president of the Western Division, was duly elected president of the ACP (Queensland). The Western Division, which had endorsed Charles Adermann (later the Hon. Sir Charles Adermann) to contest the seat of Maranoa at the 1943 federal elections, had gone into the negotiations with the distinction of seeing their candidate record the only victory over the ALP in the poll. Adermann's handsome victory was a great morale booster and a convincing argument for the policies of the Western Division.

The Australian Country Party (Queensland) was established along the successful lines of the Western Division. It demanded greater loyalty and solidarity from its elected parliamentarians and the plebiscite method of selecting candidates was enshrined. They were the foundations of the modern National Party, although in recent years the plebiscite selection method has lost favour.

Commenting in his memoirs on the Western Division's takeover of the QCP, Alan J. Campbell described the QCP as "flabby" and "effete". But he saved his sharpest criticism for the attitude of some of its politicians:

> Within a few short years of its life, the QCP was to experience distressing and disgusting actions by so many, but not all, of its pledged parliamentary representatives who are so well paid for the public service they perform. They award themselves the highest public honours, as well as the highest salaries that public opinion will stand. Many ignored bitterly the legion of hard-working organization officers, officials and members who contribute, without promise of reward, funds, time and hard work to elect representatives to Parliament. It is no wonder that it is so difficult to attract competent officers to devote their time and money for such thankless acknowledgments, whose collective organizational efforts manage to have elected enough members to Parliament to form Government, with its perks and privileges. The cynical, selfish behaviour of many of these elected representatives is reflective of the frailty of human nature.

Campbell's attitude to the responsibilities of endorsed party parliamentarians expressed in this statement has wide support within the grass roots of traditional Country-cum-National Party thinking and is considered today as one of the principles behind the National Party's success when compared with its conservative competitors.

The successful establishment of the ACP (Queensland) meant an upgrading of the party's secretariat in Brisbane and a move from quarters in the Country Press Building to Primary's Building in Creek Street. It also meant a greater effort to establish the Women's Section and the Young Country Party, and heralded the appointment of Colonel Neville

Hatton as state secretary of the party, a position he held until his replacement by Michael Evans in 1970.

If Charles Adermann's performance in Maranoa in the 1943 poll helped unite the disjointed factions of the Country Party, it was Charles Davidson's success over the Rt Hon. Frank Ford (ALP) in the seat of Capricornia in 1946 that encouraged the ACP (Queensland) to make a more determined effort to spread its influence throughout the state. Davidson, a sugar-cane farmer and an executive of the Sugar Industry Organization, was a veteran of both world wars, having commanded the AIF battalion recruited from the Rockhampton district. Frank Ford had been Minister for the Army in the Labor government during World War II. Davidson, the ACP (Queensland) candidate, beat Ford comfortably despite Ford's pre-election margin of 8,000 votes.

Labor departs Canberra

In the following year (1947), Johannes Bjelke-Petersen, then thirty-six years of age and a political protegé of Charles Adermann, contested and won the state seat of Nanango for the ACP (Queenland) and entered the Queensland parliament.

The ALP federal government of Prime Minister Ben Chifley (who replaced Curtin after his death in May 1945) won power with a reduced majority in 1946 and enjoyed initial popularity, but with the end of the war its socialist policies for economic control created unrest. The big problem for the Chifley government was the introduction of two banking Bills which were designed to abolish the Commonwealth Bank Board and eventually do away with all public company banks. These sweeping changes to the banking system were the focus of virtually all political debate at the time until they were successfully challenged in the High Court and eventually thrown out by the Privy Council in 1949.

The ALP's move against the banks was widely seen as the first move in a domino movement that would end Australia's ties with free enterprise and establish a socialist economy. First it would be the banks and then the insurance companies, the two pillars of a free enterprise economy.

It was a story that the ALP could not sell to the electorate.

Thousands of bank employees concerned about their futures did not accept ALP assurances that they would be absorbed into the Post Office Department. As a result, bank officers mobilized their ranks against the ALP in the campaign for the 1949 election. Labor was swept from office and the Menzies–Fadden coalition government came to power.

A memorable year

Nineteen forty-nine was a memorable year for politics in Australia nationally and in Queensland. Not only was it the year that Robert Menzies led to power his Liberal–Country Party coalition that would last for a record twenty-three years, but it was also the year that the House of Representatives was enlarged from 75 to 123 members and Senate numbers were doubled. In Queensland it was the year that the ALP government under Premier Ned Hanlon carried out a statewide redistribution based on the controversial zonal system which was designed to entrench the Labor Party in the state (and which, in recent years, now that it has backfired on the ALP, has become one of the bitterest of all state political debates).

Although the L–CP coalition won control of the House of Representatives in the 1949 federal election, Labor still controlled the Senate. This brake on the new government caused many problems and finally precipitated Menzies calling a double dissolution of parliament in 1951. Foremost among the issues for debate was the Bill to outlaw the Communist Party in Australia, an issue dear to the heart of the Queensland Country Party. After a bitter struggle through the Senate, the Bill was finally passed, only to be later declared invalid by the High Court. The government later submitted it to a referendum but it failed to get the support necessary, failing overall by an estimated 50,000 votes.

The consolation for the Menzies–Fadden government, however, was that it won control of the Senate at the 1951 double dissolution election.

The Country Party lost two seats in the 1951 election. In the same year, Alan J. Campbell retired as president of the party in Queensland and was succeeded by John McCormack, formerly state treasurer of the party.

QCP to the fore

The loss of two seats in the federal election was a setback to the ACP. More important to the party in Queensland, however, was that it had survived the first real test of its authority over its endorsed candidates. Charles Russell, the former ACP member for Maranoa who had "bucked" party policy and subsequently disqualified himself from membership of the party, was defeated by the party's replacement candidate, William Brimblecombe.

Charles Russell had been a vocal advocate of appreciating the Australian currency to par with sterling following the outbreak of war in Korea. The Korean War created grave inflationary fears in the economy and serious electoral problems for the Country Party federally. Returns for wool virtually trebled and the price of all basic commodities rose sharply. "Hot money" flowed into the country at an unprecedented rate in the hope of cashing in on an expected appreciation of the Australian pound. The profitability of Australia's rural industries lay in the balance. The electoral fortunes of many Country Party politicians were at stake. The ACP vigorously opposed a revaluation that would make Australian primary produce less competitive on world markets.

At the height of the debate Country Party ministers went into a crucial cabinet meeting of the coalition government with their resignations in their pockets, ready to table them should the Liberal Party decided to proceed with revaluation. The Liberals backed down and the crisis was averted, but it was to be the most serious test of the coalition in its twenty-three-year history.

The most damaging internal crisis for the Country Party was to follow, however, when Artie Fadden as treasurer introduced the 1951–52 federal budget. It was a budget designed to stifle the pressures of inflation, but in doing so Fadden had been forced to drop many rural tax concessions. Country Party supporters around the nation opposed what they described as a "horror budget". From that time and throughout the five years of rural decline that followed, membership of the Australian Country Party was to suffer. At the peak of its popularity the Australian Country Party (Queensland) organization boasted some 35,000 members throughout the state. It bottomed at 14,000.

Page's last contribution

The late fifties were the last years of Earle Page in the parliament. During his time as minister for health in the Menzies–Fadden government, he left a lasting impression on government health services in Australia. He continued to work on his cherished dream of a national health plan, which included the hospital and medical benefits insurance scheme, free pensioner medical treatment, free milk for school children and free life-saving drugs. In the six years prior to his retirement, he implemented a health system unique to the world, with an increase in federal spending from $12 million to $98 million annually.

The Queensland split

The "reds under the bed" era of the early fifties, however, had particularly disastrous consequences for the ALP government in Queensland, and by 1955 there were widening divisions within the Queensland Labor Party over the issue of the rising influence of the socialist left. By 1957 these divisions were unbridgeable and the deeply divided government was forced to an election.

The Country Party in Queensland under the parliamentary leadership of Frank Nicklin and the organizational presidency of John McCormack and Sir Howard Richter, who succeeded McCormack in 1957, had astutely assessed the failing fortunes of Labor during the lead-up years to the split, and at the time of the 1957 state election was at the height of political preparedness. In the election that followed, the Country Party won twenty-six of the seats in the Queensland Legislative Assembly and the Liberals twenty, giving the coalition a comfortable working majority. After more than half a century of struggling to establish an effective political voice in the government of the state, Queensland's primary industry interests now had control of the treasury benches.

Delivering the goods

Winning government was one thing for the party, but meeting the expectations of its supporters was another. The latter was not an easy task for the new government, especially as most of the ACP cabinet ministers were drawn from the south-east corner of the state and many were former Country and Progressive National Party members who were still not widely accepted by the party rank and file.

Within the coalition government in the early years, however, disputes were few. The only issue that persistently reared its head without any real credibility from time to time was that of amalgamation. The arguments that did occur were kept well out of the limelight.

Within ACP ranks it was a different matter. The burning issues of the former Labor Party's socialist policies, particularly those for lands and transport, created widespread debate and differences of opinion between the government and the organization. On the transport issue, there were none more vocal than Joh Bjelke-Petersen.

Labor's transport policy was governed by the railways policy which provided unfair advantage for Queensland Railways over other forms of transport in the state. The modern expansion of Queensland's highway system and the general improvement in state roads exacerbated the problem. Country Party members including Joh Bjelke-Petersen argued that the policy was outdated and archaic and should have been abandoned to allow for more vital free enterprise expansion of transport services in Queensland. Most entrenched bureaucrats and a number of influential ACP parliamentarians disagreed.

Finally, the weight of the organization of the ACP prevailed and slowly but surely the socialist protectionist policies that protected the railways against outside competition were whittled away. The state's road system, as a result, attracted greater government attention and subsequently opened up a whole new era for transportation throughout Queensland that has been essential to the expansion and improvement of numerous industries and the Queensland economy.

The land debate was largely an issue of security of tenure and investment for people who invested many years of effort and income in attempts to develop often remote and climatically difficult regions of the state. The principle of freehold title has long been of paramount importance to such people. When the Country Party-led Queensland coalition came to power in 1957 only about 6 per cent of the state was alienated under freehold title. The balance was controlled by the state. Consequently, many farmers and graziers in remote areas where tenure was uncertain could not justify the proper development and husbandry of such land that might eventually revert to state ownership. It was a major deterrent to the proper development of the country. Fences were left untended and water supplies left uncared-for and underdeveloped on leasehold land that was nearing its lease expiry date.

Finally, after long and protracted debate, the socialist policy of state ownership of all land was also overturned and the ACP-led coalition government in Queensland introduced sweeping new laws to provide for conversion of leasehold land to freehold tenure. Today it is not by accident that party president Sir Robert Sparkes himself presides over the party's powerful Lands Policy Committee, and the principles of proper land management and security of tenure are the pillars of the party's policy. Under the heading "Principal Objectives of a Sound Land Policy", the document reads: "Freeholding is the only system which will afford security of tenure that will stimulate the rapidity and intensity of land development and utilisation desired. . . . The National Party believes that the Government must do everything possible to expedite the freeholding process to provide security of tenure, and in doing so it must be Government policy that freeholding be economically feasible."

The overturning of Labor's socialist policies for lands and transport are recorded along with the abandoning of death duties in the seventies as the major milestones in the party's record of achievement.

Concurrent with the overturning of the socialist policies of transport and land tenure, membership of the ACP that had waned during the fifties and the early sixties started to return. It was clear that the policies of free enterprise initiative that many people, especially those in the primary industries sector, had long fought for were finally winning through. The foundations for Queensland's active free-enterprise economy were being established.

Stability and growth

In 1958 Sir Arthur Fadden retired from the leadership of the federal parliamentary wing of the Australian Country Party and was replaced by John McEwen. McEwen gained wide acclaim for his strength as a leader and his ability as an inter-national negotiator for Australia's rural industries. Now Sir John McEwen, he retired from the federal leadership in 1971. He was succeeded by Doug Anthony who remained the party's parliamentary leader until December 1983.

Throughout the history of the Australian Country Party, the principles of loyalty and solidarity that were enshrined in the formative years of the federal party and were later fought for so aggressively by the fledgling Queensland organizaton have been a hallmark of the party's success. Leadership changes were rare and challenges almost unheard of, apart from the difficulties of the tumultuous war years, which in reality were precipitated by Earle Page's personal intransigence rather than by a leadership coup. In sixty-three years of operating at a federal level the party has had only five parliamentary leaders. In Queensland, where the party had a somewhat shaky start, there have been but three parliamentary leaders since the party established itself in its own right in the mid-forties. Frank Nicklin held the leadership for twenty-seven years, twelve of which he was premier. He was succeeded by Jack Pizzey who passed away after only six months in office. Pizzey was elected leader on 17 January 1968 and died on 31 July the same year. He was succeeded by Joh Bjelke-Petersen.

Concurrent with the development of the mainstream organization in the post-war era was the establishment of the Women's Section of the Australian Country Party (Queensland).

The Women's Section was established in 1949 and elected its first state president, Mrs Dorothy Hawthorn, in 1950. By 1953 the organization had prospered to the point whereby the state president of the Women's Section was automatically accepted as a member of the State Management Committee of the party and women delegates were expressly elected to both divisional and electorate councils of the party.

In 1958 the Women's Section sponsored the formation of the Young Country Party in Queensland and in 1959 the Queensland Women's Section, with the assistance of state secretary Colonel Hatton, organized the first federal interstate meeting of Country Party Women's Section representatives. The Rt Hon. Dr Sir Earle Page chaired the meeting. From this meeting it was decided to make representation to the federal executive of the party for provision in the constitution to permit an annual meeting of women delegates.

The success of both the Women's Section and the Young Country Party, now the Young National Party, has been spectacular by any comparison. Both sections have added considerably to the growth and stability of the party. Seven members of the current Queensland Legislative Assembly, three of whom are now cabinet ministers in the current Bjelke-Petersen government, and one of Queensland's six members of the House of Representatives started their political careers in the Young Country Party.

The modern era

From 1957 to 1970 there were four state presidents throughout the premierships of Nicklin and Pizzey to the election of Joh Bjelke-Petersen. They were Howard (later Sir Howard) Richter, Ellis Lawrie (later a federal senator), John Ahern and Sid Roberts (later Sir Sidney).

Throughout this period, the rapidly increasing urbanization of Australia continued unabated at an alarming rate. From a rural population base of 50 per cent of the population in 1918 when the Farmers' Party was first formed, the population of rural Australia had more than halved to 20.26 per cent by the time of the 1954 census. Between 1954 and 1971, it had diminished to a mere 14.32 per cent. The writing was on the wall for the Country Party.

In 1970 Robert Lyndley Sparkes from Jandowae succeeded to the presidency of the Australian Country Party in Queensland, and Charles Holm of Ormeau was elected as senior vice-president. Late that year, Roma-born school-

teacher Michael Evans was appointed to succeed Colonel
Hatton as state secretary. Thus began the modern era of the
Australian Country Party that has culminated in 1983 with
the election of the first National Party majority government in
Australia's history.

2

The Architect

When Robert Sparkes took over the leadership of the
Australian Country Party (Queensland) in 1970, a change of
direction was desperately needed. The writing was on the
wall for the Country Party. Its traditional support base was
diminishing at an alarming rate in the wake of rapidly increasing urbanization of Australia. Support for change, however,
was not total, as Sparkes was aware:

> Quite understandably there are those in the party who object to
> change, who nostalgically wish to preserve the traditional
> character and modus operandi of the party. Let me assure you that
> I am not proposing change just for the sake of change, but because
> our very survival as a significant political force depends on our
> capacity to make correct changes.
>
> Whether we like it or not, everything on earth is subject to
> change in varying degrees – that is, everything subject to the
> process of evolution. Political organizations are no exception.
> They must adapt to changes in the political environment if they
> are to survive.
>
> The great challenge confronting us today is to determine the sort
> of adaptations we must make in our policies, our structure and our
> strategy, if we are to continue to be an effective viable political
> force in the years that lie ahead.
>
> To make the right changes we must first recognize the factors
> that make change necessary – we must face the facts of life,
> unpleasant though they may be.

Sparkes' brief in taking on the presidency was to bring about
the changes that the Country Party needed to survive. He
knew clearly what was needed and had the numbers to do

what had to be done. It was just a matter of "packaging" the change in a manner that would be acceptable to the bulk of Country Party members and voters.

The changes that were needed were electoral directional changes and not ideological changes. Sparkes may have been a "new broom" to the organization in many ways, but he was not a radically different ideological thinker. His politics was vintage Country Party, steeped in all the deep-rooted commitments that had been entrenched over half a century of political struggle. In particular, he was a strict disciplinarian who believed totally in the concept of party loyalty and unity.

Throughout the first one-and-a-half years of his presidency, Sparkes concentrated on forming his organizational team, formulating his plans for change and shoring up the party against the threat of internal unrest. In this latter regard, the Darling Downs-based League of Rights caused him considerable concern. In the initial years of his presidency, the League made a determined bid to undermine his authority.

The League of Rights

The League of Rights has been a consistent source of annoyance to Sparkes throughout his presidency, but more so in the early formative days when it operated on the fertile ground of a flagging coalition government in Canberra and the rising ALP star of Gough Whitlam.

Almost from the day Sparkes assumed the presidency, the League threatened to undermine the heartland of the party on the Darling Downs. Sparkes' campaign against the League on the issue of party loyalty was therefore also a campaign to muster support for his dreams of a more widely based National Party. The League of Rights was potentially the only organizational threat to those dreams.

Fired with this realization, Sparkes was seen at his argumentative best. In "A Message to the Rural Community" in 1971 he took the League of Rights and the "soft" sections within his heartland rural community head-on.

> Lately there have been a series of public attacks on the Country Party for allegedly doing nothing to solve, or at least reverse, the economic problems of the rural community (country towns and

districts). These unjustified criticisms are misleading the public and impairing the unity and strength of the party at a time when it has never been more urgent that the party should be united and strong. Therefore, they must be refuted.

Most of the [League's] criticisms are based on one or more of the following false grounds: (1) the Country Party in the coalition governments (federal and state) had done nothing for the rural community and that the rural community would have been just as well off under a socialist/ALP regime; and/or (2) the League of Rights' social credit economic doctrine would provide a panacea for all our ills, and the Country Party is to blame for not embracing this doctrine in its entirety and implementing it; and/or (3) the Country Party has many good policies but for some mysterious reason is stubbornly refusing to implement them.

Sparkes then proceeded to launch into voluminous argument to support his case, listing an inventory of sixteen major policy initiatives from a reduction in the rate of state and federal death duties (which he later was to have eliminated) to a stronger state government stand on law and order which he said his party had implemented.

Fabian socialists

An entire broadsheet he reserved for a direct attack on the League of Rights itself. "The League of Rights has repeatedly condemned the (coalition) Commonwealth government and especially the Country Party for allegedly pursuing wrong economic policies," he said. "In fact it is claimed that almost all the ills of the community, particularly the rural community, can be ascribed to these 'erroneous' economic policies. According to these people, the pursuit of these policies is not mere accident or incompetent oversight, but is a deliberate technique of the 'Fabian socialists'."

Linking Sparkes with Fabian socialism is akin to waving a red flag at a bull. "The Fabian socialists, so this hypothesis goes, are dominant among the government economic advisers and they are intentionally guiding the nation along an economic path that will lead to the impoverishment of an increasing number of people, especially in the rural sector. This in turn will facilitate the centralization of political power and the ultimate establishment of a socialist regime." These were the very goals that Sparkes' new directions for the Country Party were aimed at preventing.

Providing another insight into the League of Rights, Liberal backbench "ginger group" member Rosemary Kyburz was less flattering of the activities of the League in an address to the parliament on 12 December 1979, on a Matter of Public Interest.

"There is an evil and cancerous growth in Queensland, and its tentacles are spreading at an alarming rate. This evil takes many forms, but its name is the League of Rights," she said. Mrs Kyburz was, in particular, attacking the organization known as "Women Who Want to be Women". She went on to say: "I should mention other faces of the League of Rights in Queensland." (She had previously described them also as "this group of ratbags".) "It is known also as the John Birch Society, the Committed Christians Crusade, STOP, CARE, the Association of Catholic Parents, Save Our State, the Community Standards Association, Nell Madigan's Mob and the Conservative Club." She added that the League was also behind support for Milan Brych, the Anti-Fluoridation Association and the Anti-Metrication Association.

As Sparkes had suggested, Mrs Kyburz was attempting to link the League of Rights with the National Party, but she went further to suggest that the League was also active in the Liberal Party.

It was the involvement of the "well-meaning group", as Sparkes describes them, in the League of Rights that caused him the most problems. Had the League of Rights movement simply been another clearly definable political party that Sparkes could publicly identify, there is no doubt that his task of moving against them would have been much easier. As a shadowy, indefinable group within his own party ranks, he had to tread much more warily in any defensive action. This is not to say that he was reticient in his actions against their tactics. Such is simply not his style. Rather, he was particularly guarded in this area. A major breakaway faction within his organization, especially one with heartland support, would have proven a major embarrassment to Sparkes.

Struggle for the heartland

Such internal pressures on Sparkes in those early years un-doubtedly served as a spur to prove his argument. His resolve for change was strengthened, especially by those who sought to depict him as being a party to any philosophy that was designed to intentionally damage the fortunes of rural people, for this was the crux of his argument for a more dynamic National Party.

> Naturally, if the Country Party were convinced that the League of Rights had a panacea for all the economic ills of the rural community, we would very gladly accept it and try to implement it, as far as was politically possible to do so. After all, most members of the Country Party are themselves suffering from the economic problems of the rural community and would be ratbags indeed if they were to shun a sound solution to their problems. Moreover, it would be politically expedient to have a happy rather than discontented rural community. In fact, no political party would deliberately displease a large section of its supporters if it could avoid doing so.

The League was not Sparkes' only concern, however, in those initial years of his presidency. Like a good shepherd, Sparkes did not need reminding of the real wolf snarling at the heels of his flock and forever attempting to lure them away with "misguided promises". In this regard it has been a consis-tent source of amazement to him that people in his own rural heartland have at times drifted across the demarcation line to support the socialist policies of the ALP.

"We would be sadly deceiving ourselves," he said in 1971, "if we were to believe that these people [the ALP] really under-stand and care about the plight of the rural community. Of course some ALP members, especially those that hold country seats like Dr Patterson [Dawson], express pious concern and propound all sorts of miraculous cures for our ills, particular-ly on the eve of elections, to woo our votes. But don't be misled! They are only out for political capital," he warned.

The actions of the ALP, which Sparkes followed with the determination of a terrier in those years of declining fortunes in Canberra, was his greatest weapon to use against the ALP in the rural community. None of his colleagues in either the parliamentary or organizational arena handled the attack better.

ALP aids his argument

The row between ALP economic adviser Bill Hayden (Oxley) and Rex Patterson (Dawson) at the party's Launceston conference in 1971 was the evidence Sparkes needed to be convinced his argument was right. "Mr Hayden said on June 21 that 'Labor did not have a primary industry programme that gave a comprehensive and integrated approach. What we have,' he said, 'is a loose patchwork of totally unrelated propositions'."

Patterson, the author of the ALP rural policy and who was later to become the minister for Northern Development in the Whitlam government, hit back at Hayden the following day, providing further support for Sparkes' argument. "I find the statement incredible. It is also untrue," Patterson said. "It shows in fact a colossal ignorance of a person [Hayden] who should know better."

But as Sparkes was quick to further point out: "The amendments which Mr Hayden and Mr Hurford made to the committee's report were accepted by the conference." Patterson's response to this was: "I find it very hard to believe, except perhaps that very few members of the conference know anything about rural matters."

Seeing his political opponents tear themselves apart in public was the grist to the mill that Sparkes lived on.

L–CP coalition in disarray

The decline of the Liberal–Country Party coalition in Canberra throughout the early seventies and following the shock disappearance of Prime Minister Harold Holt and the void this left in the Liberal Party strengthened Sparkes' resolve for change. The internal squabbling over leadership of the federal Liberal Party and the subsequent downfall of the McMahon–Anthony coalition in 1972 provided the final evidence and the platform he needed.

"Disunity in the Liberal Party associated with selfish political ambitions that placed personal aggrandisement above the welfare of the party – and the coalition government. This factor manifested itself in leadership struggles and conveyed the impression to the public that the party was too preoccupied with infighting to govern properly," Sparkes told the Australian Country Party federal executive's post-mortem meeting on the 1972 federal elections which swept Gough Whitlam's Labor Party into office.

"After all, if leading Liberals could find so much fault with the government and the prime minister, it might well have been time for a change," he went on to say. "Clearly, the Liberal Party organisation should have disciplined those responsible for these repeated acts of disloyalty, even, if necessary, to the point of expelling them. The immediate adverse effects of the ensuing uproar would have been more than compensated for by the long-term effect of improved party solidarity."

Sparkes had made his move. He had the clear proof that the Liberal Party was failing its traditional urban support base and that there was ample room for the Country Party to follow the rural drift into the cities. Eighteen months of pondering, preparation and patience was now ready to be put into practice.

To properly gauge the extent of his political vision and the success of his efforts to bring his dreams to fruition, it is important to appreciate the dreams he brought with him to the presidency which launched the Queensland Country Party down the road to the state and national recognition that it enjoys today.

Sparkes' vision

In 1973 Sparkes revealed his dreams in a lengthy submission to the federal executive of the Australian Country Party. He said that the party was at the crossroads (an expression he uses often). "Which path we take in the future will largely depend on how we answer this all-important question." And while others at the conference leafed through their papers and wondered what this brash, forceful fellow from Queensland was talking about, Sparkes positively put his case.

"There can only be one answer, and I have been saying it for some time now. If we are to survive as a significant political force, we cannot remain essentially rural based. We must expand the basis of our support by projecting ourselves as a truly national party with a stable, middle-of-the-road philosophy." Interestingly, this was Sparkes' first real promotion of the name "National Party", even though it went over the heads of some of the delegates. From his point of view, it was intentional.

> We must exhibit a concern for a whole spectrum of human affairs. By doing so, we will attract increasing support from a wide range of people in all walks of life – people who eschew political extremism of both the left and the right – people who want change for the sake of change – people who believe that the happy medium course is the best approach to life.
>
> I believe that the paramount role – in fact, the responsibility – of the Australian Country Party in the future is to propound and pursue the happy medium course in politics.

Sparkes realized even then that this statement would not be readily accepted by some "dyed-in-the-wool" influential sections of the Australian Country Party. Premier Joh Bjelke-Petersen was later to comment on this middle-of-the-road attitude, saying: "You know what happens to people who walk down the middle of the road?" Still, Sparkes persisted because the political ground he was seeking for the National Party really had nothing to do with wishy-washy, indecisive politics that could have been the interpretation of his "happy medium" statement.

"We must face the harsh reality," he said, "that with the rapid growth of big cities the proportion of the rural population to the total population is dwindling quickly. Although the Australian Country Party has succeeded in retaining smaller quotas for country seats against the 'one vote, one value' principle advocated by the ALP and the Liberal Party, urban seats outnumber rural seats and with every succeeding redistribution this ascendancy of urban seats over rural seats will increase. Therefore, as surely as night follows day, if the Australian Country Party endeavoured to remain solely a rural-based party, it would be destined for oblivion. We would not even hold the balance of power and we would be a futile voice crying in the wilderness."

And so Sparkes launched the campaign to lead the Australian Country Party, at least in Queensland, out of the rural political wilderness that he astutely realized was developing.

Achievement

A decade later it can be seen just how successful Robert Lyndley Sparkes has been. The promised land that he predicted in 1973 is now clearly visible. But how were the goals achieved? How has Robert Sparkes led his rural-based Country Party out of the wilderness and into the streets of Brisbane and the major provincial areas of Queensland where today it is seen as a major political threat to both the Liberal and Labor parties?

To demonstrate that it was all part of a brilliantly conceived and orchestrated plan, let us again look further at the prophetic 1973 speech to the ACP federal executive.

> In Queensland we've been proving a policy of broadening the party's image, and with some success, as evidenced by our victories in such urban seats as Surfers Paradise and the fact that in the last state elections we polled ahead of the Liberal Party in thirteen of the thirteen seats we contested with them. [Already the push into Liberal and Labor heartlands in Queensland had begun.]
>
> It is now imperative that the party should accelerate the process of broadening its image on a national scale. However, in this broadening process we need not and must not neglect our traditional role of protecting the interests of the rural community and, similarly, we must ensure that the increasing urban component in the party does not dominate to the detriment of the rural community.

Quite accurately, even at this stage, Sparkes was pinpointing the biggest obstacle that he would need to overcome in his plans to shift the political base of his organization. Even today the problem of fairly accommodating the demands of increasing numbers of city members in the same political bed as the numerically lesser, but influentially more powerful, rural membership is a constant headache for the party administration. "I am confident that both these criteria can be met, however," Sparkes predicted. "In determining the future stance and action of the party we must consider several important aspects, namely, (a) policy and philosophy, (b) organisation and strategy, and (c) collaboration with the Liberal Party."

New policies

Sparkes was never happy with the limited policies of the Australian Country Party. In the area of more appropriate policies, he wanted to see the party further expand its social conscience. "I strongly recommend that the party appoint committees of experts on various subjects, for example, social issues, education, environmental equality, economics and so on."

To launch the Country Party into these new and un-charted waters for many of its members, Sparkes suggested the establishment of policy committees chaired by party members but including "outside" experts in various fields from the community at large. His purpose in bringing in outside help on these committees was twofold. "By involving a cross-section of the community, especially in the bigger urban areas, these committees would assist in overcoming the misconception, unfortunately still widely current, that the Australian Country Party is merely a narrow-minded, rural pressure group."

Not only was Sparkes concerned with the diminishing importance of the rural vote in Australian politics, but he was also at that stage acutely aware of the increasing importance of the youth vote. "Already approximately 33 per cent of voters are under thirty. With the inevitable reduction in the voting age to eighteen, this percentage will be increased," he realized, and wanted the ACP then and there to set about to capture an increased proportion of this important vote. "They must be convinced that the Australian Country Party is not a moribund rural pressure group, but an alive and dynamic broadly based national party, concerned with all aspects of life." Again Sparkes intentionally dropped the words "national party", astutely linking his party with where he believed their future lay.

To ensure that the party gained the best-possible advice and insight into the interests and opinions of young people, Sparkes proposed the undertaking of regular attitude surveys of young people. In this area he accepted the advice of media entrepreneur Frank Moore, an influential party supporter in Queensland, who was to play an increasingly important role in working with Sparkes to implement his expansionist policies. He also initiated a wider role for the Young Country Party in the operations of the senior organization, "without giving them undue influence" and to "bridge the generation gap".

Professional marketing and fund raising

When the party developed new and more dynamic policies, Sparkes foreshadowed that they should be professionally packaged and marketed to the electorate. "Our Queensland policy booklet is both obsolete and unattractive," he said. "We are selling political policies and it is just as necessary that they should be presented in a form that encourages assimilation and acceptance as it is to present a commercial article for sale in a properly prepared brochure." And Sparkes concluded: "In fact, the devising of a satisfactory format warrants the cost of an advertising agency" — a remark it seems difficult to believe was said only ten years ago, considering the thousands of dollars now spent on advertising.

Sparkes realized even then that his proposals could not be achieved by relying solely on the meagre finances available from ordinary party membership fees. He was planning to establish the most efficient political machine ever seen in Australian politics and that required money. "Generally speaking, party membership income is no longer sufficient to maintain an effective organisation with all the necessary facilities, nor are periodic election-fund donations sufficient to enable us to mount the most effective political campaigns," he said, no doubt laying the foundations for the Bjelke-Petersen Foundation that was to come almost a decade later. The days of the old Country Party being able to fund itself

These three men held the keys to the National Party's future in Australia. Queensland Premier Joh Bjelke-Petersen has led the way, while Sir Robert Sparkes has organized the most formidable political organization in the history of Australian politics. Doug Anthony was federal leader throughout the Queensland party's meteoric rise to power. He retired in January 1984. (Photograph courtesy of Queensland Newspapers Pty Ltd)

A rare occasion when a Queensland cartoonist gave Sir Robert Sparkes the limelight. An interesting aspect is the depiction of Sparkes as a well-dressed, conservative business man – a sharp contrast to the hayseed image often given to Premier Joh.

Smiles all around on this occasion, at a function in support of the Iwasaki project at Yeppoon. Premier Joh, his friend and supporter and Minister for Water Resources, Neville Hewitt (second from left), and the later expelled member for Callide, Lindsay Hartwig, pose with executives of the Iwasaki company. Japanese millionaire Iwasaki is third from the left.

from the contributions of ordinary members, no matter how high their membership fees might be, were coming to an end.

Sparkes was particularly concerned with the party's ability to match performance in the urban areas with the superior financial resources available to the Australian Labor Party. "The ALP's funds are massively augmented by increasing union contributions and income from commercial enterprises operated through tax-exempt union fronts; for example, in Queensland it is estimated that the ALP receives about $200,000 annually from 4KQ Radio Station. Moreover, the Whitlam government's announced intention to grant improved conditions such as four weeks annual leave to those public servants who are members of their union will mean millions of extra dollars more in union dues over the next few years. Undoubtedly the unions concerned will express their gratitude by passing on some of this enormous rake-off to their benefactor — the federal ALP."

Sparkes at that time considered that the party should itself purchase a radio station. He also proposed increased membership fees although the rise was relatively modest compared with the demand he forecast for his expensive programme. He also called for an expansion of the party's cattle and commodity scheme whereby rural supporters could give in kind rather than in cash.

Involving the pollies

The best of political strategies devised by backroom generals like Sparkes have little hope of implementation without the involvement of the parliamentarians who have to take them into the public arena. Sparkes realized this, and his 1973 blueprint for the future of the Country Party included increased involvement of the parliamentary wing with the policy makers of the organization.

"Parliamentarians, both state and federal, should be invited to attend meetings of Central Council, parliamentary duties permitting," he said. "By doing so, not only would they be more conversant with the thinking of the people they represent, but also they would have the opportunity to influence that thinking by speaking, though not voting, on issues." It is interesting to note in this statement the reference to parliamentarians attending, so long as their duties permit. It is a further hallmark of Sparkes' attitude to government that all parliamentarians should first honour their commitments to their elected responsibilities. It is also noteworthy that, today, all Queensland National Party parliamentarians are members of Central Council with full voting rights.

And further on the subject of his vision of Country Party politicians of the future, Sparkes recognized the increasing importance of television in the presentation of politics to the masses. "In fact," he said, "the personality or charisma of the party leader — or his lack of it — has such a big electoral effect today that I am convinced our strategy must place increasing emphasis on exploiting the qualities of our leaders. In fact, we must cultivate the personality cult whenever our leader's personality lends itself to this treatment."

Finally, Sparkes came to the question of future relations with the Liberal Party. "Whilst I agree that we must retain our separate identity and that the disadvantages of continuing in coalition with the Liberal Party in opposition would outweigh the advantages, we must collaborate with the Liberal Party to provide the most effective parliamentary opposition and to convince the public that the two parties are quite capable of providing a united federal coalition government again. In the final analysis, both parties must realize that public bickering and squabbling will seriously impair their prospects of regaining the federal government."

As conceptually brilliant as Sparkes' expansionary programme for the then Country Party was at that time, especially now with the benefit of hindsight, it was not accepted federally, and only with persistent bludgeoning was it finally accepted in Queensland.

To understand how the battle was won, appreciation of the political philosophy and style of R.L. Sparkes is as important as appreciating the close working relationship that has been forged between Sparkes and the premier. For if Premier Joh Bjelke-Petersen is the builder who constructs the final fabric of political life in Queensland, Sparkes is the architect of most of the plans.

Sparkes in context

Robert Lyndley Sparkes, president of the Australian Country Party (Queensland) from 1970 to 1974 is today Sir Robert Sparkes, knighted in 1980 for his distinguished services to the state and to local government, president of the National Party of Australia (Queensland). He is the power behind the throne of Queensland's seemingly indomitable National Party. His is the steady hand on the helm of the Bjelke-Petersen–National Party juggernaut that has been described as the most effective political "war machine" in the history of the nation. Whereas former press secretary Allen Callaghan gave Joh Bjelke-Petersen the media spit and polish, Sparkes has given him the grass roots political organization and stability so essential to success.

Ironically, it was instability that brought the two men together in their seemingly inseparable political alliance that endures today. Bjelke-Petersen went to Sparkes in 1970 to seek his help in settling dissidents within his parliamentary ranks who wanted to oust him from the leadership. Sparkes, in his first year of the presidency, read the riot act and threatened disendorsement to any who would put personal ambition before party solidarity, and further trouble was aborted.

The son of prosperous Jandowae grazier, grain grower and former state parliamentarian Sir James Sparkes, Bob Sparkes had known Joh Bjelke-Petersen previously from his early days when Joh was an aerial seeding contractor, but it wasn't until this worrying period of instability for his party in 1970 that their now-famous alliance was forged. It was an alliance that was destined for success from the start.

Sparkes, the expansive thinker with a vision for a greater Australia but without the desire to enter the parliamentary arena himself, needed a strong, reliable parliamentary leader if he was to see his dreams become reality. Bjelke-Petersen, the political survivor with his deeply rooted dedication to the cause and the zeal of a religious crusader, needed the solid, reliable organization base that Sparkes now indicated he could provide. It was a political alliance of mutual benefit with each man's territory clearly defined. Sparkes did not want Bjelke-Petersen's job and vice versa.

It was to be a political alliance built on solidarity, unity and loyalty to the cause – a belief that both men share with total conviction. "Whether we like it or not, the party system is here to stay, and no member can expect to enjoy – nor can the party afford to allow him to enjoy – the privileges of party membership and at the same time the freedom of an independent," is more vintage R.L. Sparkes from those formative years. "The lesson for the Australian Country Party is quite clear – our parliamentarians must be given every opportunity at party meetings to voice their views and criticism without fear or fetter. But once the vote is taken they must abide by the majority decision and refrain from any public attack on the party or the coalition government in which it may be a partner; the only exception being in matters of conscience. To put it bluntly, we must only wash and hang out our dirty linen in private! And this applies to both the parliamentary and organizational wings of the party. No matter how repugnant restraints of this kind may be, we cannot afford to play the game of politics any other way."

These were deliberately strong words from a man determined to set a standard by which he expected his organization to be run. It is a line from which Sparkes has not wavered during his thirteen years in the presidency.

Commitment to loyalty

Throughout his presidency, party unity and an unpreparedness to accept disloyalty to the cause have been pillars of Sparkes' beliefs. At any hint of disunity within his own party ranks, he has moved quickly and decisively. Witness the 1971 threat of disendorsement made to the organizers of the coup to oust Bjelke-Petersen and the 1981 decision to expel the sitting member for Callide, Lindsay Hartwig.

The state bank issue was another that required such firmness. "I do not wish to be embarrassingly specific, but I think you would all agree that we have witnessed incidents, too many incidents, in which some party members have acted wittingly or unwittingly in a manner most detrimental to the party," Sparkes told the Caloundra conference of the party in 1982 when he moved to head off disquiet in party ranks over the setting up of a state bank in Queensland, a move Sparkes firmly believed was backed by the League of Rights.

"It has been put to me that the motivation of both groups is mischievous, even malicious, but in view of the fact that both groups include some decent people, I prefer to think they are well meaning but misguided," Sparkes added. (He was referring to "The Enterprise Queensland Association" and "The Rockhampton Anti-Inflation Study Group" which had sprung up in support of the state bank proposal.) "I strongly suspect that both groups are League of Rights 'fronts'," he said. "Both groups certainly include persons with a sympathy for League of Rights philosophy and policies, especially their economic policy which is sheer social credit theory" — which, on the matter of a state bank, Sparkes described as "making funny money".

Then came the cruncher, which the 600-odd delegates at the convention hall knew was spoken with purpose and intent: "If the persons concerned so acted wittingly, then they deserve the utmost censure [expulsion]. Most of us spend a lot of time, effort and money in building up this party. We cannot and will not tolerate a situation where all the good work done by the many tends to be undone by the irresponsible conduct of the few." He then laid down the law for National Party solidarity – a carbon copy of his advice to the federal executive almost a decade earlier.

Exacerbating Sparkes' difficulties with the League of Rights was their forthright backing of the premier and, at times, his interpreted leanings in their direction, such as was widely suggested in the state bank debate. Sparkes' only defence was his seemingly inexhaustible ability to aggressively argue his case within the guidelines of the party structure. A talented exponent of the frontal attack in politics, Sparkes' tactic with the League has simply been to wear them down with forcibly presented argument at every opportunity he is given.

As authoritarian as Sparkes has been throughout the term of his presidency, he has, like Bjelke-Petersen, demanded and received almost total loyalty from the vast National Party organization in Queensland. It has at times been given begrudgingly, but he has always won through in the end. He has always known the limits of his power and influence, and never missed the opportunity in the heat of debate to humble himself to the organization, which in any final showdown holds the reins on the considerable power that he exercises.

Demonstrating such political astuteness at the same Caloundra conference, Sparkes reassured his followers and any who might suggest that he was overstepping his mark: "It is not the prerogative of the premier or the president [himself] to say that a certain policy shall or shall not be amended or revoked. Neither of us can dictate policy matters though we may argue forcibly against them. Indeed, if either of us could dictate, it would be a sorry day for the party. In the final analysis, it is your decision and that's how it should be and will continue to be as long as I am your president."

Rumours were rife that a possible challenge would be

mounted against Sparkes' presidency over this issue. It didn't eventuate. But just in case any of the delegates hadn't understood the full impact of his demand for loyalty and party unity, Sparkes went on to say: "The claim of one group that it comprises loyal National Party members is nonsense. Loyal National Party members do not vent criticisms of their party publicly like the ALP. To avoid damaging the party, loyal members use the constitutional avenues within it to argue their case, and if they can persuade a majority that they are right, then their view will prevail." The message is always the same: deviants from the party line cannot and will not be tolerated in the interests of the success of the organization.

Then with direct reference to the group promoting disunity over the issue of the state bank, Sparkes delivered the final word: "Setting up another political faction or organization as a vehicle to attack our party not only indicts these people as being disloyal, but of course under Rule 3 (c) it automatically expels them from the National Party. Clearly their action is designed to divide and fragment our party and that we will not tolerate."

Hartwig's expulsion

In Sparkes' defence, it is important to point out that members accused of wrong-doings against the party line have been given ample opportunity to explain and repent. Witness the case of Lindsay Hartwig. "No doubt you have heard various reasons why the party took this drastic action, including Mr Hartwig's own quite erroneous explanation," Sparkes said in an explanation of the case in April 1981. "Hence the necessity to put the record straight by giving you all the facts and circumstances." Sparkes went on to further preface his nine-foolscap-page statement: "At the outset I want to stress that I have dedicated my political life to building up the parliamentary representation of the National Party, so that the party has the capacity to implement its policies for the good of its members and the state and nation generally. Hence you will readily appreciate that the last thing I would wish to do would be to reduce our parliamentary strength by expelling a parliamentary member."

The statement then went on to detail ten separate areas where Sparkes claimed Hartwig had breached party rules. He pointed out that he had first reprimanded Hartwig over his disloyalty in September 1979 and that his actions had been supported by the State Management Committee meeting on 21 September that year. That meeting accepted an unequivocal assurance given by Hartwig to Sparkes that he would in future refrain from public criticism of the party and its leadership. The Management Committee's actions were supported by Hartwig's own electorate council which also carried a resolution asking him to refrain from further such public criticism. On 12 March 1981, however, Hartwig, under parliamentary privilege, again attacked the party and in particular the Central Zone vice-president, George Robertson. Sparkes said the party was left with no alternative.

The Sparkes–Bjelke-Petersen alliance

The strategic importance to the National Party of the Sparkes–Bjelke-Petersen alliance has not been overlooked by the party's detractors or by those who might seek to bring either of them down. "Put Sparkes and Joh at each other's throats and you bring the National Party to its knees" has long been recognized by many of their political foes and attempted by some. Both men are, however, constantly alert to such tactics and throughout their numerous differences of opinion, some of which have been extraordinarily heated, there has been one factor that has brought about many a successful settlement to a dispute – a simple matter of not wanting to give the common enemy the satisfaction of splitting them after so many years.

Joh Bjelke-Petersen's controversial style of leadership, variously described as dictatorial, intransigent and draconian, and earning for him the sobriquet of "Jack Boots Bjelke", is one that even his closest allies and supporters at times have found difficult to live with, including National Party president Sir Robert Sparkes. Sparkes and the premier have clashed on numerous occasions on issues such as abortion, Aboriginal land rights, street march legislation and the 1977 federal referenda. Both men have had to give ground at one time or another, and their score would be about 50–50 in wins and losses.

Sparkes sums up the Bjelke-Petersen style thus: "Of course, strong political leadership of the kind Joh Bjelke-Petersen exemplifies inevitably becomes embroiled in controversy from time to time." But Sparkes believes that the inscription that adorns Joh's office desk very aptly depicts the alternative: "To avoid criticism – Say nothing! Do nothing! Be nothing!"

"Even though Joh is often controversial," Sparkes says, "I say – thank God for his strong, honest, purposeful leadership in these turbulent times." It has been a line that the National Party has sold over and over to the electorate and has firmly believed is the cornerstone of its growing electoral success.

Sparkes' explanation of the premier's rigid style was given at the 1978 State Conference of the party in Brisbane. It was contained, in fact, in a peace offering by Sparkes to end the stand-off that had developed between himself and the premier over the 1977 referenda debate and which spread to other minor issues in what was a very difficult year for internal National Party relations. "There has been, and there still is, a concerted campaign by the ALP, aided by significant elements in the media, to denigrate and destroy the premier, and through him the National Party," Sparkes said. "We have probably aided their campaign of denigration sometimes by inadvertently projecting an authoritarian style of government. This is a problem that has been contributed to by a breakdown in public relations and in communication and consultation between the premier, cabinet and the parliamentary wing," he said. "As leader of the party organization, I accept my share of the responsibility for this unfortunate development." The coolness of the relationship warmed soon afterwards.

It was Sparkes' speech in 1978 that prompted a concerted effort by the National Party as a whole to rally behind the premier and squash the anti-Joh "Jack Books Bjelke" campaign, which had originated in the 1971 Springbok Rugby Union tour of Australia when the premier declared a State of Emergency and was continually being used to denigrate his warnings about socialism.

Sparkes' speech to the 1978 State Conference calling for greater party support for the premier to combat the campaign was something of a history lesson, just in case some of the delegates weren't aware that law and order had been an issue long before Joh Bjelke-Petersen came on the scene. "Violent militant pressure groups and the danger to law and order arising from it bring to mind a theory on evolution of governments propounded by the Greek philosopher Plato," Sparkes said. "Firstly, there is a monarchy or dictatorship. Secondly, the monarchy or dictatorship breaks down into an oligarchy. Thirdly, the oligarchy breaks down into democracy. Fourthly, democracy breaks down into violence, mob rule and anarchy. Fifthly, the people become tired of violence, mob rule and anarchy and accept a monarchy or dictatorship and the cycle commences afresh."

Sparkes specifically drew the attention of delegates to the fourth stage of Plato's cycle — the breakdown of democracy into violence, mob rule and anarchy. "I do not think," he said, "that it is an exaggeration to suggest that we are witnessing the commencement of that cycle in some democracies today, for example Italy." The inference was there also that similar developments were occurring in Australia. "Accordingly, we must fully support our premier, Joh Bjelke-Petersen, and the state government in their determination to uphold law and order in the state. Although probably not a politically popular or expedient stand, it will be judged by history to have been wise and far sighted."

Thus, Sir Robert Sparkes and Joh Bjelke-Petersen work together like a well-oiled machine. Since 1970 when Bjelke-Petersen's leadership was seriously threatened and he survived on proxies, his own vote and Sparkes' support, Joh hasn't really had to look over his shoulder to see where the knives are coming from — while others worry about protecting their political backs, Joh has had the stability of Robert Sparkes.

Again, in the state bank debate at the Caloundra conference in 1982, Sparkes' detractors sought to drive a wedge between the two. Astutely, despite the fact that he knew that the premier had a great interest in the concept of a state bank and would like to believe it was economically and political possible, Sparkes was determined that the issue would not be used to divide them in public.

"Now let me refute another lie being propagated, namely, that I am constantly at loggerheads with the premier," he said. "The fact is that we agree most times, but, Ladies and

Gentlemen, as you may have perceived, we are both fairly strong-willed, independent-thinking individuals. Therefore occasionally we disagree." Both men glanced at each other with just the slightest hint of a smile to themselves as Sparkes continued: "That is not bad! That is a good healthy thing! If we were otherwise, we would not be the effective leaders we seek to be. Anyway, if there is a difference between us on some major matter that we can't sort out, then we should submit it to you people for resolution. Once you have decided, whether or not we like your decision, we are bound to abide by it! That's democracy! Ladies and Gentlemen, this tactic to try to divide Joh and myself is not new. It has failed in the past and will fail again this time, I assure you."

Sacking Sullivan and Tomkins

In December that same year, however, two of Sparkes' most senior state parliamentarians were very nearly successful in driving home a wedge that would split the president and the premier apart.

To some, Sparkes had overstepped his mark when he moved to have deputy parliamentary leader Vic Sullivan and Aboriginal and Island Affairs minister Ken Tomkins step down from their cabinet posts after their much publicized "fishing" trip in Torres Strait. Sparkes had been under considerable party pressure for many months to get new, young talent into the aging Bjelke-Petersen cabinet, but Joh, the astute political survivor, was unwilling to sacrifice any of his tried and proven supporters, regardless of the minor misdemeanour that Vic and Ken may have committed.

In the hurly-burly of day-to-day politics where nothing is certain, the greatest asset any leader can have is the numbers. And now Sparkes, with the backing of the organization, was insisting that two of Joh's most senior and trusted ministers should stand down. Exacerbating matters even further was the long-standing feud between Sparkes and Sullivan which dates back to their early days in organizational politics on the Darling Downs. Some even suggested that Sparkes wanted Sullivan's seat of Condamine as his entree into state politics as Joh's successor. The following excerpts from an ABC "Nation-

wide" interview with deputy leader Vic Sullivan at the height
of the issue explained the tension that existed:

> Interviewer: Are you saying that Bob Sparkes really made the
> decision and not Joh Bjelke-Petersen?
>
> Sullivan: Well, Bob Sparkes in his position as president. Any
> decisions that have come out of my ministries of Lands,
> Primary Industries, Mines, Commerce and Industry I accept
> responsibility for. So Bob Sparkes as president of the party has
> got to accept responsibility for what comes out of his organiza-
> tion. Now last night on television, you know, I think it was
> Jane Singleton [ABC interviewer] asked the premier why
> would you sack Mr Sullivan, Mr Tomkins, and he said: Oh,
> well, you know the media and everybody were pressuring me
> to.
>
> Interviewer: You don't believe him, though, do you?
>
> Sullivan: I have no reason to disbelieve him, but if he did OK.
>
> Interviewer: But he said in the paper yesterday, was quoted in
> fact, he said at the news conference that when you were made
> a cabinet minister after the last election, you did so on the
> undertaking that you would quit the post in around twelve
> months.
>
> Sullivan: That is not true.
>
> Interviewer: But he says that you said that.
>
> Sullivan: Oh well, he said it, but I am saying that it is not true.
>
> Interviewer: Well, that means you are accusing the premier of
> saying an untruth.
>
> Sullivan: Look, let me say this, the people of Condamine in the
> 1980 elections re-elected me with an almost 6 per cent increase
> in my vote and the day the party re-elected me unanimously as
> deputy leader that was the day when the reshuffle was taking
> place. Now Sparkes as president of the party said to the
> premier, the premier told me this; he said: you know Vic
> Sullivan considers himself lucky to even be in cabinet.
>
> Interviewer: There has been a long-standing feud between you
> and the president of the party, Mr Sparkes, hasn't there?
>
> Sullivan: Well, if there is, it's not of my making. Some blokes like
> power without glory they call it. Apparently Bob fits into that
> category. But you know what a slap in the face it is for the
> thirty-five members of state parliament, to say that after having
> re-elected me unanimously as deputy leader, for the organisa-
> tion to say he's lucky to be in cabinet.
>
> Interviewer: Are you saying that Sparkes was behind the media
> campaign against you?
>
> Sullivan: Keep the pressure on, keep the pressure on Sullivan and
> Tomkins.

Interviewer: Are you saying it?
Sullivan: Sure! And you know.
Interviewer: That's a serious charge.

Aboriginal and Islander Affairs minister Ken Tomkins was interviewed on the same programme, and he likewise criticized Sparkes and the organization's involvement in pressure being placed on the premier to have the two ministers step down from cabinet. When asked to name names of people who were responsible for the ministers' demise, Tomkins did not hesitate: "I'd say Sir Robert Sparkes for one, probably Charlie Holm, too. And they've got a few others who I won't name."

Tomkins went on to put the pressure right back in the Sparkes–Bjelke-Petersen court when asked by the interviewer to implicate Joh in their demise.

Interviewer: What does it say about the rule of Premier Joh Bjelke-Petersen. Is he losing his grip?
Tomkins: That's very hard to answer. I really haven't a great deal of . . . I've got nothing to say against Premier Joh. Really I haven't . . . I don't . . .
Interviewer: Even though he forced you to resign?
Tomkins: Yes that's right, yes, yes. I've got to say that he's got a very nice way of doing things, always has had. And I must admit that although I'm not very pleased with him, I rather admire his style.

The Sullivan-Tomkins issue cut deep into traditional National Party Territory and feelings. Both were extremely popular politicians in their own areas and both were known strong numbers men for the premier. And yet, in the end, it was Sparkes who won through. Furthermore, his credibility remained intact; he did not seek preselection for Condamine when Sullivan finally announced his retirement, a point of contrast to be compared with Liberal president Yvonne McComb's controversial actions leading up to the destructive separate Senate ticket decision of which she was to be a beneficiary.

Sparkes' brand of industrial relations

The politics of responsibility to the common good that Sparkes extolls throughout the organization of the National Party also permeates his political thinking. At times in the public arena, however, it has not received the widespread community understanding and support he could have expected from within his party ranks. Such was the case when he suggested in 1982 that the Queensland government move to establish an elite military-style organizaton to intervene in industrial disputes in the Queensland power industry.

"What is proposed is that there be a specially trained and very mobile force of people with the necessary technical skill to step in and operate the power stations. The basis of this proposal, of course, is that it's very clear that, whilst the community can probably weather most strikes out, strikes by a relative handful of people who operate our power stations can fairly quickly bring the whole community to its knees with enormous economic costs. Costs in terms of human hardships when power is cut off to hospitals, aged persons' homes, lifts, air-conditioning and of course the health of the ordinary citizen who gets affected by the breakdown in sewerage and effluent disposal."

"Some people would see it as something of a stranglehold on the right to strike, do you see it that way?" the interviewer at the time inquired.

"I don't think in a modern civilized society we can conceive that a very small group of people in the total population have the right to bring the complete community to its knees," Sparkes retorted.

Ken Blanch, writing in the *Sunday Sun* at the time, didn't agree with the Sparkes solution. "National Party president Sir Robert Sparkes should start brushing his hair down over one eye and growing a toothbrush moustache," he said. "They would go well with his views on industrial relations."

Sparkes' style

Although these are but a sprinkling of examples of the philosophy, style and vision of Sir Robert Sparkes, they clearly indicate the rigid adherence to organizational discipline that has existed during his dynamic term in office. They also provide an excellent example of National Party leadership to be compared with other political parties in Australia today.

Dogged determination and the authoritarian style of Sparkes, however, are but the outside expressions of the man that the public at large has come to associate him with. Ironically, within the National Party, some suggest that Sparkes is too soft on some issues such as abortion and human relations. Neither assessment would seem correct. His slow, sometimes dull and monotonous style of presentation often adds further to the misconception that he is little more than a heavy-handed, country-styled hatchet man for "Jack Boots Joh". In reality it is clearly evident that Sparkes is one of the most expansive thinkers in the upper echelons of political power in Australia today. Methodically he has set about to place his stamp on Queensland and Australian politics, and through sheer and utter persistence and ability he has been considerably successful.

In achieving the dream of wider acceptance for the Country-cum-National Party, Sparkes' personal drive and determination have been major determining factors, but it wasn't achieved by Sparkes alone. The political "war machine" that he brought together over the past thirteen action-packed years has included many significant contributors. And there is considerably more to the story of how the Nationals came out of the political wilderness.

3

Winning Brisbane
and the Bush

Former Queensland Country Party state president Alan
Campbell described the Country Party in his memoirs as a
party which "represents all primary industries, particularly
the rural section with its industrial organizations and country
folk generally. All are mutually dependent upon a common
political policy for their well-being. The rural people are
divided into three sections, namely: (a) the producer who is
entitled to a fair return upon his investment and for his
initiative and enterprise, (b) the worker who is entitled to the
best wages and conditions his industry can afford, with adequate educational facilities and social services, and (c) the
country townsman who will prosper if his customers are
prosperous."

This was the "cows and corn" image that the Country Party
wore in the eyes of the increasing urban electorate in
Australia. Through increasing mechanization of rural
Australia and the consequent exodus of Australians from the
"bush" in the years following World War II, the farmers,
graziers, farm workers and country townsmen and women of
Alan Campbell's era simply no longer existed in the numbers
necessary for his Country Party to survive as it had since
1920. It was the party that R.L. Sparkes inherited when he
acquired the presidency in 1970. That was the image he knew
had to be changed if the party was to survive.

Bob Sparkes' vision for an expanded, more dynamic image
for the Country Party in Queensland publicly manifested
itself at the State Conference in Townsville later the same
year, when a resolution empowered the State Management

Committee of the party to investigate the advisability or
otherwise of a new name for the party. Shortly after the
Townsville conference, the Federal Council, to which Sparkes
was a delegate, decided to make the project a national
investigation. The move that would bring the new-image
Country Party into direct conflict with its coalition partner,
the Liberal Party, for the hearts and minds of urban voters
was officially under way. Many Liberal supporters would
argue that this was the day the coalition died.

A new name

Seeking to base their final decision on the soundest possible
political bases, the State Management Committee of which
Sparkes is the chairman moved to appoint the nationally
renowned public relations consultancy firm of W.D. Scott and
Company Pty Ltd to undertake a national survey of public
opinion. The Roy Morgan Research Centre Pty Ltd was also
commissioned to make a further and more detailed survey of
opinion based on the findings of the W.D. Scott survey. In
particular, the Roy Morgan survey was to determine public
acceptability of a range of suggested names for the new-look
Country Party. Some of the names suggested by party
members included: Australian Conservative Party, the
Democratic Party of Australia, the National Democratic
Party, the Centre Party, the New Australian Country Univer-
sal Party, the Australian Democratic Centre Party, the Big
Country Party, the Decentralization Party and the National
Party of Australia.

The Management Committee sought to determine the
answers to four principal questions: (1) whether a change of
name would be likely to lead to a broader understanding and
acceptance of the party and its policies, (2) whether a change
of name would lead to greater electoral support in both the
federal and state political spheres, (3) whether a new name
might attract new members, and (4) whether a new name
would encourage greater financial suport for the party.

When the results of the surveys were finally available, the
federal executive met to consider the findings but decided to
leave implementation of the recommendations to the respec-

tive state bodies involved. It was a disappointing decision for Sparkes who had hoped that the federal organization would adopt the proposal nationally. Undaunted, Sparkes came back to Queensland and strongly recommended to his State Management Committee that Queensland proceed alone.

Detailed, lengthy and confidential submissions were then compiled and dispatched to all branches for consideration. The party's eleven vice-presidents around the state were asked to act as "expert witnesses" on local branch discussions and report back to a further meeting of the State Management Committee before a final decision was made. A special meeting of State Conference was called for October 1973 to consider the Management Committee's final recommendations for a name change. Delegates attended from branches throughout the state where the submissions had been primarily discussed.

The final decision of the State Conference was an overwhelming vote of 420 to 22 in favour of the Management Committee resolution to change the party's name to the National Party of Australia – Queensland. The actual date for the launch of the new name was then left in the hands of the Management Committee. The Management Committee subsequently decided on April 1974 for the launch, a decision that would enable the party to get maximum benefit from the change in the half-Senate election expected in May. A series of gala functions planned by branches around the state would provide maximum exposure to state and federal National Party politicians in the lead-up to the half-Senate election. An April date would also avoid clashing with school holidays and Queensland's notorious wet season, two important criteria as far as the rural-based Country Party was concerned.

Launching throughout the state

Saturday 6 April was finally decided as the day for the official launching. A gala dinner function was held at Lennons Plaza Hotel in Queen Street, Brisbane. Mr Sparkes' Country Party was coming to town.

To launch the decision, the state executive director of the party, Mike Evans, issued the following media release:

> On Saturday April 6, the Australian Country Party, Queensland, will officially become the National Party of Australia − Queensland. The Federal Leader of the Australian Country Party, the Rt Hon. J.D. Anthony, MP, will proclaim the name change during a reception/luncheon ceremony at "Talk of the Town Restaurant" at Lennons Plaza Hotel, Queen Street, Brisbane. Also taking part in the ceremony will be the Hon. J. Bjelke-Petersen, MLA, Premier of Queensland and State Parliamentary leader and Mr R.L. Sparkes, State President, who will also be the official host. In addition, Senators, Federal and State members of Parliament, Party branch executives and members from Branches in Brisbane and adjacent regions, as well as a widely representative cross-section of community leaders will attend. During the following two weeks special name-change functions will also be held at Toowoomba, Longreach, Mackay, Nambour, Ingham, Innisfail, Cairns, Mount Isa, Blackwater, Moranbah, St George, Roma and Charleville. Street meetings will also be held at Maryborough, Bundaberg, Rockhampton and Townsville. Federal and State Parliamentary leaders, Senators and members will attend these functions on a rostered basis. Private and chartered light aircraft, scheduled commerical aircraft and a chartered bus will be used during the name-change campaign to convey a party of about 20 officials and musicians. The National Party singers and accompanying musicians will present the specially written Party anthem and entertain with selected items at the official functions and street meetings.
>
> In commenting on the name change, Mr R.L. Sparkes, State President of the Party said, "Delegates to our special conference last October voted overwhelmingly (420 to 22) in favour of the new name of National Party of Australia. They saw this as an essential first step towards achieving a much greater general public awareness of the breadth of the Party's policies and achievements. Changing our name will not in itself change the picture that people have of us but will give us the opportunity to re-present ourselves and re-state our policies and our principles in contemporary terms. The Party will shortly afterwards commence a comprehensive press, radio and television campaign throughout Queensland to outline our message to the widest possible audience," Mr Sparkes concluded.

The touring party included the premier, Robert Sparkes, federal leader Doug Anthony, Queensland senator Ron

Maunsell, M.G. Evans, the immediate past president, Sid
Roberts, Young National Party president Gary Pike, state
secretary Jim Gillan and various state and federal politicians
who joined the band wagon along the way. No expense was
spared in conveying the message across the state that a new
era in Queensland politics was dawning. The promotional
campaign for the Toowoomba "Name-Change" Function held
on the night of 6 April in the centre of blue-ribbon old
Country Party territory on the Darling Downs was typical of
the extent of the promotion. Full-page advertisements were
taken in the Toowoomba *Chronicle*, the Dalby *Herald*, the
Warwick *Daily News* and the Gatton *Star* proclaiming the
party's new name and direction. Numerous radio spots were
also taken on stations 4GR and 4AK and prime-time commer-
cials appeared on DDQ television. Handouts to the party
faithful and supporters included 400 records of the National
Party song and copies of the lyrics, 400 policy booklets,
balloons, sashes and blow-up posters of Premier Joh Bjelke-
Petersen and Doug Anthony.

Wherever the National Party band wagon rolled it was
welcomed with enthusiasm. There was little doubt that
Sparkes and the Nationals had a winner on their hands. In
Mount Isa, for example, 600 people packed into the pro-Labor
stronghold of the local Irish Club to be entertained by international entertainer Ted Hamilton and receive Sparkes' message
that the "old cows and corn" days of the Country Party were
over. A new dynamic political force was out to capture seats
like Mount Isa and other provincial city seats across the state.
"The old cows and corn connotation in the name Country
Party has hampered the party's efforts to expand into urban
areas," Sparkes said. "When it was established in 1918, [the
ACP] was essentially a sectional party to look after the
interests of the rural community. However, in the last couple
of decades the party has ceased to be sectional. It has broad-
ened its membership and interests and is in fact, a truly
National Party concerned with the whole spectrum of human
affairs." And in a bid to re-establish the bonds between the
rural and urban areas of the state, essential to the future
success of his new party, Sparkes added: "It is extremely unfortunate that the Australian community has been fragmented
into two sections, urban and rural, in seeming conflict. All

sections of the community are interdependent and the
National Party is dedicated to achieving better understanding
of this basic fact of national life which is essential if all
Australians are to be able to work together for the maximum
mutual benefit." The National Party singers then broke into
the party anthem:

> Across Australia coast to coast,
>   a nation proud and strong,
> A country where the air is blowing free,
>   the air is blowing free,
> Where the leadership and national pride
>   go hand in hand and side by side,
> The National party stands for you and me.
>
> So sing it loud — be proud of the National Party
> We're a nation, Australians everyone
> Stand tall and call for the National Party,
> Australians who want to get things done.
>
> We don't have time to stand in line,
>   Our country's moving on,
> Growing larger, getting greater day by day,
>   getting greater day by day,
> Prosperity and harmony, a better life for all,
> Let the National Party lead us on our way.

Subsequently, in recognition of the masterful public rela-
tions performance involved in selling the new party name, the
National Party was awarded the Public Relations Industry
Association Award for 1974.

First electoral successes

In the early federal election that followed later that year, the
National Party in Queensland won the seats of Capricornia,
Dawson and Leichhardt against the national tide which saw
Gough Whitlam's Labor Party returned to office. In the state
election held in December that year, the National Party won
the seat of Mount Isa with a massive swing of 14.5 per cent
against the ALP and recorded a state-wide swing of 10.5 per
cent away from the ALP, and reaped a record total of thirty-

nine seats in the state parliament, only three short of a majority in the party's own right. The ALP in Queensland was reduced to a meagre eleven members in the state parliament. Most importantly for the party, it held its ground on the Gold Coast and won the Brisbane seat of Wynnum and the near-Brisbane seat of Ipswich West. The party's first-ever Aboriginal candidate, Mr Eric Deeral, also won the marginal Labor seat of Cook.

In the following federal double dissolution election in 1975, the party lost Capricornia to the ALP. In the following state election in 1977, the party lost Surfers Paradise to the Liberal Party when the Labor Party switched the direction of its preferences, and the marginal seats of Wynnum, Ipswich West and Cook went back to Labor. Overall, however, the party recorded a state aggregate vote of 26.24 per cent compared with 24.62 percent recorded by the Liberal Party, consolidating the party's position as the rightful major partner on both a seat and state-vote basis. The party's vote gave it thirty-five state seats compared with twenty-four held by the Liberal Party. In the federal election, however, the Liberal Party had polled 27.9 per cent of the state vote compared with 25.7 per cent by the Nationals, indicating that many Queenslanders were voting Liberal in the federal arena and switching to the Nationals in the state.

Liberals retaliate

The 1977 campaign was a satisfying result for the National Party. It did not receive the metropolitan vote it had hoped for, but it did consolidate its positions in a number of key provincial cities. However, it was a campaign marred by dispute between the Liberal and National parties over the issue of three-cornered contests.

The Liberal Party, under pressure from the Nationals for the support of its traditional heartland vote, had decided to hit back with three-cornered contests against sitting National Party members in seven seats, namely, Cooroora, Ipswich West, Isis, Redcliffe, Redlands, Surfers Paradise and Townsville West. Sparkes and the National Party were furious about what they termed was a misguided waste of anti-socialist resources. "This Liberal Party three-cornered assault against the National Party did not add a single solitary seat to the anti-socialist parties' parliamentary representation, but it did involve an appalling waste of manpower and money, and in addition created such serious friction between the two coalition parties – friction which continues to strain relations between us," Sparkes said. In public the Liberal Party supported their stand by claiming that their involvement in such three-cornered contests would boost the anti-socialist vote. The National Party dismissed this as pure party political propaganda and even went to the stage of suggesting that the Liberals had in fact run "dead" in Wynnum, where they recorded a meagre 7.28 per cent of the vote, as had been the case in Capricornia at the previous federal election where the Liberal candidate had polled only 5.88 per cent and the National Party lost the seat.

The battle for the near-Brisbane seat of Redcliffe on the north coast, which was held for the National Party by the Speaker of the House, Mr Jim Houghton, was the most bitterly contested. Notably, the Liberal candidate at the time was Terry White. Sparkes hit out at this aggressive effort by the Liberals: "If some of the thousands of dollars spent by the Liberal Party in the futile attempt to take the seat of Redcliffe from the sitting member and Speaker of the parliament, Jim Houghton, had been spent on the Liberal seat of Maryborough, Gilbert Alison [Liberal] may not have lost that seat by a handful of votes to the ALP."

"Surely the most blindly committed supporter of three-cornered contests involving sitting coalition party members must now perceive their utter futility and folly," Sparkes told the 1978 State Conference of the National Party in Brisbane. "Certainly the vast majority of business organisations that contribute election funds to the National and Liberal parties now realize that three-cornered contests do not advance the anti-socialist cause one iota. In fact, they bitterly object – and quite rightly so – to their money being squandered on fights between the two anti-socialist parties instead of being used against the common enemy – the ALP socialists." This statement by Sparkes was specifically designed to hit at the hip-pocket nerve of the Liberal Party. The battle for urban electoral support is heavily dependent on out-Liberalling the

Liberals in the area of attracting the big financial backing needed to wage the increasingly expensive campaigns. A dyed-in-the-wool conservative, Sparkes correctly realized that wasting hard-to-get supporters' funds was the quickest way to lose friends in the big-business sector of city politics.

Separate Senate ticket

In 1978, the Liberals also took the bold decision to run a separate Senate ticket, a decision seen in some quarters as another knee-jerk reaction to the Nationals' intrusion into Liberal Party territory and in other quarters as pure political opportunism. This decision gravely concerned the National Party at both state and federal levels and brought the Queensland Liberal Party into direct conflict with its federal parliamentary organization which staunchly opposed the separate Senate ticket proposal. Sparkes hit back: "I am seriously concerned that the Liberal Party's policy of attacking its coalition partner in three-cornered contests and its recently announced decision to run a separate Senate team instead of the traditional National–Liberal team indicates a declining support by the Liberal Party for the concept of coalition government."

Sparkes continued to assert that there remained ample opportunities for both the coalition partners to win seats from the ALP. In such contests he believed that the partners should work together in three-cornered contests and support each other. He believed, however, that once one of the partners won a seat, in the interests of coalition harmony the other partner should not attempt to take that seat away. The validity of this argument is not widely accepted, however, outside National Party ranks, and is considered more in the area of "coalition ethics" rather than valid political argument, because there can be no doubt that in some cases the involvement of the two coalition partners in a contest is needed to maximize the coalition vote. In such cases, Sparkes argues that the sitting member must first accept the involvement of a candidate from the other coalition party. Again, it is a matter of "political ethics" and is purely in the interests of fostering harmonious coalition relations. Most Liberal coalitionists share

Queensland National Party boss Sir Robert Sparkes and his Liberal Party counterpart, Dr John Herron, sharing a joke. Throughout the 1983 state election campaign the two presidents had little to joke about, however. (Photograph courtesy of Queensland Newspapers Pty Ltd)

this view, the most notable being Kevin Cairns who called on the Nationals twice to assist in holding his marginal inner-Brisbane seat of Lilley.

Providing further ammunition for Sparkes' attack on the Queensland state Liberal Party for their increasing divisive tactics was the post-election decision by Malcolm Fraser in 1975 to continue the federal coalition with the National Party despite the fact that he had won sufficient seats in his own right to govern alone. This decision angered many Liberals in Queensland who saw it as an opportunity to stem the tide of National Party advancement. "If it were not for the close rapport which Malcolm Fraser had with Doug Anthony and other senior National Party ministers, I do not think we would be in the present Federal Government at all — a very unsatisfactory situation, but still one to be preferred to the total impotence and ineffectuality of sitting on the crossbenches," Sparkes acknowledged in 1976. He added the belief that, unless the federal party did not soon emulate the lead set by the Queensland party and shed its rural sectional image and generally broaden its image, it would be doomed.

Despite its lack of members in the federal government, there were some notable achievements for the party federally that year. The Queensland National Party initiative of abolishing death duties had been carried through federally and the re-introduction of the fuel price equalization scheme had been implemented — both personal triumphs for Robert Sparkes.

Financial difficulties

The rash of elections and the federal referenda from the time of the name change had placed the National Party in serious financial straits by 1978. The operations of the party were slipping behind at the rate of about $2,500 a month, in addition to a sizeable shortfall in the previous federal election budget which still had to be cleared. The situation annoyed Sparkes and leading Nationals more than anything at the time. "When one considers the millions of dollars that people we represent have at stake in the free enterprise democratic system, it is as incredible as it is deplorable that we suffer a chronic shortage of funds," he said. "This shortage not only restricts our capacity to mount effective election campaigns, but now threatens the viability of our organization."

The cost of the National Party's push into the city was certainly more than the old Country Party stalwarts had ever envisaged. Defending blue-ribbon rural seats is a comparatively inexpensive exercise by comparison with mounting statewide campaigns to include urban areas of the state. There were still some within the party, however, who continued to believe that the city push was a colossal waste of time and funds. To this Sparkes replied: "You should remind the cynics and the critics that support for the party is not only warranted by our many positive achievements, but also by the fact that the party has prevented the occurrence of many things that would have been positively harmful."

It was the spiralling cost of running their now metropolitan-based statewide political machine that worried the Nationals. Despite the handful of critics, there was no turning back. So Sparkes hammered home the message to the party faithful: "The future of our party is at stake! Make no mistake, if our party fails through lack of finance, we will all suffer incalculable harm."

The matter of financing the National Party's Queensland operation continued to plague the party through 1978 and 1979. During 1978, however, the party moved positively to overcome, in a lasting sense, the continuing worrying state of its financial instability. The party's membership was the most extensive of any political party in the state, but membership fees alone were not sufficient. An increase in membership fees and a statewide drive undertaken by the specially appointed membership director, Neville Harper, did improve the situation but still not sufficiently to provide a lasting solution. The establishment of the Sir Francis Nicklin Fellowship and life subscriptions at $300 each helped a little further, but still the problem of long-term financial security was unsolved.

At this point the party once again looked at the possibility of a major statewide drive for funds. They had previously considered such a move but thought it too ambitious. Finally, they decided to again discuss the matter with fund-raising consultants Compton Associates Pty Ltd, to advise them on how such a drive could be undertaken. Everald Compton, the managing director of the company, addressed the Management Committee meeting held in the party's rented accommodation on the corner of Leichhardt Street and Upper Edward Street in Brisbane.

The Bjelke-Petersen Foundation

It was later decided to engage Compton Associates to conduct a statewide survey on the prospects of mounting a major drive for funds. Compton described what eventuated in an article written for the *Fundraising Australia* publication issued in March 1981:

> It became very evident during the feasibility study that the personality of the Premier was, among Free Enterprise believers, the key issue in their support of the National Party at that time. There were influential people who were not party members, who felt that the Premier was good for the State and they said that they would support any campaign that would help to keep his political philosophy alive in the State. While there were many wealthy people who wanted to support the Premier, I found that his support covered people in all income brackets and, in fact, there were many little old ladies who idolized him. I would have had to have been totally blind not to be able to see that a vast amount of money could be raised in a fund-raising program that was based on the Premier's name, and it could be raised from a relatively few people. It was therefore my own personal recommendation that the Bjelke-Petersen Foundation should be established and it was I who recommended to the Premier that he should go along with the concept. If I had my time over again, I would still recommend the same thing because it was the personality of the Premier which drew the support which came to the Foundation.

Everald Compton's other recommendation was that the funds of the Bjelke-Petersen Foundation should be invested in bricks and mortar — buildings around the state of Queensland that would carry the National Party name as symbols to local contributors who supported the Foundation.

Compton then set up a state network of committees aimed at approaching a target group of a couple of thousand potential donors. Prominent citizens who were known supporters of the premier and who were prepared themselves to donate were approached and asked to chair local committees. Each of the people recruited on to the local committees was then asked to go out and find five others who would be prepared to donate — the simple but effective technique of pyramid selling based on prominent centres of influence. For many party people (even the top office bearers), who were unused to asking for funds at this level, it was a shock to the system. Some like Sir Robert Sparkes were to be surprised at how easy it was.

In an attempt to avoid any criticism, which was recognized as inevitable anyway, Sparkes and the premier with the support of the State Management Committee empowered Everald Compton to personally retain the authority to accept or reject any donation that was received. Compton revealed in his *Fundraising Australia* article that he did in fact reject several offers which he considered were quite clearly undesirable. Despite this precaution, however, the criticisms inevitably flowed. The criticism from the party's political opponents was expected. A statement by expelled former party member Lindsay Hartwig, MLA, that he was asked to contribute $10,000 to the Bjelke-Petersen Foundation received wide publicity but little credence in National Party ranks. Hartwig was reported to have said in a Rockhampton *Morning Bulletin* article, published on 11 September 1982, that he had been asked by a person whom he declined to name to write to 250 people in his electorate seeking donations of $500 each for the Foundation, but he refused to do so. In the same article Hartwig was reported to have said: "I feel now that because I didn't donate any money to the Foundation, it was probably one reason why I was eventually squeezed out of the party." Sir Robert Sparkes described Hartwig's claims as "rubbish", adding: "He is embittered about not being made a cabinet minister and that's all." Hartwig was expelled by the party in May 1981 for alleged disloyalty after a running battle with the State Management Committee of the party over many months.

At the height of the uproar over the Bjelke-Petersen Foundation, the now Labor Party leader in Queensland, Keith Wright, who was emotionally described in a *Sydney Morning Herald* article as a "devout Baptist and the Labor member for Rockhampton", said that the Bjelke-Petersen Foundation was "an example of extortion at its worst". Two Liberal members of parliament, Dr Norman Scott-Young (Townsville) and Terry Gygar (Stafford) said that they wanted to see a Royal Commission which would at least clear the air. Queensland Liberal Party state director Stephen Litchfield was reported to have said: "The claim being made is that if you support the National Party you will get somewhere. People are frightened to be anything but National if they wish to do business with the government." Litchfield later said that the National Party was "selling itself and the government to the highest bidder". In a further statement, Keith Wright said, "If we are going to make analogies here, it was the analogy of the Mafia and the Godfather. It's an offer you can't refuse."

Throughout the weeks that followed, the Foundation received sensational nationwide media coverage as political opponents of the party sought to bring the Foundation into disrepute. Everald Compton in his *Fundraising Australia* article, however, probably best sums up the realities behind all the noise: "Now that the dust has finally settled, it is clear that no one took any notice of the Bjelke-Petersen Foundation until it was successful. The other political parties ignored it, even joked about it, saying there was no one in Queensland who would want to give any money to the Premier. When the word got around that more than a million dollars had been pledged, a panic started among the other parties and it was found to be politically expedient to try to find something wrong with the Foundation at all costs." Compton went on to say: "When allegations were made that people had been blackmailed and forced to make gifts, I asked all informants to give me names and addresses so that I could personally ensure that their gifts were returned. Despite constant requests, no names were ever supplied."

In judging the Bjelke-Petersen Foundation it is important to note that among Compton Associates' clients prior to the firm establishing the Bjelke-Petersen Foundation were a number of prominent church groups, the ALP's John Curtin House fund-raising programme and the Social Credit Political League of New Zealand. In addition to this, the ALP in Queensland has since launched its own Alpha Foundation and the Liberal Party has had its Menzies Foundation. Everald Compton was also engaged by the Liberal Party to head its fund-raising effort for that party's Brisbane City Council election campaign in 1982.

In the Bjelke-Petersen Foundation issue, the National Party has had the last laugh, and the long-term financial security that Sparkes sought for the party has been realized. The Foundation today owns a three-storey building in the main street of Southport, its party headquarters (Bjelke-Petersen House at 6 St Pauls Terrace, Brisbane), a two-storey building in Rockhampton and a similar structure in Townsville. In addition to this, the Foundation owns a prime block of real estate in Cairns. The Foundation's assets are conservatively valued today in excess of $1 million, taking into consideration the increase in value of the properties from when they were originally purchased.

One negative point to come out of the Bjelke-Petersen Foundation which caused concern to the National Party was the damage done to the reputation of some individuals who were named under the privilege of parliament as having supposedly bought favours with donations. "Seldom in my thirty years of political involvement have I seen the misuse and abuse of parliamentary privilege more openly, more blatantly, or more often than in recent times," Sir Robert Sparkes commented on the way the parliament was used to attack the Foundation.

What damage the attacks from the Liberal Party had on turning away future donors from their own fund-raising campaigns is a matter of conjecture. Under a system in which all political parties rely on the generosity of many anonymous donors to continue their activities, it was surprising how little regard was given to this aspect. From a National Party point of view, however, there appears little indication that the public criticism has damaged the party's fund-raising activities; in fact, there is one school of opinion that believes that it has had the reverse effect.

Florence Bjelke-Petersen's endorsement

Few "sour grapes" issues survive the test of time in politics. There is always something more important that arises, and public attention is subsequently diverted. And almost guaranteeing this is the reality that in the past decade life in

Queensland politics has never been short of new and explosive issues. In this instance, it was the decision by Florence Bjelke-Petersen to nominate for preselection on the party's Senate team. This followed the announcement by the Liberal Party that it would be fielding a Senate team separate from the Nationals for the first time and that the party president, Yvonne McComb, would be seeking endorsement on that team. "If Mrs McComb wants to break tradition, we'll see what she thinks about running against Florence," Premier Joh said in response. And so yet another heated chapter in Queensland politics was launched and, conveniently, the Bjelke-Petersen Foundation was moved off the front pages.

Florence Bjelke-Petersen was undoubtedly then, as she is today, the best known of National Party women. A private survey commissioned at the height of the arguing and used to support her bid for preselection in fact gave her a 90 per cent-plus recognition rating compared with 10 per cent for the party's no. 1 senator, Ron Maunsell. In addition to this she was also the wife of the premier, arguably the most effective numbers man in the party, second only to Sir Robert Sparkes if he is second to anyone.

In the cold, hard facts of political life, there was much to argue in favour of Florence Bjelke-Petersen gaining endorsement for the Senate team at the expense of one of the party's sitting senators, but there was the extremely difficult matter of actually dumping a senator. Someone would have to lose and it didn't look like being Florence Bjelke-Petersen. Now the boot was really on the other foot for Sparkes and his state management team who had long preached loyalty to the rank and file. It was to prove one of the most difficult and internally damaging debates of the past decade. The senators in the hot seat were Ron Maunsell from Cairns in the far north of Queensland and Dr Glennister Sheil from Brisbane. The subsequent federal election campaign, however, spearheaded by Florence Bjelke-Petersen in the no. 1 Senate spot as leader of the National Party Senate team, soundly indicated the wisdom of the decision. The defeat of senators Maunsell and Sheil, however, caused considerable resentment.

72   *In Their Own Right*

Worsening problems in the north

The 1980 state elections again saw the Nationals hold the ground won in 1974 and consolidated in 1977. For the first time there were signs of a increasing party vote in the Brisbane metropolitan area, although the party did not win any Brisbane seats. The party did, however, regain Surfers Paradise from the Liberal Party in a clean sweep of the south-coast seats from Redlands and Fassifern through to the Queensland–New South Wales border seat of South Coast held by Russell Hinze. The North Queensland seats of Mourilyan (Vickie Kippin) and Townsville West (Hon. Max Hooper) were, however, lost.

The loss of Max Hooper's seat of Townsville West exacerbated problems in the north which had flared over the relegation of Ron Maunsell to further down the Senate ticket and his subsequent defeat. Making matters worse in the north, two senior ministers, deputy leader Ron Camm and Minister for Police Tom Newbery, resigned prior to the state poll. The National Party held their seats but the north had now lost three ministers and a senator in the space of a couple of months. The only remaining minister in the north was Val Bird, MLA (Burdekin), Minister for Northern Development, but he had decided through pressure of his portfolio responsibilities to move residence to Brisbane.

The north's dissipated cabinet strength was immediately pounced upon by the northern media and political opponents of the National Party. In 1981, before he was expelled by the party, Lindsay Hartwig even suggested that the north's lack of representation in the new Bjelke-Petersen cabinet was grounds for a breakaway re-formation of the old Country Party in the north. Lindsay Hartwig had few supporters for his proposal, however, and after a run in the media the issue fizzled. The problem of not having what the north described as "fair representation" in the cabinet, however, continued to be a running sore in the north.

The problems of the north were not helped either by the inability of former senator Ron Maunsell to gain a prominent position on the 1983 Senate team. He and former senator Glen Sheil were beaten for the favoured third place on the team behind Senator Florence Bjelke-Petersen by little known

Wynnum businessman and party zone vice-president Ron Boswell. Former Young Nationals president Mike Behan won the third, active position on the ticket.

The remarkable success of Florence Bjelke-Petersen throughout her first term in the Senate, however, over-shadowed the problems of the north. It was hard to criticize success, especially as she was making inroads into Brisbane, where no previous National Party candidate had succeeded. With Florence Bjelke-Petersen at the head of the Nationals' Senate team, the party's vote leapt from the order of 25–26 per cent to 33–34 per cent. Much of the gain was in the Brisbane metropolitan area. The added vote was enough to win back the Nationals' third Senate seat in the poll that was eventually held on 5 March 1983. From a state National Party point of view, it was now just a matter of converting the Senate vote for Florence Bjelke-Petersen into votes for National Party state candidates in the Brisbane city area.

By the end of the decade of expansion in 1983, there was no doubt that Mr Sparkes' National Party had arrived in the cities of Queensland. They were still a long way from the ideal they sought, but the "cows and corn" image of the sixties was gone.

4

The Coalition

History has recorded that the twenty-six-year coalition between the Nationals and the Liberals in Queensland, which finally shattered in August 1983, has indeed been a restless coalition for most of its duration. One could expect, in fact, that the Queensland electorate had by this time become immune to the periodic eruptions within the coalition ranks, which in the past had always been settled without any real damage to the government of the state. However, this time it was different.

The National Party (the then Country Party)–Liberal Party coalition in Queensland was established in 1957 in the wake of the historic split in the Queensland Labor Party over the issue of three weeks annual leave. On 24 April 1957, the then ALP premier, Vince Gair, was expelled by the Queensland Central Executive of the Labor Party for refusing to implement Labor Party Convention decisions on the issue. On 12 June 1957, the Gair government was refused supply by forty-five votes to twenty-five when the Liberal and Country parties voted with the ALP. Gair was forced to an election, and on 3 August 1957 his government was defeated. The Country Party won twenty-four of the seats in the state parliament to eighteen by the Liberal Party. And on 8 August the first coalition ministry was formed under the leadership of Frank Nicklin (ACP). The Country Party took the premiership because of its greater numbers.

Early agreements and disagreements

The general concensus of the coalition agreement reached between the two parties at that time was that, for parliamentary purposes, the two parties in government should act as a united force. It was accepted that the Country Party, because of the make-up of its parliamentary representation, "essentially" represented the interests of people living outside the capital city of Brisbane, while the Liberals "essentially" represented the interests of the people living in the metropolitan area. Throughout the twenty-six years that the coalition endured up to the 1983 split, this situation "essentially" did not change very much. It was really the *threat* of change that continually rocked the boat and muddied the waters. In the lead-up to the 1963 state elections, the two parties actually did agree to a seat entitlement, which not only protected sitting members from being challenged but also "defined" the seats which each party would contest based on the distribution of candidates in 1960.

In April 1965 the Liberal party, however, decided to break with the 1963 agreement and announced that it would contest seats against sitting Country Party members. The following state elections in 1966 witnessed the first of three-cornered contests involving sitting Country Party members in Albert, Murrumba and Redcliffe. The National Party held all three seats contested by the Liberals. The experience, however, left deep and bitter divisions and its mark on future coalition relations.

In 1969 the Liberals renewed their efforts to win Redcliffe and Albert and this time the seat of South Coast, but again the Country Party held its ground. In 1972 the Liberals again contested Redcliffe against Jim Houghton and again ran against the sitting National Party member, Russ Hinze, in South Coast and also against Mike Ahern in Landsborough. Again they were unsuccessful.

In 1974, the concern over the common enemy in Canberra restored harmony to the coalition ranks and, for the first time since 1966, the Liberal Party did not stand candidates against sitting National Party members. It is interesting to note, however, that the two parties did contest nineteen seats together in 1974, indicating that there was still adequate fertile ground to farm without encroaching on each other's turf. Staunch coalitionists were quick to herald the landslide 1974 result for the coalition in Queensland as clear evidence of the importance of working together. Dissident Liberals, however, were still not convinced, and preferred to believe that it was public opinion against the Labor Party in Canberra that caused the massive swing in Queensland. In 1974 also the Liberal Party argument was weakened by the request from the Liberal member for Lilley, Kevin Cairns, MHR, for the Nationals to field a candidate in Lilley to assist in holding off a Labor challenge.

Kevin Cairns repeated his request for assistance from the National Party in 1977 and, although he did hold the seat in his own right, the National Party spent considerable funds and effort to assist.

In 1976, the state saw by-elections in Lockyer (Sir Gordon Chalk) and Clayfield, two seats held by the Liberal Party. As far as the Nationals were concerned the tradition of "defined" areas of interest, established in 1963, had already been ripped to shreds by their coalition partners when they had repeatedly campaigned against sitting National Party members. As there was now no sitting Liberal member in either of these seats, the National Party felt justified in seeking to win both. Surprisingly for the Nationals, they won neither, despite the fact that they ran two exceptionally well known candidates: Neville Adermann (son of Country Party stalwart the late Sir Charles Adermann and brother of the then federal minister Evan Adermann) in Lockyer, and party executive director Mike Evans in Clayfield.

The four-day government

The coalition up to 1968 under Frank Nicklin and later Jack Pizzey had its moments, but it suffered from none of the tensions that have beset the alliance throughout the premiership of Joh Bjelke-Petersen. During the fifteen years to the 1983 split, through the terms of four Liberal parliamentary leaders and four party presidents, the rifts have progressively deepened.

Bjelke-Petersen's premiership got off to a bad start and,

knowing the man he is, it is almost certain that after such a rocky start he was unlikely to allow himself to be placed in that situation again. Firstly, it was the matter of the Governor of the day nominating minority Liberal leader Sir Gordon Chalk to form a government until the Country Party got its act together after the surprise death of Jack Pizzey in 1968. Chalk had long cherished the thought of being premier, and rumours were rife that he would go to any lengths to hold on to the position, even against the odds. He had the substantial backing of the influential Brisbane-based business community, and general public opinion at the time supported his claim that he was the best-qualified man to lead the state. There was even talk that he would join the Country Party to ensure his numbers. His reign in the top job, however, lasted only four days. He did not join the Country Party, and when the vote was taken the Country Party voted en bloc and Bjelke-Petersen was elected. From that day onward, Premier Joh Bjelke-Petersen never let Gordon Chalk's ambitions stray far from his mind. In the words of long-serving, colourful independent Tom Aikens (Townsville South): "If your enemy be an ant, think of him as an elephant."

Unquestionably, the tensions have been largely due to the ambitions and success of the Country Party since the days of the name change to the National Party. As the Nationals won increasing public support throughout the state, the coalition that started with two parties of equal political stocks became increasingly like a business partnership between a prince and a pauper. The Liberals were simply not matching the Nationals' electoral success, and in the business where might is always right they were placed under greater and greater pressure from within their own ranks to survive. Throughout the period of deteriorating relationships, the Liberals, like the Labor Party, continually struggled to find reasons for their weakening position. The supposed gerrymandering of the Queensland electoral system became the favourite excuse, but under scrutiny it was an excuse that could not be substantiated. The Hanlon Labor Party government in 1949 had introduced the zonal system of electoral distribution and only on rare occasions were the Liberals able to gain political capital outside of the extreme south-east corner of the state.

Internal and external tensions

The tensions have increased since 1976, when Yvonne Mc-
Comb succeeded to the state presidency of the Liberal Party
after John Moore won the seat of Ryan in the 1975 federal
election. Moore and Sparkes had a good rapport dating back
to their youth. In fact, Sparkes had been a senior prefect and
Moore had been a junior prefect at Southport College. (An interesting aside to their relationship is the story that John
Moore often told about how Sparkes had Moore make his bed
for a week on one occasion, after Sparkes, the senior prefect,
had disciplined the younger Moore for some minor schoolboy
misdemeanour.) This was to be different under Yvonne Mc-
Comb. (Sparkes has often said jokingly − but there could be
some truth in the comment − that he finds it "difficult to deal
with females in politics".)

Mrs McComb publicly declared during 1976, "I'm strong on
competition. Electors are just as well served by having a
choice; competition in seats is important," foreshadowing her
commitment to wider competition with the National Party
during her term as state president. Yvonne McComb's senti-
ments were not totally accepted within Liberal Party ranks,
however, and the new parliamentary leader, Bill Knox, was
one who was not in favour of increasing tensions within the
coalition. But Yvonne McComb had the numbers.

In 1977 more tensions arose in the Queensland coalition
following the decision by the Fraser government to hold
referenda on a number of issues, including casual Senate
vacancies and votes for Territorians in referenda. Surprisingly, this caused most problems for the Nationals. The party
split down the middle over the referenda and prominent State
Management Committee member and Joh man Bill Siller
subsequently resigned his position. It was a severe setback for
the party in the metropolitan area and caused grave concerns
throughout the state. On the one hand the premier and his
supporters were opposed to the referenda questions, while on
the other Sparkes and his supporters were prepared to go
along with Malcolm Fraser and Doug Anthony for a "yes" vote.
In a compromise decision, the Central Council of the National
Party carried the following motion in an attempt to accom-
modate the two factions: "That this Council notes that the

State Management Committee has decided to support a 'yes' vote in the forthcoming Referenda and that the National Party State Parliamentary wing has decided to adopt a contrary stance; and further this Council recognizes that both these components were constitutionally entitled to so decide; and further the Council affirms its complete confidence in and support for the leadership of the Premier and the State President." This was a masterful display of political compromise. Sparkes moved the resolution and Bjelke-Petersen seconded it. Until the referenda were decided, however, that was about the only agreement reached on the issue by the two sides.

In proposing the referenda, the federal Liberal Party was asking the National Party to support issues which were not dissimilar to ones, only a short time previously, the parties together had rejected when proposed by the Whitlam Labor government. The premier and a substantial section of the rank and file of the National Party did not buy this move, which they interpreted as being for pure political convenience. The same people were surprised that Fraser and Anthony were able to sell the idea to Sparkes and the State Management Committee. On this point, however, it is probably worth remembering Sparkes' comment that it is better to stay in government than to sit on the crossbenches. Sparkes would also argue that Malcolm Fraser's decision to accept the Queensland National Party's proposal to abolish federal death duties in July 1977 more than compensated for any support he might have had to give the referenda debate against Bjelke-Petersen's best advice. The premier had championed the death duties issue in the Queensland parliament a year earlier.

The referenda issue caused a serious deterioration of the relationship between the premier and Sparkes which was to endure for many months. Throughout this period, the premier continued to attend State Management Committee meetings, but at times you could have cut the air with a knife. It was obvious that the premier believed very deeply that there was a need for the top echelons of the party to realign themselves in his direction. He has always seen his role as the political front man for the party in Queensland, and he believes that his first responsibility is to the people of the state. That position often required him to stand against decisions taken in Canberra, regardless of who was in power at the time. It was a difficult time for the Nationals — both Sparkes and Bjelke-Petersen are determined men when they believe they are right.

Liberal revival and more problems

Aggravating matters for the Nationals throughout 1977 was the revival of spirits within the Liberal Party following their successes in Lockyer and Clayfield. Lockyer in particular was a great boost to their pride, despite the fact that Gordon Chalk had held the seat for many years. The Nationals long believed that they held a mortgage on this blue-ribbon rural electorate and it was only a matter of waiting until Chalk retired before returning it to the fold.

In Lockyer the Nationals waged an aggressive campaign on the issue of law and order, while in Clayfield Mike Evans thumped the stump on the widely popular issue of the Nationals' support for the abolition of death duties which the former Liberal leader and treasurer, Sir Gordon Chalk, had opposed. The Nationals had everything going for them to win, but they didn't.

That year also saw the continuation of the political drama over the police raid on the hippie commune at Cedar Bay, and the aftermath of the resignation of Police Commissioner Ray Whitrod who claimed that copies of his reports on Cedar Bay had been destroyed by National Party police minister, Tom Newberry.

So concerned was Sparkes at the developments within the party that he was prompted to deliver one of his most notable speeches at the tense Mount Isa State Conference held in July that year. It was another "at the crossroads" speech from Sparkes. "Periodically, in their destinies, all individuals and organizations come to crossroads where they have to make momentous decisions as to their future course of action," Sparkes said. "The National Party reached such a crossroad in this state a few years ago, when it had to decide either to remain as it was, or broaden its image and character and become a truly 'national' party concerned with and acceptable to all sections of the community. Now we have reached another major crossroad, and decisions we take will deter-

mine not only whether or not the party continues as a powerful political force, but in fact whether or not we survive as a
significant force at all."

It was shock treatment to the 400-plus delegates assembled
1500 kilometres from Brisbane in the remote north-west. "Unfortunately," Sparkes continued, "history reveals all too often
the pinnacle of power is the point at which decline begins."
Sparkes was aiming his remarks squarely at dissident factions
within the party who had been upset by the amount of money
fruitlessly spent in the attempt to win Clayfield and whose
activity within the party indicated that they felt there should
be a return to old Country Party ways. "Our capacity to survive," Sparkes drove home his point, "depends very largely on
our ability to perceive and assess these fateful crossroads
situations and to make the right decisions at the time."

He then pressed on to resell the decision for the name
change and the success it had brought the party. "In short, we
must always endeavour to hold sufficient seats to ensure that
we are included in all anti-socialist governments by right and
not merely by invitation; and with the ever-increasing
preponderence of urban seats that simply means we must get
in and win and hold our share of these seats."

Solidarity against criticism

It is notable that Sparkes, in the above speech, avoided saying
that the party had to be the dominant partner in any such anti-
socialist government — a reference to the fact that in the
federal government his party was there by invitation and not
by right. "Politics is a numbers game. Never let us forget, and
as long as I am your leader I will never let you forget, that in
the final analysis politics is a numbers game," Sparkes said at
Mount Isa. "Good politics and objectives are nothing more
than pious verbiage unless we have the numbers in parliament to translate all or at least some of them into reality."

From his shock tactic, Sparkes launched into the party standard of unity and solidarity, and then proceeded to the matter
that was to prove to be his greatest concern for the next three
years — the matter of the National Party's growing ultra-
conservative image. "I come now to the most serious danger —

the concerted and determined campaign by our political opponents, aided by some hostile sections of the media, to portray the National Party as an ultra-conservative, almost fascist party totally opposed to any worthwhile social, political or economic changes." He later concluded, "Right-wing people will naturally support us, but in addition we must secure the support of a significant proportion of 'middle-of-the-road' people. To achieve this support we must get rid of our propaganda-created, ultra-conservative and fascist image. We must be innovative and, short of compromising our fundamental principles, we must studiously avoid any statements or actions which suggest an extreme right-wing posture."

The Nationals' concern about being cast in the mould of ultra-conservative and even fascist was made more difficult by the rising tide of union and social unrest across the nation during 1977 and the divisive uranium debate. Premier Bjelke-Petersen was at the forefront of government action against militancy, and was thus clearly an easy target for the more liberal elements of the media who sought to cast him in the role of a "jack boots" authoritarian.

In his address to the Mount Isa State Conference, the premier reported confidently the good news that at his level the coalition was working well. "Bill Knox and myself work very closely on all issues," he said. He offered no hope, however, that he would be softening his stand against the unions. "The militant and communist union leaders must be halted as they are bent on dominating and destroying our economy with unrealistic demands they make and the subsequent stoppages and strikes. The unrest is affecting everyone." Using the achievements of his coalition government over the years since it came to power in 1957, he justified the need for his continued strong stand. His only deviation was to distinguish the militant leaders from other sections of the union movement. "We must stand behind moderate union leaders, the rank and file and employers who refuse to be stood over and intimidated by the Hamiltons, Carmichaels, Halfpennys, Mundys, Elliotts and other communist union bosses," he said. It is a tack that he has used often and which has won him wide support among conservative unionists.

Militancy continued after the Nationals' State Conference

and, in fact, worsened in the run-up to the 1977 state election. The controversial "street march" debate was a rallying point for the growing campaign against Joh Bjelke-Petersen and his style of government. It was also a rallying point for Liberal Party efforts to distance themselves from the "authoritarian image" of the Nationals. It did nothing to foster improved relations between the two coalition partners.

Crows and blackmail

As the campaign for the 1977 election hotted up, it seemed to all that things were going from bad to worse for Premier Bjelke-Petersen and the Nationals. His widely publicized press secretary, Allen Callaghan, was unavailable to tour with him as his principal media adviser, and on the northern and western tour that he undertook it seemed that he was really starting to encounter serious problems with the media. In Mount Isa he was baited on the funding of the Lake Julius dam, and in his normal forthright style he said that if the people of Mount Isa wanted support from his government then he expected their support in return. "Blackmail" was the headline. Then it was on to central Queensland to the electorate of Warrego, where a former Miss Australia questioned the premier on his stand against uranium protestors. The premier responded with his widely used jibe: "If you fly with the crows, squark like a crow and look like a crow, don't complain if you get shot at." The headlines read: "Joh Calls Miss Australia a Crow." One reporter even went on to ask if Joh really intended to shoot people who didn't agree with him. Such was the mood of the media at the time. The "Jack Boots Bjelke" campaign was sure-fire sensational copy.

In the light of these developments, the Queensland Liberal Party sought to distance itself even further from Premier Bjelke-Petersen and the National Party. Campaign advertising showing Liberal leader Bill Knox and Joh Bjelke-Petersen together was dropped.

Aboriginal backlash

On top of all this, a national "scandal" was being fuelled by the media over the supposed ill-treatment of Aboriginals in Queensland. The Bjelke-Petersen government had moved in to stop a federally financed trachoma treatment campaign among North Queensland Aboriginals in the politically sensitive seats of Mount Isa and Cook, both held by the National Party. Two Aboriginal workers on the programme were known Labor Party sympathisers. Quite amazingly, the tide turned almost overnight for Bjelke-Petersen. This Aboriginal issue virtually wiped out the entire anti-Bjelke-Petersen campaign. Aboriginal issues have never been election winners in Queensland, and whatever problems had been created for the premier in the preceeding weeks this issue tipped the scales back in his favour.

In the state election that followed in 1977, the National Party lost three seats and the Liberal Party four — to Labor. The Nationals were to claim that their three seats, Murrumba, Ipswich West and Wynnum, were lost because of poor Liberal Party performances in three-cornered contests against sitting National Party members.

Liberals "get on top"

Buoyed by the nagging image problems that the Nationals experienced during 1977, the Liberal State Convention held in Toowoomba in 1978 re-elected Mrs McComb unopposed and launched into a "get on top" campaign. It was a campaign initiated by the Young Liberal organization with the support of the small "l" section of the party aimed at making the Liberals the dominant partner in the coalition after the 1980 state elections. It was a campaign that many have suggested was falsely based — the tide of the anti-Bjelke-Petersen campaign had already turned. The ALP knew this after the 1977 campaign and confessed as much in a tactically revealing article in the *Labor Review* in March 1982 headlined "Llew's Liberals the Likely Losers". The article read: "Neither Labor or Liberal can expect to blow the National Party away with a lot of huffing and puffing in or out of Parliament, nor any amount of sniping about the Nationals' wealth or the alleged Eldorado, the Bjelke-Petersen Foundation."

The "get on top" campaign was not fully supported by a

number of Liberal coalitionists, including parliamentary
leader Bill Knox. Later that year, Knox paid the price with his
job. Knox was deposed and replaced by Dr Llew Edwards.

The remnants of the image problem which endured for the
Nationals through 1978 and 1979 was sufficient to strengthen
the Liberals' resolve to push ahead and Yvonne McComb's confidence that their "get on top" ambition would be achieved.
Part of the strategy was not only to launch into wider three-
cornered contests against the Nationals but also to break with
coalition convention and field a separate Senate team for the
elections due in June 1981. So concerned were the National
Party about the development of the separate Senate team proposals that, in the lead-up to the Liberals' 1979 State Convention on the Gold Coast, the party launched an extensive advertising campaign through the media, aimed at rank-and-file
Liberals, seeking to deter them from the course of action proposed by their executive. It did not work. Yvonne McComb
was again elected unopposed and the thrust continued.
McComb emerged from the 1979 State Convention of the
Liberal Party as the undisputed "High Priestess" of Liberalism
in Queensland. She could no longer be written-off as "that
dame in a Jackie Howe singlet", as one prominent National
Party member called her after she had appeared in public
wearing a popular tank top in vogue at the time. She had considerable support within the Liberal Party for her way of
thinking and the National Party had to accept this fact of life.
To this stage, it was a common belief within the upper
echelons of the National Party that "commonsense would
prevail" in Liberal ranks and that "Malcolm (Fraser) would
pull Mrs McComb into line, once the full ramifications of her
actions were realized in Canberra".

Malcolm Fraser wasn't able to "pull Mrs McComb into line",
however, as the Nationals had hoped. In fact, Mrs McComb's
influence became such during this period that she led her
party in a decision to break convention and to run a separate
Senate ticket in the planned 1981 federal elections and later
announced that she would be a contender for preselection on
this separate Senate team. This move, together with the
deposing of Bill Knox by the new, trendy, small "l" faction
within the Liberal Party, seriously undermined her credibility
in conservative political ranks. Knox had substantial support

among the traditional Liberal Party big business community and his axing did not weigh well with these people, regardless of the reasons put forward by the small "l" faction or by Mrs McComb. The conservative sections of the Liberal Party were also increasingly of the opinion that Mrs McComb was feathering her own future parliamentary nest. Her Senate bid fuelled such speculation. What the Nationals had been unable to achieve themselves, Mrs McComb was about to bring about by her own actions.

On the ABC programme "AM", broadcast on Monday 17 September 1979, Mrs McComb argued her case for a separate Senate team. Firstly, she was asked if she thought she would get Malcolm Fraser's support for the separate Senate ticket. "Mr Fraser has said publicly that he understands that we do have problems to live with. I believe he also understands that it is an organizational decision which was made at our Convention in June 1978," she said. "The Liberal executive met last Friday, not specifically to discuss this issue, but it came up as a matter of course. The executive resolved again to go ahead and of course we know that the decision cannot be overturned unless by another convention which is due next June."

The interviewer then asked why Mrs McComb believed that a joint ticket with the National Party would be "uncomfortable" for the Liberal Party. "Because we are different in many ideological ways," she replied. "The media have picked up three — (1) is the matter of redistribution, (2) is the right of appeal [on the street march issue] and (3) is a public accounts committee." Mrs McComb continued her statement: "Now these three factors, for instance, are accepted as the norm in federal legislation. Not only the Liberal Party agrees with this, but the National Country Party [federally] also agrees with it. Of course we must remember that the Senate is particularly a states' house. Now it is somewhat uncomfortable if these matters such these three and others are of such great difference between the two parties. And I believe it up to Mr Anthony, as he federally agrees with the line that the Liberals take in these areas, to speak with his Queensland National Party and get them to become more democratic, even to join the Liberal Party and make one party throughout Australia."

The interviewer picked Mrs McComb up on the point that

she had previously rejected Mr Fraser's right to intervene in a state party matter, and asked: "Is it reasonable to expect Mr Anthony to deal with state affairs and not expect Mr Fraser to deal with state affairs?" Mrs McComb replied: "Mr Fraser has, of course, discussed the matter with us at length and I would hope that Mr Anthony would discuss it with his party too."

The differences widen

There was little hope of a National Party backdown on the three issues of contention that Mrs McComb raised, although there has always been some room for discussion on the issue of a public accounts committee. It is therefore somewhat ironic that in 1983 this should have been the issue that finally led to the coalition split. The question of a change in the zonal system of electoral redistribution has never been negotiable, and it is impossible to believe that Premier Bjelke-Petersen would accept any weakening of his stand against the militants involved in the street march issue. The main argument against a public accounts committee is one which suggests that the government should agree that it was not doing its job of properly husbanding the state's funds and resources. This was a matter of principle in which there could have been negotiable movement. The premier is opposed to the suggestion, but a number of Nationals have indicated a willingness to at least debate the issue.

The important aspect of Mrs McComb's statement was that it confirmed the Liberals' strategy of distancing themselves from the National Party. Mrs McComb could hardly have believed that all three of these issues were negotiable. As Bob Sparkes would have said, the Liberals had reached a crossroad and made a decision. Now they had to live with the repercussions — good or bad. A number of prominent Liberals thought the decision was wrong, to the extent that they were prepared to go public with their opinion. The most vocal was Jim Killen, the articulate member for Moreton (Qld) and a minister in the Fraser government. Killen suggested that the party should call a special convention to discuss the matter. In a statement released at the time, Killen said: "It is quite clear that all of the implications of a separate Senate team have not been adequately considered. It is simply not sound to contend that the executive is now merely implementing a Convention resolution. Politics is more than just a matter of wielding power. There are clear responsibilities. There are clear duties." Killen was convinced that the State Executive of the Liberal Party were over-stepping their mark. "There was precisely nothing in the decision of the 1978 Liberal Party Convention to field a separate Senate team which gave the executive the right to treat and bargain over state issues with respect to that decision."

Killen based his continuing argument on the Liberals' ability to adequately support a separate Senate team. "Away from the cities and provincial towns, Liberal Party organization in Queensland is sparse. In many areas it is simply non-existent," he said. "It is clear to ready demonstration that if the Liberal Party fields a separate Senate team approximately 800 polling booths would not be manned. That would mean that approximately 600,000 electors in Queensland would not receive Liberal how-to-vote cards." Killen went to the point of addressing the State Council of the Liberal Party at Gympie on 22 September 1979 in a last-ditch effort to have them reconsider the move.

Killen's action was supported by Prime Minister Malcolm Fraser who had called a special meeting of Queensland MHRs and senators to discuss the matter on 14 September. He stated after that meeting in a comment to the Melbourne *Age* that persistence with a separate ticket could harm the coalition and endanger seats. In the *Courier-Mail* that day the prime minister was also reported to have said that it would be intolerable if he and Mr Anthony campaigned in Queensland with separate policies for separate candidates. In the same article he said that the Liberal Party state executive was "lighting a bushfire in Queensland which would be difficult to put out".

Liberal Party deputy leader Philip Lynch, who earlier in the month had said of the Victorian Liberal Party move against the National Country Party minister Peter Nixon (Gippsland), "We need this sort of thing like a hole in the head", also added his weight to Fraser and Killen's appeal for a joint Queensland Senate ticket. "Liberals should not lose sight of their national priorities this weekend. We must not allow rivalries on the state scene to impinge on the coalition's unity and purpose at the federal level," he said in an article published in the Rockhampton *Bulletin* on 22 September.

Former Liberal senator Ian Wood (1950–1978) was another to speak out against the decision. In a letter to the editor published in the *Courier-Mail* he said: "'This might look good to some Liberals, to secure another Senate seat, but the complexity of the Senate vote can mean the loss of a seat through the donkey vote, for instance, if the National Party is at the top of the ticket and the Liberals are at the bottom, with other teams sandwiched in between." In the same letter Wood said: "Liberals such as Mrs McComb and especially Mr Litchfield and now Eric Robinson, and other state liberals are taking every opportunity to criticize the Premier and the Nationals, but not the Labor Party." He continued: "Wouldn't it be great if the Liberals ceased being in opposition, and if Mrs McComb and Mr Litchfield devoted their attention to assisting the falling Liberal membership in Queensland."

Supporting the concern of Fraser, Lynch and Killen was the fact that, at the height of the Queensland debate over the separate Senate ticket, the federal coalition government was experiencing the worst mid-term public opinion slump in twenty-five years. They trailed the ALP by 40–50 per cent. Ringing in the ears of all Liberals were the words of Sir Robert Menzies, who broke his political silence for the first time in 1973 to speak against a Victorian move for a separate Senate ticket in that state. Sir Robert had described the Victorian move as a "cardinal blunder". After his statement, the Victorian move was abandoned.

Mrs McComb and the Queensland Liberal executive were not convinced by the argument of their federal parliamentary leaders, and the party continued its commitment to a separate Senate ticket. Yvonne McComb was subsequently elected to the second position on the Liberal Party separate Senate team behind Senator Neville Bonner and ahead of Mount Isa mayor Franz Born.

The decision by Yvonne McComb to seek endorsement on the party's separate Senate ticket smacked of opportunism to many political pundits who saw the move for the separate Senate ticket in the first place being the opportunity for Mrs McComb to pick up the possible fifth Senate seat that appeared to be up for grabs between the two parties. On previous voting figures, the Liberal Party had reason to believe they were favourites. Political journalist Anne Summer, writing in the *Financial Review* of 14 September 1979, summed up National Party beliefs when she said that Mrs McComb "wants a Senate seat". National Party state president Sir Robert Sparkes, who had the task of negotiating with Mrs McComb on the issue, summed up the difficulties that he faced. "Could Mrs McComb possibly be objective in her participation in . . . negotiation, how could she genuinely seek a joint Senate ticket? – harmony between the two parties. If she is going to be a Senate candidate . . . she obviously will have the incapacity to be objective and impartial in the negotiations."

So upset were sections of the National Party by this action of alleged political opportunism, where an individual might be prepared to sacrifice the future of the coalition for short-term political ambition, that no stone was left unturned in the effort to thwart the Liberals' push for the fifth Senate seat.

Lobbying for Flo

Out of the blue, in the search for a counter to Yvonne McComb's campaign for the Senate, the suggestion was made by a Brisbane news reporter that maybe Joh should consider nominating his wife, Florence, to counter Mrs McComb. Joh liked the idea, and so started another round of exciting possibilities and problems for the Nationals.

Florence Bjelke-Petersen's bid for preselection was given its first real test of party opinion at the National Party's Central Council meeting held in the Murrayfield Room at the headquarters of Queensland Rugby Union at Ballymore on Saturday 20 October 1979. The premier and his supporters were convinced that Flo was the answer to Yvonne McComb. Surprisingly, this opinion was not enthusiastically supported by a number of Management Committee members at that time. In the final discussion Joh did not kick the goal he wanted at Ballymore that day. One of the principal speakers in favour of a Florence Bjelke-Petersen-led Senate ticket on the day was the vocal minister for Police, Racing and Main Roads, Russ

Hinze. The executive won the day, however, and had the decision held over until a special meeting of the Council at the Rydge Motel on Friday 14 December.

Between the Ballymore and Rydge Motel Central Council meetings, the question of Florence Bjelke-Petersen winning a spot on the National Party Senate team became a secondary issue. The burning question now was whether or not she would command the no. 1 position. Joh was convinced that Florence would be an outstanding vote-catcher for the party and therefore, in customary frankness, believed that the party should not hesitate to put her at the top of the ticket. It wasn't as simple as that for Sparkes and the executive. Sitting senator Ron Maunsell was the automatic choice for the no. 1 spot, while another sitting senator, Dr Glennister Sheil, was also up for re-election. A separate Senate ticket from the Liberals would make it difficult enough for Maunsell and Sheil to hold their seats, let alone for the party to win a third. Someone would almost certainly be sacrificed if Florence Bjelke-Petersen was given the no. 1 spot, and perhaps even both. It was a very difficult dilemma for the party.

The smiles weren't always there. Liberal leader and treasurer Sir Gordon Chalk dearly wanted to be premier throughout his term in office. Premier Joh was his stumbling block.

Premier Joh and his trusted deputy premier, Liberal leader Dr Llew Edwards. Even when the curtain came down on Edwards' parliamentary career, the friendship continued.

Premier Joh, Queensland's "Minister for Everything" Russ Hinze, and Brisbane Commonwealth Games chairman, Justice Ned Williams. Having men about him who could get the job done has been a hallmark of the premier's leadership.

The State Management Committee meeting prior to the December Central Council meeting at the Rydge considered the question of positioning on the Senate ticket, and finally opted to buy time for themselves to further consider the question. In a resolution moved by the now Attorney-General, Neville Harper, and seconded by Central Zone vice-president George Robertson, the question of positioning the Senate team was left unresolved until a further meeting. Subsequently, the Central Council chose Senator Maunsell, Senator Sheil and Florence Bjelke-Petersen to comprise the party's 1980 Senate team. They would have to wait seven agonizing months for the final decision on their fate.

Another important milestone in coalition relations was posted in 1979. Terence Anthony White was elected as the Liberal member for Redcliffe in a by-election held on 1 September, following the retirement of the National Party Speaker of the House, Jim Houghton. It was White's second attempt at the seat and ended a long and bitter struggle by the Liberal Party to wrest this seat away from the Nationals.

The positioning of the Senate team was left for decision until the State Conference meeting of Central Council at Surfers Paradise on 28 July 1980. Ironically, it was to be the first State Conference not to be attended by the president, Bob Sparkes, now Sir Robert Sparkes. Sparkes was in London attending his investiture. The senior vice-president, Charles Holm, presided. In the Senate preselection ballot, each candidate was again given the opportunity to address the Council before the meeting, and then the ballot was taken. The order of address was Senator Maunsell, then Senator Sheil and finally Florence Bjelke-Petersen. The order of the vote was Bjelke-Petersen, Sheil and Maunsell. For the first time in the history of the party, a sitting senator (two, in this case) had been replaced by an ordinary candidate, although there would be few who would say that Florence Bjelke-Petersen was just another ordinary candidate.

Flo turns the tide

The election of Florence Bjelke-Petersen to the head of the National Party Senate team was a turning point for the

Nationals, another crossroads where, however, for once Sir Robert Sparkes did not have to be involved in making the decision. In the final analysis, he is probably pleased that he didn't. There were continuing coalition tensions during the year and these were tightened somewhat by the surprise shift of Senator Bernie Kilgarif (N.T.) from the National Country Party to the Liberal Party. Paul Everingham had only recently taken over as chief minister in the Northern Territory and there was concern that the pro-NCP Country Liberal Party might be about to veer off towards the Liberal Party. The CLP has never liked to show a high public profile on a preference between the two coalition parties, although its members have traditionally sat with the NCP in the federal parliament.

The 1980 federal election held on 18 October was a severe setback for the Liberal Party and the federal coalition. Florence Bjelke-Petersen was elected to the Senate, but the vital fifth seat finally went to the Australian Democrats after a long, drawn-out distribution of preferences. Senators Sheil and Maunsell were not returned. Heightening tensions between the two parties on the day was the Liberal Party legal action to have the National Party remove photos of Liberal candidates from National Party Senate tickets in electorates where no National Party candidate for the House of Representatives was involved. The seat of Herbert in North Queensland was one such area where the local National Party executive sat up throughout the night to physically cut their Senate how-to-vote card in two. The National Party had opted for this move in the hope of maximizing the Senate vote, but the Liberals, on their separate Senate track, did not appreciate it.

The election was also marred by coalition squabbles over claims by the then finance minister and former Liberal state president, Eric Robinson, that the independent candidate for McPherson, former test cricket umpire Lou Rowan, was in fact a National Party "stooge", planted there to unseat him. Rowan had been a National Party member and had sought endorsement by the National Party to contest the seat as a National against Eric Robinson. There was considerable party support for the action, as Robinson was unpopular in National Party ranks, but the move was resisted. Rowan subsequently resigned and ran as an independent. A further extension of the Robinson affair was his surprise resignation from the Fraser ministry after the election.

Speaking after the Senate poll was declared, Sir Robert Sparkes soundly criticized Mrs McComb and the Liberal Party decision to run a separate Senate team. "So much for the Liberal Party claim that its separate Senate ticket strategy would maximize the coalition vote," he said. "The Senate poll highlighted the gross irresponsibility of the Liberal stance. The progressive Senate count showed that the coalition parties had the votes overall to win the fifth Senate seat in Queensland . . . but the 18.78 per cent drift of preferences from Mrs McComb, away from the coalition, has given the seat to the Democrats." Sparkes also hit out at the stance taken by Eric Robinson: "The real truth of the Liberal Party's Senate strategy was spelt out by former minister and Liberal Party state president Mr Eric Robinson, who said (quote): 'The real reason behind this is that on the night of 18 October, there it will be for all to see — the true figures showing what percentage supports the National Party in Queensland and what percentage supports the Liberals.' Well, Mr Robinson has had his way." Sparkes continued: "The National Party recorded 4 per cent more primary votes than the Liberals in the Senate election in Queensland . . . and the coalition lost a senator and the government lost control of the Senate in the process." It was the move that Prime Minister Malcolm Fraser would later say finally cost the federal Liberal–NCP coalition the government.

Dr Herron's inheritance

With Mrs McComb's move to contest the Senate elections, her position as state president was taken over by Dr John Herron. Dr Herron's approach to the Liberal leadership differed little from his predecessor. He was a strong supporter of the separate image espoused by Yvonne McComb. The only difference was his preoccupation with the supposed National Party gerrymander.

Herron inherited the problem of brushing up the Liberal image after the federal election in readiness for the state poll in December 1980, a task that wasn't helped by worsening coalition disharmony.

November was a particularly bad month for the coalition that year. Importantly for the Liberal Party it was the month that the small "l" section of the party came in for severe criticism. It now seemed that the party was splitting down the middle, with the traditional Liberal conservatives lining up on one side and the trendy small "l" section on the other. Prime Minister Malcolm Fraser, Victorian premier Dick Hamer, Hamer's predecessor, Sir Henry Bolte, and former Liberal state president A.W. Hartwig were among the conservative section that called for commonsense to prevail. The former state secretary of the Liberal Party and the minister for Aboriginal and Islander Affairs in the state parliament, Charles Porter (Toowong), publicly bucketed the trendies in the Liberal Party. "This present madness between the coalition anti-Labor parties must stop before it grows out of hand," he said. Mr Porter, whose statement appeared in the Bundaberg *News* on 14 November, also said that he was not sympathetic to the politics and methods of former Queensland Liberal Party presidents Mr Eric Robinson and Mrs Yvonne McComb, the present president, Dr John Herron, or the party's executive director, Stephen Litchfield.

It was a savage attack by Porter on his party, but it didn't stop there, for he had a sideswipe also for National Party boss Sir Robert Sparkes. "The Liberal organization, through McComb and Herron and that bunch, and the Nationals through Sparkes are trying to orchestrate the parliamentarians to do what the executive says." Ironically, Porter himself was seen as something of a "trendy" when he entered politics in 1966. What had changed his mind? "There was a vast difference between the Liberal and Country parties where we represented the country," he said. "The Country Party were agrarian socialists with their marketing boards and the Liberals represented free enterprise. Now both parties represent similar policies – private enterprise, anti-Labor – with the Liberals in the city and the Nationals in the country."

Coalition relations in November 1980 were also marred by the Liberal Party onslaught against National Party minister Russ Hinze in his seat of South Coast. The Liberal Party waged a particularly strong campaign against Hinze during which candidate Ross Woods was reported to have said that with such a large field against Mr Hinze the preferences were likely to drift everywhere, although he (Woods) expected to get his share. "But one thing most candidates seem united about is that their last preferences will go to Russ Hinze. This is what the preferential system is all about."

Hinze didn't lose his seat and National Party supremacy was not dented by the Liberal onslaught. The Nationals "got their own back" to some degree by fielding dual candidates in the seat of Lockyer, finally taking that seat away from the Liberal Party. The point of no return had been passed, with the Nationals winning three seats away from the Liberal Party in these elections: Surfers Paradise, Southport and Lockyer.

A call for sanity

The 1981 State Conference of the Young Liberals held at Kooralbyn Valley on the Australia Day weekend was the platform used by Liberal Party parliamentary leader Dr Llew Edwards to launch his bid to restore some sanity to coalition relations following the difficulties for both parties in 1980. His move put him in direct conflict with his organizational executive. Dr Edwards said that in his opinion there were no votes for the Liberals in knocking the Nationals, but Dr Herron disagreed, as he had done earlier in the year when he had disagreed with Edwards' move to go quickly back into coalition government with the Nationals after the 1980 elections. It was the beginning of the end for Dr Edwards. He was clearly out of step with the Liberal organization led by Dr Herron and the small "l" backbench section. In a letter to all branches, Dr Herron pointed out: "Although the initial attempt has been unsuccessful, there will be no turning back from this policy." In the same letter Dr Herron said that he was "sick and tired of hearing that the implementation of policies of the party is 'dictation' by the organization". A month later, however, the premier was reported in the *Courier-Mail* of 2 February as saying that he and Dr Edwards had held informal discussions about a possible merger between the two parties after approaches from the business community. This suggestion only further exacerbated the widening rift between Dr Edwards and the Liberal "trendies", who were not in the mood for accepting any amalgamation initiated by the National Party. Stephen Litchfield, the state executive director, dismissed the merger suggestion, saying that the Liberals had approached the Nationals ten times in the past to amalgamate, but nothing had ever come of it. "It would be better if there was only one free enterprise party," Litchfield said, and then with a backhanded swipe at the National Party added: "Sooner or later the National Party will get to the stage where it becomes ineffectual and has to amalgamate." Liberal Party backbencher Terry Gygar (Stafford), another who has been described as one of the "ginger group" on the Liberals' backbench, also bought into the debate. "We stand far apart on many issues," he said. "The Liberal Party has a philosophy but the National Party only represents the mining companies, speculators and fewer and fewer farmers."

As Stephen Litchfield said, there have been numerous attempts to bring about a merger between the two coalition partners to fight their common foe, the socialists. Merger proposals have gained widest support at the federal level of the two parties where there has long been concern about the ALP's plans to restructure the voting system in Australia in such a way that it would be impossible for the two conservative parties to win as separate identities. The federal Labor plan, which has gained considerable renewed credibility under the Hawke government through the activities of Special Minister for State Mick Young (before he was sacked), involved a redistribution of electoral boundaries on an equal numerical basis and the introduction of optional preferential voting. The pragmatic Nationals have been quick to realize the dangers. Sparkes in particular has been a consistent advocate and promoter of such a merger if the ALP plan is put into practice.

These merger plans have not been as enthusiastically welcomed by the Liberals, despite Mr Litchfield's suggestion to the contrary — particularly in Queensland where, undoubtedly, many Liberal officials would wonder if they could survive in the same party as the more aggressive and successful Nationals. It is a very interesting point to speculate;

who among the organizational heavies on either side would survive such a merger?

Merger discussions

In the wake of the 1972 success at the polls of the Whitlam Labor government, merger suggestions emanating from the federal coalition sparked off a whole round of discussions and concerns about this very point. Federal Country Party leader Doug Anthony initiated the discussion with the suggestion the Liberal Party, the DLP and the Country Party enter into an alliance to oppose the Whitlam government. Sparkes immediately supported the proposal with his idea to "push the scheme to its fullest extent". "Obviously the alliance would be for all anti-socialists," he said. "The Country Party and the DLP could be expected to join as whole parties and some disgruntled Liberals could join, if the whole party stayed out." Sparkes even fostered hope that some right wing ALP supporters might also join the new alliance. The scheme had been discussed with DLP leader and former ALP premier of Queensland Vince Gair, and already had the enthusiastic support of DLP senator Condon Byrne. As had happened during the 1962 merger talks, however, the fundamental differences between the two parties and the political importance of swapping preferences in some marginal seats, so long as compulsory preferential voting survived, won out in the end. The merger talks came to nothing.

The National Party and the DLP in Queensland did go very close to merger in 1972–73, but finally the idea was scrapped.

Dr Edwards and the premier's 1981 suggestion was the next serious raising of a possible merger, but it was little more than kite-flying by both leaders anxious to demonstrate their own desires for a closer working relationship.

Following the election of the Hawke federal Labor government on 5 March 1983, merger discussions, at least within National Party ranks, once again became serious. Sir Robert Sparkes raised the matter publicly in July 1983, when he said in a *Courier-Mail* article that he saw the amalgamation of the anti-socialist forces as almost inevitable and said this process could be expedited by Labor Party moves to either first-past-the-post voting or the introduction of optional preferential voting. "I'm not sure what we'll see will be an amalgamation of the Liberals and the Nationals as we know them today or whether a new conservative party will emerge," he said. "If that was to happen," he added, "you'd probably find that the little 'l' Liberals would form a breakaway party." Sparkes was serious about the suggestion. He had floated the idea earlier at the State Management Committee and, although it caught most members of the committee by surprise, the practical inevitability of such a necessity, if Labor were to proceed with its proposed changes to the electoral system, was well appreciated. Sparkes' hope of a possible new conservative party gained considerably wider capital during the hectic final days of the 1983 coalition crisis, when a number of staunch coalitionists in Liberal Party ranks indicated an interest to join such a new political force.

New difficulties

Dr Edwards' calls for coalition harmony and closer ties early in 1981 were mere whispers in the wilderness by the end of that year when a new rift between the partners had emerged. This time it was over the appointment of the chief justice to fill the vacancies to be created by Sir Charles Wanstall's retirement and that of the senior puisne judge, Mr Justice Lucas, in February 1982. The Liberal Attorney-General, Sam Doumany, believed that the appointments should be made on his recommendation. The premier believed that the cabinet should make the decision, and in cabinet he had the numbers.

In November a Liberal Party backbench revolt over tenancy conditions at shopping centres further threatened the coalition. It was only swift action taken by the cabinet that headed off what looked like certain defeat for the government over the shopping centre issue. Cabinet short-circuited the problem by agreeing to introduce new legislation governing shopping centres and gave shopping centre owners six months to get their house in order. The same day that the rebel Liberal backbenchers pushed the shopping centre issue, they also forced the government to postpone action on proposed amendments to the Education Act. So concerned was the government of possible defeat on this issue that the Speaker of parliament, Sel Muller, took the unusual action of voting with the government himself.

In January 1981, the former state president of the Liberal Party and finance minister in Fraser's ministry prior to the 1980 elections, Eric Robinson (McPherson), died suddenly from a heart attack. Eric Robinson had been an active supporter of the "ginger group" section of the Liberal Party and gave their cause considerable credibility. His death prompted another coalition struggle over his vacant seat of McPherson. The Liberals subsequently chose former Liberal Party state parliamentarian Peter White to contest the seat. White had been an outspoken member of the small "l" section in the state parliament and had lost his seat of Southport to the Nationals in 1980. The Nationals endorsed former senator Dr Glennister Sheil. White won the seat easily.

In the McPherson campaign the National Party vigorously promoted its concept for replacing the present graduated tax scale system with one of a flat rate of taxation, an issue that the Nationals never really got off the ground and Prime Minister Fraser was to later suggest even helped the Liberal Party comfortably retain McPherson. National Party opinion was that it was a solid sympathy vote for the Liberals because of the circumstances of Eric Robinson's death that had the greatest influence. The poorer-than-expected National Party performance in that McPherson by-election did knock a lot of wind out of the "flat rate tax" campaign for the National Party.

Federal Liberal tension

In the lead-up to the campaign, the circumstances of Eric Robinson's departure from the Fraser cabinet and his subsequent untimely death were widely debated. The bitterness between the two internal factions of the Liberal Party finally flared publicly in June, when Prime Minister Fraser was asked by former Liberal Party state executive director Keith Livingstone not to attend the official opening of the Eric Robinson Airport Terminal at Coolangatta. Mr Livingstone said in his letter to Mr Fraser:

> It would be unacceptable that Mr Anthony or you should officially

open the terminal in light of the events which led to Mr Robinson's departure from your ministry following last year's elections. No matter how often you deny that you manoeuvred Mr Robinson out of your ministry because of his support for the expansionist moves of the Liberal Party in Queensland, I and others do not accept that account of events.

National Country Party federal leader and deputy prime minister Doug Anthony finally officiated at the ceremony along with a close friend of Robinson, Sir Philip Lynch. Robinson's widow did not attend the ceremony which was interpreted by the media as a boycott.

Nineteen eighty-one was also the year of the splitting away of Andrew Peacock from the Fraser ministry over the matter of National Country Party influence in the cabinet. Peacock's resignation and return to the backbench was yet another widening of the gap between the so-called trendies and the conservatives in the Liberal Party.

In December, Angus Innes (Sherwood) attempted to replace Dr Edwards as leader of the Queensland parliamentary Liberal Party. Although unsuccessful, this was seen as a strategically important move by the Liberal Party "ginger group", of which Mr Innes was recognized as the leading parliamentary light. In the light of later events, this move was seen as the testing of the waters by Innes and the "ginger group" — a counting of heads to determine the lie of the land for the moves ahead. A Melbourne *Age* article on 12 August 1983 headlined "How Bjelke Planned to Dump Liberals" claimed that this move by Innes also tied in with plans by the premier to split with the Liberals, even at this early stage, if the Innes bid succeeded.

"Even though Mr Innes was given no chance of defeating his leader, who was also deputy premier," writer David Broadbent concluded, "Mr Bjelke-Petersen went out of his way to declare that he would not accept as his deputy anyone who rolled Dr Edwards." The article continued: "Those who took any notice of the warning rejected it as yet another attempt by the 72-year-old premier to interfere in the affairs of the Liberal Party to protect his loyal but subservient treasurer."

Silver anniversary

The Queensland coalition celebrated its "silver anniversary" year in 1982 and, as Sir Robert Sparkes told the Young Nationals' State Conference in Mackay in May, the Nationals were planning to celebrate the anniversary in August. He was hopeful then that the Liberals would participate fully.

It was also the year that the Nationals decided to widen their political scope and move into local government elections — a move that had been strenuously resisted by influential sections of the party for many years. It was, however, a logical extension for the expanding National Party. The Liberal and Labor parties were both active in Brisbane City Council politics, and local government throughout the state was increasingly falling to Labor Party influence.

The move was badly handled by the Nationals, however. Following approaches from the anti-Labor independent Local Government Group in Townsville, the party agreed to extend the ward system that operates in Brisbane to Townsville and Rockhampton, and to introduce preferential voting in these areas. The move was poorly sold by the National Party and created considerable public unrest in the areas concerned. At the polls that followed the party did badly. It limped away from its first sashay into local government, embarrassed and much wiser for the experience.

In July, at the State Conference of the National Party in Caloundra, Sparkes continued his promotion of better relations within the coalition. "We are fully aware of the continuing attempts by our opponents to drive wedges in the coalition . . . to try to create division and to make it less effective . . . to destroy it," he said. "These attempts have been obvious for virtually all of the past twenty-five years . . . and still the coalition endures — why? Because collectively it has men and women of sincere good will and purpose, with Queensland's and Australia's best interests at heart, people who want it to work, who work at making it work and who are prepared to subordinate their own parochial personal desires and viewpoints in working together for Queensland."

Sparkes then turned his attention to the next federal election and made the observation on the prospects of the Liberals again fielding a separate Senate team: "With two Liberal senators coming up at the next Senate election (assuming that it is a normal half-Senate election) and only one National, one would have thought political expediency, apart from the more worthy motivation of the best interests of the coalition government, would have induced the Liberal Party to return to the traditional joint ticket approach." Sparkes' words fell on deaf ears at Liberal Party headquarters in Brisbane.

In September 1982, the federal Liberal Party moved to crack down on tax avoidance and in particular "bottom of the harbour" tax avoidance schemes. The prime minister and the treasurer proposed retrospective tax legislation to recoup lost revenue from these schemes. The move created tension for Mr Fraser right across the entire spectrum of his own organization and brought him into conflict for the first time with National Party state president Sir Robert Sparkes. Sparkes said that the suggestion of retrospective taxation was "utterly repugnant" to the National Party and he pressed the prime minister to review his decision. The prime minister did not and pushed on with his proposals which cut deeply into his own Liberal organization across Australia as well as alienating many Nationals. It was an unsettling issue that Fraser would carry with him into the 1983 elections.

On Saturday 4 September, five hundred people dressed in evening dress packed into Brisbane's Crest International Hotel to celebrate the twenty-fifth anniversary of the Queensland coalition. It was a night of celebration and backslapping. Sir Robert pumped his familiar line that despite the critics the coalition has been good for Queensland. Even Joh Bjelke-Petersen was in a generous mood, commenting that the coalition could not have achieved as much as it had without the Liberals.

Liberal leader Dr John Herron was closest to reality, however, when he said that the coalition was like two campers who were unrolling their sleeping bags for the night when they saw a bear approaching. One started putting on his running shoes and the other said: "Why are you doing that; the bear can outrun you." At that the other fellow said: "My friend, all I have to do is outrun you." Dr Herron then went on to predict that the successful partner in the coalition over the next twenty-five years would be the one with the running shoes. Considering the style of Dr Herron and Sir Robert

Sparkes, however, it was difficult not to think that it might just end up being a re-run of the great tortoise-and-hare event.

Casinos and an election gamble

Nineteen eighty-two was also the year of the great casino debate. After several false starts the government finally got around to acting on its 1980 election promise to establish two casinos in the state to boost tourism. One was to be on the Gold Coast and the other was to be in Townsville. In a worsening economic climate nationally, both casinos appeared doomed to difficulties from the start, and throughout 1982 and into 1983 they were a continuing saga of embarrassment to the government and in particular to Dr Edwards who was finally given ministerial responsibility for guiding the casino legislation through the parliament. Dr Edwards, a lay preacher and deacon of the Raceview Congressional Church, was opposed to all forms of gambling and did not drink or smoke. He was known to be opposed to the introduction of casinos into Queensland in the first place, but for that matter so was the premier.

Malcolm Fraser's manoeuvring for a possible early federal election, and plans by both coalition partners to prepare for the event, quieted major wrangles in the latter months of 1982. It was also the time of the exceptionally successful Brisbane Commonwealth Games, which started out threatening all sorts of problems for the government over the Aboriginal land rights issue, but ended up as a public relations bonanza for the Queensland government. Even Malcolm Fraser got into the act.

The land rights issue and the protests planned to embarrass the Queensland government were swamped by the overall success of the games. To an extent they backfired on the Aboriginal community that was hoping to focus worldwide attention on their cause. The tide of public opinion against their disruptive actions had even wider political implications.

With a federal election on the horizon, the Liberal Party had the problem of coming to terms with having an Aboriginal as their Senate team leader opposed to the increasingly popular Florence Bjelke-Petersen. In a swift, orchestrated move, the party dropped Aboriginal senator Neville Bonner from the top of their ticket to the precarious number three position and replaced him with Senator Kathy Martin. The move caused an uproar, with Senator Bonner finally resigning from the Liberal Party and standing unsuccessfully as an independent. Senator Martin was also close to resignation. It was a no-win situation for the Liberals. They copped flak for dumping Senator Bonner and ended up with a Senate team leader who really didn't want the job.

It is now history that Malcolm Fraser gambled on an early election on 5 March 1983 hoping to catch lacklustre Labor leader Bill Hayden unprepared and with "his pants down". Labor, however, had another surprise. Popular former union leader Bob Hawke came to Queensland for a crucial caucus meeting on the day Malcolm Fraser announced the election and came away leader of the Labor Party after a surprise move against Hayden. The election on 5 March saw the federal Liberal–NCP government ousted from government with a massive swing back to Labor.

In Queensland, the Nationals were the only ones with anything really to smile about, although they had lost the far northern seat of Leichhardt to Labor. Senator Florence Bjelke-Petersen had polled a remarkable 33 per cent of the vote and had wrested the fifth seat away from the Liberal Party for former National Party Metropolitan Zone vice-president Ron Boswell. The Liberals lost Fadden (Don Cameron), Bowman (David Jull) and Petrie (held by minister John Hodges).

Former prime minister Malcolm Fraser stood down from the leadership of the federal parliamentary Liberal Party following the defeat of the coalition on 5 March and later resigned from parliament. The leadership was taken over by Andrew Peacock, a decision that was welcomed by the small "l" section of the Liberal Party in Queensland and not so enthusiastically heralded by the Nationals. There had long been an understanding with Malcolm Fraser — after all, he was a man from the land himself. Andrew Peacock, on the other hand, had on occasions not been so well disposed towards his coalition partners.

Defections

With the federal election behind the coalition, the round of normal pre-election endorsement of candidates for the 1983 state election created the first signs of the coalition crash that was to occur. The Liberal "ginger group" was anxious to use the opportunity to increase its numbers in parliament, having carried out the 1981 "head count" when Angus Innes (Sherwood) challenged Dr Edwards and been found wanting.

First the member for Windsor, Bob Moore, and then Bill Kaus (Mansfield) lost party endorsement to younger candidates. These moves seemingly would guarantee that after the 1983 election the "ginger group" would have the numbers. Little did they expect, however, that their position would deteriorate so quickly.

After being dumped by their party, Kaus and Moore initially decided to contest the 1983 election as independents. There had been initial suggestions that they would attempt to join the National Party but these were not encouraged by the top echelons of the party. Finally, however, Sparkes and Bjelke-Petersen were convinced that it was in the party's interests to accept Kaus and Moore and made the recommendation to the State Management Committee in July, prior to State Conference in Brisbane.

The recommendation was extensively debated by the meeting and required considerable selling by Sparkes and the premier before it was finally accepted. There is strong support in the National Party against accepting candidates that move from the Liberal Party. Their record in the past has not been good. But as Sparkes and Premier Bjelke-Petersen argued, this was different. Kaus and Moore were sitting members and it was unlikely that the party could field better candidates in either of these seats. Bill Kaus and Bob Moore were welcomed into the National Party and duly endorsed as National Party candidates for the 1983 state elections. Liberal leader Llew Edwards had lost two votes and the balance tipped in favour of the "ginger group". It was now just a matter of when they would make their move.

5

Strange Bedfellows

"There was a long-standing federal minister who said about relationships with the Country Party: the only thing they understand is a lump of four-by-two between the eyes. I say this and I have many friends in the National Party. This is our lump of four-by-two."

So spoke John Angus Mackenzie Innes, member for Sherwood and leader of the backbench Liberals who came to be known variously as the "ginger group", "the trendies" and the "small 'l' Liberals". He was commenting on the ABC current affairs programme "Nationwide" on backbench Liberal support for Terry White in August 1983.

The endless stream of problems between the Queensland coalition partners – the National (Country) Party and the Liberal Party – over the years came to a head with the rise of the small "l" Liberals. Innes represented the new wave in the Liberal Party, and provided the focal point for the gathering of the Liberal "trendies", described by their archenemy in the state parliament, Russ Hinze, as "Peacock-type Liberals" as opposed to "Fraser-type Liberals".

Peacock-type Liberals

Former barrister Angus Innes was elected to state parliament in 1978 after the surprise death of the then minister for Welfare Services, John Herbert. Privately, many people wondered if he wasn't more interested in federal politics. Some suggested that through his association with Sir James

Killen (as Sir James' campaign director) he would move into
Killen's seat of Moreton when Sir James retired, but considering the safety margin in his own seat of Sherwood and the
marginal uncertainty of the federal seat of Moreton others
found this difficult to believe. Innes made his first bid for the
leadership of the Queensland Liberal Party in December
1981, when he carried out what many observers believed to
be a "testing of the waters" exercise against Dr Llew Edwards.
The bid was unsuccessful, but it lined up the numbers for
Innes, and that was a vital first step to take. The reported 14 to
8 voting margin was an impressive "dry run".

In addition to Innes, the small "l" faction included three
other lawyers – John Greenwood, QC (Ashgrove), a former
minister sacked by Dr Edwards, Guelf Scassola (Mt Gravatt),
and Ian Prentice (Toowong) – as well as former law student
Terry Gygar (Stafford) and the husband–wife team of
Rosemary Kyburz (Salisbury) and Rob Akers (Pine Rivers).

"The trendy Liberals do things the ALP would never do,"
Hinze said in an interview on 22 August 1983. "They are un-
controllable. You have to understand that in party politics at
all times the party comes before your own feelings. Otherwise
you become an independent."

To a man and a woman, the "ginger group" were prepared to
vote against their party and their government to emphasize
what they believed in. This is the vital area in which they differed from the National Party. In this regard, Sir Robert
Sparkes' 1973 statement, when outlining the blueprint for the
National Party, is particularly relevant: "Whether we like it or
not, the party system is here to stay, and no member can
expect to enjoy – nor can the party allow him (her) to enjoy –
the privileges of party membership and at the same time the
freedom of an independent." This is basic, enshrined National
Party philosophy.

Teamwork and individuals

Under the leadership of Joh Bjelke-Petersen and Sir Robert
Sparkes, the National Party has conscientiously opted for a
teamwork approach to state politics, in the belief that a
champion team will beat a team of champions any day. A

significant number of senior Liberal ministers and members
have agreed with this style and approach to government; that
is how the coalition survived for as long as it did. The dissident Liberal backbench believed otherwise.

Rosemary Kyburz typified the group's attitude in this
regard: "I think that the greatest problem in the Queensland
parliament is the National Party in general; the backbench
and the ministers refuse to allow the implementation of any
Liberal policy." When questioned about the number of times
that she had crossed the floor in state parliament to vote
against the government, and if enough was enough, she
replied: "No. I think we've just started. I was particularly
angry at the principle which was displayed . . . by the premier
when he said that if Liberal backbenchers were going to keep
pursuing motions, we would have to close the parliament
down, because, after all, if the parliament didn't run the way
he wanted it, then there wasn't much use. I would remind him
and those bovine members of the National Party who moo at
his heels that in fact we are elected as private members. We
are only formed into parties once we are elected and I consider myself a private member primarily and first of all." Mrs
Kyburz went on to say that she thought her own Liberal
leader at the time, Dr Edwards, also mooed at the heels of the
premier, and suggested that he should "look for a surgery"
after the next election.

Again, Kyburz's statements typified the vast difference of
political style between the National Party and the small "l"
Liberal group. Public attacks on the leader or the party are
grounds for expulsion in the National Party, as Lindsay
Hartwig found out and as Sparkes threatened dissidents at the
Caloundra conference in 1982. Such antics deepened the rift
between the Liberals and the Nationals.

Differences of opinion

The National Party's style of representation is based heavily
on work in the electorate. Ordinary members are encouraged
to establish themselves in their electorates and thus give
parliamentary "grandstanding" a secondary priority. There are
no parliamentary broadcasts, few voters read Hansard, and

with unemployment and inflation worrying people and the everyday histrionics of parliament providing the sensationalism that the media feeds on, who really cares about a new scheme to give parliamentarians more opportunity to travel and to talk?

Parliamentary reform is hardly one of the raging issues that arise in public opinion polls in Queensland. As far as the average voter is concerned, as long as he has a job and food on his table and prospects for the future he has the confidence that his government is doing its job. Liberal leader Dr Llew Edwards realized this when he said: "Ninety-nine per cent of the people wouldn't even understand what a public accounts committee is, let alone the people of Queensland, and what we've got to do now is . . . get on with the job and win the election." It's basic "bread and butter" politics but it's a formula that has been exceedingly successful for the Nationals and Queensland. Party-system government has its critics, but in Queensland it has given the state twenty-six years of unprecedented growth and stability. Understandably, Premier Joh Bjelke-Petersen and the National Party are reluctant to abandon the formula and throw open the parliament to wholesale, uncontrolled debate.

The "legal eagles" and academics on the Liberal backbench describe as trivial the grass roots antics like campaigns for "dunny" doors to swing the right way, or non-slip bathroom floors, as have been championed by National Party member Vince Lester (Peak Downs). Almost since the day they arrived in parliament, the small "l" group believed that singlehandedly they could reform parliament and break the back of Bjelke-Petersen's party-system government. It was an honourable crusade, but one hardly steeped in widespread public support or likely to promote coalition harmony. It was a stance, however, that attracted popular media support, but for all the wrong reasons as the Nationals saw it. The easiest way to get your name in the headlines in politics is to attack your own party, and in this regard the Liberal dissidents gave the media a field day, so much so that a virtual cult following within the media developed for the trendy Liberals over the past three years. Their good looks and university-polished presentation were a television producer's dream to contrast with the roughhouse likes of the Nationals' Russ Hinze and the simple antics of Vince Lester. So fascinated was the media with the comparisons, that academic studies on the subject were written, not to mention the reams of newspaper column inches. Queensland University political commentator Paul Wilson described the run-of-the-mill Queensland politicians as "bar room politicians". Writer Frank Robson said that "their behaviour in public can be monstrous". The Queensland parliament was described as "rough and brutal" and Joh was said to be in the mould of Bolte and Askin, appealing to the uneducated masses. The aside was thrown in for good measure that Queensland just so happened to have the lowest standard of education in the nation. But in the end Robson had to admit that these were the politicians that the people trusted: "They might put their foot in it, but you know they're talking from the heart."

The continuing public attack on the government by the "trendies" earned the displeasure of Premier Bjelke-Petersen. On an ABC "Nationwide" programme he said: "The damage will be done to the members concerned. They are the people who like to stand up alongside of me and. Dr Edwards for a picture at election time — I have done it so often for them over the years — who like to say they are a member of the coalition team, the National and Liberal Party team when election time comes. As soon as the election is over you can notice a tremendous difference. They run around in all directions, pleasing themselves what they do."

As vehemently as he rejected the campaign by the Liberal "trendies" to publicly attack the government, there were occasions when Bjelke-Petersen was impressed with their performance. The 1983 Constitutional Convention in Adelaide was one such occasion. "If they acted that way all the time, everything would be all right," he said. In the lead-up to the Constitutional Convention, the Liberal lawyers, Innes, Scassola and Prentice, did a considerable amount of work to assist Attorney-General Sam Doumany to organize the numbers to oppose the federal government's campaign to water down states' rights in the Constitution. The end result was a most impressive defeat for the Hawke government constitutional team, led by the confident federal Attorney-General, Senator Gareth Evans. Joh Bjelke-Petersen was impressed by the Liberal "trendies" on that occasion.

Parliamentary reform

Joh Bjelke-Petersen was the stumbling block in the parliament for the impatient Liberal Party backbenchers and the worried Liberal executive members who emerged in 1978 with a new direction for the Liberal Party in Queensland. His intransigence and unpreparedness to allow what they called "Liberal philosophy" to be projected through the government caused much of their criticism.

"To mention an all-party committee in this state is considered to be heresy, not democracy," the Liberal member for Townsville, Dr Norman Scott-Young, was prompted to say in parliament in April 1981. Parliamentary reform and change of style away from that of Bjelke-Petersen was the crux of the

Keeping up with Premier Joh in an election campaign is a big enough task for a fully fit politician. Liberal leader Bill Knox had the added handicap of a broken leg when he had the job in 1977. (Photograph courtesy of Queensland Newspapers Pty Ltd)

Three prominent players in the Queensland Liberal Party's demise at Barcaldine's tree of knowledge under whose branches the Labor movement was spawned in the days of the Great Shearers' Strike: Brian Austin, Terry White and Dr Llew Edwards.

issue. In the eyes of the Liberal backbench dissidents, Joh was "too tough", "too unbending". In Joh's opinion, however, "If they don't like it, they can go and join the Labor Party."

The problems boiled down to one issue — the belief held by a small group of Liberal backbenchers that parliamentary reform (to allow wider debate) would somehow, miraculously, bring about revitalization of the Liberal Party in Queensland. Joh Bjelke-Petersen, however, sticks rigidly to his belief that control of parliament by the government of the day is vital to continued stable government.

It has been suggested that the parliamentary reform campaign was really a front for a leadership struggle within the Liberal Party, but it has to be realized also that parliamentary reform was really a veiled challenge to Joh Bjelke-Petersen's style of leadership. The premier's style was the "red herring" that distracted public attention from the real issues. Parliamentary reform and public accountability were the words that gave it all a ring of respectability. Joh's controversial style was the only vehicle on which such a credible diversionary campaign could have been mounted and sustained; after all, it was widely sold during the Whitlam years that there was "something devious" about Joh. It was therefore easy to suggest that it carried through into the parliament. And there was a ring of chivalry about young men and women striving to bring about reform from dictatorial control. There were enough journalists around who grew up in the anti-Joh era to ensure widespread sensational press coverage and, well, there just might have been the chance that this would be the issue to bring Joh Bjelke-Petersen down. The prize for that would surely be recognition in the annals of Australian history.

The claim by Ian Prentice (Toowong), when speaking on parliamentary reform on 24 November 1982, typifies the somewhat political naivety of their crusade: "Today I wish to put forward what some people may consider to be a rather revolutionary step in Queensland concerning the need for this parliament to be the governing body, the body making decisions on the future of the state and the fact that it should play a role in government and the way it works." An opposition member summed up the feeling of the majority of members: "Impossible!"

The campaign by the Liberal dissidents to bring about parliamentary reform largely centred around the issue of a public accounts committee. It was an issue that Terry White was linked with from the time he first came into parliament. In April 1980 he spoke at length on the subject: "The role of Parliament and the faults of Parliament in Queensland are matters which I would like to discuss briefly," he said. "We can distinguish six roles of Parliament. They are: firstly, enforcing accountability, that is, making the Government, through questions to Ministers, debate and discussions on Legislation, accountable for its actions; secondly, scrutinizing administration; thirdly, granting supply; fourthly, providing a forum to focus public issues; fifthly, forming a government; and sixthly, selecting ministers." He went on: "It is in the area of rationale debate of Government policy, scrutinizing public administration and assessing the effectiveness of Government policy choices that this Parliament is weak." Hardly soul stirring stuff that captures the imagination of the poulation, but it was an indication of Terry White's early parliamentary inclinations.

National Party member for Southport Doug Jennings, who also sat in the Victorian parliament and was deeply involved in exposing the land scandal dealings of the parliament in that state, is one who doesn't believe in public accounts committees. "Public Accounts Committees in five other governments over the last two decades elsewhere in Australia have proven to be ineffectual," Jennings said in a *Gold Coast Bulletin* article on 5 August 1983. He said that public accounts committees in the Askin Liberal government, the Wran Labor government and the federal Whitlam government did nothing to stop southern land scandals. "A parliamentary public accounts committee in Victoria did nothing to curtail some of the biggest and most corrupt deals this country has ever experienced," he said. "Even after the corrupt land deals were first exposed in June 1974, the parliamentary public accounts committee did absolutely nothing to investigate them." There was not one question asked in the Victorian parliament about the doubtful land deals until Doug Jennings raised the matter in 1977.

It was an argument, however, that the dissident Liberal backbench would not accept. From the beginning, the parliamentary reform campaign had been a political minefield for the Liberal Party, despite the fact that on 16 March 1983 the parliament finally voted by a margin of one vote to carry the following resolution sponsored by Guelf Scassola: "That the House expresses its gratitude for the work already performed by the Standing Orders Committee and requests the committee report to the House, on the first sitting day after 30th June 1983, on the proposals placed before the Standing Orders Committee for the establishment of a Public Accounts Committee and other committees of review and accountability." Notably, Terry White was not in the House that day; conversely, a number of coalitionists were also not there to vote on the issue. If they had been, the issue might never have got off the ground in the first place.

The orchestrated Labor Party campaign to embarrass the Liberal Party and to undermine their credibility following their decline in the wake of the "McComb–Separate Senate Team Affair" in 1980 was built almost solely around the issue of parliamentary reform. The hardened old heads in the Labor Party quickly realized that they had the trendy Liberals on a line and it was only a matter of pulling the strings to see them dance. As Labor Party heavy Kevin Hooper (Archerfield) pointed out, when asked to described the political acumen of the trendies: "Some of the legal people in parliament are duds, to put it bluntly. In boxing parlance, I could give most of them six straight lefts before they put their guard up."

Labor Party traps

The Labor Party campaign of baiting the Liberals on their reformist attitudes got under way in the lead-up to the 1980 elections. In May 1980, the then deputy leader of the Labor Party, Bill Darcy, started the barbs. "We have seen the posturing of the Liberals in crossing the floor on abortion, street marches, education, the Bellvue, SEMP, MACOS, essential services, Tarong and electricity charges," he said. "The government proposals would have been defeated if the Liberal Party had crossed the floor. Liberal Party members were supposed to have opposed these various matters, but all we have in Queensland is a couple of Liberals who are trying to save face in their electorates. It happens on issue after issue in this parliament." It was divisive, damaging criticism for the Liberals, but they had gone looking for it. As Joh Bjelke-Petersen would say: "If you sit on the fence with crows, you can't complain if you get shot at," or, in a similar vein, "There's no hope for you when you've got one foot on the fly paper."

In August the baiting of the Liberal Party by the Labor Party on this issue continued. In response, Guelf Scassola hit back with an attempt to regain control of the issue. "In recent days the Opposition has attempted through its leader to give the impression that it is the champion of the cause of parliamentary reform in this state." Like a pup tugging for possession of a piece of cloth, the Labor Party responded: "What has concerned Queenslanders and me [Warburton–ALP, Sandgate] over a long period is the absolute hypocrisy displayed from time to time by the Liberals in this parliament. Outside the House they indulge in an exercise of deception, pretending that they agree with the principles contained in our proposals. How many times, for example, have the Liberals said that they believe in the establishment of a parliamentary public accounts committee and that they support electoral reform? Yet in the parliament where it counts, where honourable members have to put up or shut up, political expediency takes over from their so-called principles and the hapless marriage of convenience continues to flounder along."

Despite the continuing sniping between the Liberal and Labor parties over parliamentary reform that raged on and off over the last three years, it was an issue that the National Party did not become involved with. While the Liberals copped the stick from the Labor Party in the parliament on an issue they could hardly hope to win, the Nationals were out farming the electorate. Parliamentary reform was an issue the Liberals insisted on pursuing, and one which the Nationals let them chase. In that context, it kept both the Liberal and Labor parties happy and away from the real issues of the state. Little wonder the National Party's stocks rose dramatically during this period.

Premier Bjelke-Petersen did, however, make one substantive statement to the parliament in 1980 on public accountability. "The wise husbandry of public money has always been of highest priority to my Government," he said. "We have in this State a measure of the Parliament, namely the Financial and Administration Audit Act 1977–1978, which has been acknowledged both in Australia and overseas as leading legislation in the field of accountability of the executive and the administrative arms of Government to the Parliament. The whole pattern of the Act is to govern the management and control of the moneys appropriated by Parliament from the public accounts. All departmental expenditure is therefore subject to the controls prescribed by the Financial Administration and Audit Act."

After three years of watching the Liberals tear themselves to pieces over public accountability, and of having the opportunity to see the lack of success of such committees elsewhere, Bjelke-Petersen is even more convinced that such committees don't work. "Every other state is in a frightful mess financially. They are broke; got massive unemployment. Queensland is on the surge forward. Every department has an audit account where all accounts are audited and that man and that department is responsible in turn to the Auditor-General – every department."

Doubts about Joh

This issue of parliamentary reform has been at the centre of the problems between the coalitionists and the small "l" Liberal reformists. There were, however, peripheral issues that have been hived off this central theme. All were in the same vein, and related to parliamentary behaviour – all tried to suggest that there was something wrong with the National Party-led government. The Bjelke-Petersen Foundation, misuse of the government aircraft, the "Joh Show" (Joh's television campaign to promote the government), jobs for "the boys", the letting of government contracts, and law and order issues such as street marches and the Essential Services Act have all attracted the condemnation of the small "l" Liberal group, without any real evidence of lasting public sympathy for their efforts.

In the final analysis, the most intriguing aspect of the struggle between the National Party-led coalition group and the small "l" Liberal dissidents is in trying to identify the political benefit for the agitators. It was a politically damaging exercise for the Liberal Party in Queensland. Prior to the 1983 election, it cost the party three leaders, a senator, several members and about 10 per cent of its popular vote. Former prime minister Malcolm Fraser believes it also cost him his government. So what was it all about?

It has been suggested that it can only have been an internal power struggle, a struggle similar in style to the way Andrew Peacock finally got Malcolm Fraser's job. In this instance, however, the plan backfired. ABC current affairs commentator Janine Walker hinted at this underlying issue in her commentary on 9 August 1983. "I wonder, and surely many Queenslanders must be wondering too, just what Liberal backbenchers are looking for from a leader? If they are looking for an immediate implementation of their platform, or a potential leader is promising that to them, then surely he must be flying under false colours, because not Mr White, not Mr Doumany, not Dr Edwards can deliver that to the Liberal backbench."

Liberal backbench member Guelf Scassola, who has been described as one of the dissidents, disagrees that a leadership struggle was involved. He said as much in a communique to voters in his electorate dated 15 August 1983. "Other people," he said, "with strong political motivation from other parties, have suggested that that whole exercise was a stunt and have suggested a variety of motives, from conspiracy by some Liberals to put Mr White into leadership, to a National Party plot to run the state alone. All such statements are false. [It] has resulted from the reaction of those who are embarrassed by, or opposed to, the conscientious pursuit of sensible parliamentary reform by members of the parliamentary Liberal Party."

6

Bones of Contention

Generally assessing the twenty-six years of the National–Liberal coalition, it seems that there has been an endless stream of problems between the Queensland coalition partners. In reality, however, when the surface is scratched, they all boil down to four main areas: (1) electoral distribution (the supposed gerrymander), (2) three-cornered contests involving sitting coalition members, (3) parliamentary reform, and (4) issues of style (street marches, government appointments, contracts and the like).

The gerrymander

Liberal leader Terry White launched his 1983 campaign with the promise of a "bobby-dazzler" of a redistribution – after the election and if his party had the power and influence to deliver. Labor leader Keith Wright went on record as saying that if Labor won they would carry out a redistribution that would keep Labor in power, not for three years, but for thirty-three years. Both were priming the electorate for what they believed would be the central issue of the 1983 election: the issue of Queensland's supposed "gerrymander".

"You don't give votes to sheep and cows and machines – only to people," Dr John Herron, president of the Liberal Party, said prior to the 1980 state elections. He was referring to the size imbalance that exists between urban and non-urban electorates, which the Labor and Liberal parties consider to be a gerrymander in favour of the National Party. Dr

Herron's suggestion is that the National Party gives votes to "sheep, cows and machines". "I'm not against country people having better representation, but I believe times have changed with television and aeroplanes, so that distance is no longer a great barrier to good representation." Dr Herron was speaking in favour of the Liberal Party's "one vote, one value" redistribution proposals which it shares in common with the Labor Party.

Loss of seats

Although they differ somewhat marginally, Labor and Liberal Party proposals are based on the premise that every electorate in Queensland should have the same number of voters, without the consideration for remoteness, sparsity of population or inequality of opportunity that the National Party formula provides. The Liberal and Labor parties admit that equal-size electorates will mean that existing northern, central and western Queensland seats will be moved to the more heavily populated south-east corner of the state, but disagree with National Party claims that this will downgrade the parliamentary representation that these areas now receive. Labor state secretary, Peter Beattie, while touring North Queensland during 1983, said that what the area lost in parliamentary representation would be more than made-up for by an increase in public servants. This argument has been supported in the past by suggestions that larger electoral allowances for country area parliamentarians would also assist in overcoming any downgrading of the areas. The issue has been at the crux of deteriorating coalition relations throughout the five years leading up to the 1983 state elections. Ironically, it's an issue that the Nationals have defended poorly, but there are reasons.

Political realities

Central to the issue, of course, is the question: Are the Liberal and Labor parties unjustly treated by the existing method of distributing electoral boundaries in Queensland? Two of Australia's foremost commentators on electoral matters, Malcolm Mackerras and Dr Colin Hughes (ANU), say no. "Of the seven fairest elections that have been held in the

Commonwealth and the three largest mainland states since 1949, Queensland accounts for three of them, New South Wales 2, the Commonwealth 1 and Victoria 1," says Dr Hughes. "The Queensland electoral boundaries provide . . . more fairness than do the Commonwealth or New South Wales or Victorian boundaries." Malcolm Mackerras, writing in the *Bulletin* magazine on 23 August 1983, said: "People have this strange idea that Queensland has some kind of unique gerrymander which guarantees that Labor cannot win. Not so." Mackerras went on to predict that a landslide swing to Labor was in fact possible in the 1983 state election.

The facts are that the Labor Party hasn't polled the numbers under any system to win government in its own right in Queensland since 1957. (Labor's share of the vote since 1957 is as follows: 1957 − 28.9%; 1960 − 38.8%; 1963 − 43.8%; 1966 − 43.8%; 1969 − 44.9%; 1972 − 46.7%; 1974 − 36.0%; 1977 − 42.8%; 1980 − 41.6%; 1983 − 44.01%.) The Liberal Party has lost seats through previous redistributions and consequently has probably the most reason to complain about redistributions of the past. What has to be recognized, however, is that during this time the Liberal Party has had exactly the same conservative vote to appeal to as the Nationals and still it has found it difficult to win acceptance outside the main Brisbane metropolitan area. In the lead-up to the 1983 election, it held only one seat, Townsville, in provincial Queensland. In the important recent years since 1971, the Liberal Party has simply failed to capitalize on the opportunities, even if they have been less than those available to both the National and Labor parties.

Again, in 1983, the Liberal Party misread the signs with their belated decision to make "one vote, one value" redistribution a central campaign issue. Whereas there could have been grounds for complaint in the past, these are rapidly diminishing as the north and west of Queensland develop, especially as a result of the opening up of the Bowen coal basin.

By opting for the "one vote, one value" policy as a central campaign theme, they effectively wrote themselves off in the country − not only in that election, but almost certainly for many to come. This latter point is most interesting in relation to the clash between the Queensland Liberal Party executive and former prime minister Malcolm Fraser prior to the 1983 election.

Ironically, Malcolm Fraser's appeal to traditional National Party voters in Queensland was of major concern to many Nationals during his term in office. Fraser's style of conservative Liberalism, which has proven so successful in rural Victoria and Tasmania, was considered by many National Party strategists as a "sure-fire" winner for the Liberals in Queensland.

What happened with the passage of time, however, is totally the opposite. In assessing the failing electoral appeal of the Queensland Liberal Party, determining the electoral cost of the shift away from the traditional "Fraser-type" Liberal approach to the small "l", "Peacock-type" Liberals, as so succinctly defined by Russ Hinze, is an important political and academic exercise. Many hard-nosed political realists will undoubtedly come to the conclusion that "you can take a horse to water, but you can't make him drink".

The most favourable electoral boundaries possible will not help if the parties concerned fail to make the most of their opportunities.

In the 1980 state election, Labor polled only 41.59 per cent of the total vote in Queensland, compared with 54.78 per cent polled by the coalition partners. On these figures, one can only wonder what perversion of democracy would be needed to produce a Labor Party victory. The only system that could improve Labor's chances is one which abolishes preferential voting. On a first-past-the-post basis, Labor's chances would be improved, but if this happened and the National and Liberal parties amalgamated, as has so often been rumoured, it is likely that Labor would still not win. The abolition of preferential voting and a counter Labor Party gerrymander is the only way that Labor could swing the numbers. That's possibly what Labor leader Keith Wright had in mind when he said his redistribution would keep Labor in power, not for three years but for thirty-three.

Brisbane influence

A redistribution of electorate boundaries on a "one vote, one value" basis as suggested by the Liberal and Labor parties would have its greatest influence in the Brisbane metropolitan and near-Brisbane areas. This is where the Labor and Liberal parties have traditionally held greatest influence. This is the area the National Party has been so anxious to penetrate. More electorates in this part of the state and fewer in the provincial and country areas would theoretically improve the chances of the Labor and Liberal parties to win the numbers to govern. This is the real basis of the arguments of the Liberal and Labor parties for redistribution on a "one vote, one value" basis, and thus makes it difficult not to interpret the issue as pure political opportunism, even if, to a large degree, that's what politics is all about.

The catchy slogan "one vote, one value", purposefully designed to appeal to the inherent "fair play" instincts of Australians, has been brilliantly used to sell the campaign for the redistribution of electoral boundaries in Queensland on the basis of each electorate having the same number of voters. If awards are handed out for mass deception in public relations, it would have to be an all-time winner. At first hearing, it sounds a totally fair proposition to the average, not-so-interested voter. Everyone's vote should be equal; that's what democracy is all about. The reality of life in sparsely and unevenly settled Queensland (and Australia as a whole) makes it impossible for votes to be equal in value. It is true that each vote can be counted only once. It is not true, however, that the value of each person's vote can be the same in Queensland if based on demographic grounds alone. It is simply not true to suggest that the value of the vote of a person living in a remote area of the state such as Burketown, Windorah or Coen is equal to the vote of the person living in the suburbs of Brisbane or the Gold Coast. It is akin to saying that a hundred hectares of land in Burketown is worth a hundred hectares of land in Queen Street, Brisbane, or downtown Surfers Paradise. Both are the same size, but the return from each area is vastly different. Built-in economic protection for these areas, such as adequate and indexed zonal tax concessions and across-the-board compensating additional expenditure to equalize the degree of disadvantage, would alleviate the disparity, but the overwhelming numbers of "my-survival-first" politicians in all parliaments of the Commonwealth almost guarantees that this does not happen. Therefore, electoral "weightage" is the only hope for such areas. It gives them some chance of sharing more equally in the "cake" of government.

Exploding the myths

The principle of "one vote, one value" has been so brilliantly sold to the Queensland electorate over the past five years that the supposed Queensland "gerrymander" is as widely believed as the Barrier Reef is beautiful. A wide cross-section of Australians, including many Queenslanders, believe that the National Party governs because it holds all the numerically small country seats, while the Liberal and Labor parties hold all the (numerically) largest south-east corner seats. This is not true, however. In fact, prior to the 1983 election, the National Party held eight of the ten largest seats in the state, and all of them in the heavily populated south-east corner. The top seven largest seats in the state, prior to that election, were all held by the National Party. Agreed, the National Party also held all the smallest seats in the state, but surely that is what should be expected from a party that seeks to represent the entire spectrum of the population in any state.

In the public relations area, the "gerrymander" has been an issue that the National Party has never really been able to get on top of. With most to lose from the implementation of such a system, the National Party has been beaten hands down by the Labor and Liberal parties' media-sell campaign on the "gerrymander". In the areas that it affects most, such as central, northern and western Queensland, it should have been a crushing electoral winner for the Nationals. These areas would lose several parliamentary seats to the heavily populated south-east corner of the state and, as every politician worth his salt should know, you don't win votes taking things away from people.

The reason for the National Party's poor defence of the "one vote, one value" attack is fourfold. Primarily, their biggest problem is that they haven't seriously applied themselves to commercially marketing their "defence" in the same manner as the Labor and Liberal parties have sold their criticism. Even in the 1983 election, when the party seemingly had everything going for it on the issue, the defence campaign was more of an after-thought than the pre-meditated political kill it might have been. One reason for this is the National Party has felt somewhat "hobbled" by "seemingly" conflicting statements made by Joh Bjelke-Petersen, during his early days in parliament, on redistribution proposals introduced by Labor when they were in power. This position has been confused and conveniently misconstrued by the premier's political opponents, and poorly understood by his followers. Joh Bjelke-Petersen said at the time, in criticism of Hanlon's redistribution proposals, that they would enable a "minority" party to govern. Political opponents of the National Party have jumped on this statement and used it as criticism of the National Party's position in governing Queensland. The vitally important difference that is conveniently overlooked is that Joh Bjelke-Petersen was talking about one party operating on its own which could poll less than 50 per cent of the vote and, through an electoral gerrymander, could still win enough seats to govern – as the Labor Party did in 1946 when they polled only 43.58 per cent of the vote and stayed in power and again in 1950, after Hanlon's redistribution, when they polled only 46.87 per cent. As former independent member for Townsville South Tom Aikens (who was there when Bjelke-Petersen attacked the Hanlon proposal) pointed out when asked about the Hanlon redistribution: "Hanlon's only objective was to keep the Labor Party in power, nothing else."

To defend its position, the National Party has relied on long and often boring statistical defences, which quite simply haven't attracted the attention of the masses who hear the catchy "one vote, one value" propaganda and say: well, that sounds fair. Reams and reams of National Party counter-propaganda has been compiled on the issue, but still the electorate is confused.

Secondly, and probably the real reason the Nationals have never really put marketing thought into their defence, it has never previously become a major election issue. In the past it has been an issue that the Labor and Liberal parties have talked about and threatened to make the central theme of their campaign, but have not done so. So, in National Party thinking it has probably also been a matter of "letting a sleeping dog lie". This happened again in 1983.

In not making "one vote, one value" a major issue, especially in the decentralized areas of the state, one can only wonder at how many seats in these areas the National Party still has the potential to win.

Thirdly, the issue has gained momentum at a time of declining political influence in the most affected areas of the north and the west within the National Party.

Fourthly, and converse to the latter suggestion, this period of promotion of the "gerrymander" myth has gained recognition at a time of increased political influence within the National Party in the Brisbane metropolitan and near-Brisbane areas. Many Nationals in these areas have simply been wary of the issue, fearing that it could in fact backfire on them in areas which would obviously be direct beneficiaries of any redistribution on the basis of equal electoral franchise, a matter of the "hip pocket" rule in reverse.

Importance of weightage

The importance or validity of "weightage" is the aspect of the electoral system that most people do not understand. In a nation that prides itself on "fair play", it is also the biggest selling point for the present system. It is the element in the system which provides for one electorate to be bigger than another. It is provided for in the Westminster system for the purpose of balancing out the inequalities between areas. Such inequalities stem from: (1) the ability of a member of parliament to effectively service his/her constituents, taking into consideration area, transport facilities and density of population; (2) the ease with which people in the electorate can contact their parliamentary representative when it is necessary; (3) the maintenance of community interest; and (4) the opportunity for all areas to achieve their potential.

If a state or a nation were evenly endowed, evenly developed and evenly populated, there would be no need for such considerations. It would be expected that all electorates would be of the same size and would subsequently get an even distribution of the "cake". However, when we have a state such as Queensland or a nation such as Australia, where there are such vast differences between regions, resource endowments, the services areas received and population distribution, it is obvious that under any democratic system of government some consideration has to be given for the less fortunate.

Why is this so? Quite simply, it is because democracies are largely about self-interest. The democracy we enjoy in Australia survives on the balance of politically marginal seats. The first law of politicians in such electorates and of the governments that depend on them is survival and survival depends on self-interest. Such a situation does not encourage statesmanlike concern for the problems of the electorate next door, or for that matter a thousand kilometres away in decentralized Australia. The only chance for this to happen in political Queensland/Australia today is if some "equalization of opportunity" or "protection" of the less-fortunate areas is built into the electoral system, and this is what is called "weightage". This is the consideration that is built into the Queensland system that creates some numerically larger and some numerically smaller electorates. The numerically larger electorates are in the heavily populated, well-serviced areas, where the member of parliament could ride around his boundaries on a bike in a day, while the numerically smaller electorates are located in the sparsely populated, poorly serviced parts of the state, where the local member wouldn't be able to ride his boundaries in a month of Sundays.

If "weightage" were a device that was used exclusively by the National Party in Queensland, there would be grounds for concern. It is not, however. It is widely used throughout the democratic world, wherever the Westminster system of government is followed. In Britain, the home of the Westminster system, the size of electorates vary to the order of 113,000 voters in the largest to 22,000 in the smallest. In Canada, the largest electorate in a recent survey had 139,000 voters and the smallest, 22,000. In the U.S.A., the same survey revealed a differentiation in electorate sizes of between 951,527 and 177,431 voters. In Western Australia, another sparsely populated state similar to Queensland, the electorates differ in size from approximately 15,589 electors in the largest to 2,101 in the smallest.

The Australian Senate is another area in which "weightage" consideration is given. If the Senate had been proposed on a "one vote, one value" basis when federation was proposed, it is extremely unlikely that the Federation of Australian States would ever have been formed. To provide for the fair representation of the states, the Senate provides for an equal number of senators to be elected from each state, regardless of area size or population. The United Nations is another organization that would not exist if "weightage" were not given to the smaller, less-populated nations. If "one vote, one value" representation existed in the United Nations, countries such as the United States and China would totally dominate.

Even the Australian Labor Party, within its own federal organization, recognizes the need for "weightage". If it were to form its federal organizational body on the basis of a "one vote, one value" system, the states of New South Wales and Victoria would totally dominate, and it is extremely unlikely that the organizations from the less-populated states would ever be heard. And as was said previously, the Hanlon Labor government introduced the Queensland system anyway.

A sour grapes issue

In the final analysis of the Queensland "gerrymander" it is difficult not to see the argument of the Labor and Liberal parties as pure "sour grapes" for their electoral failures of the past, and an exercise in public deceit aimed at bringing about circumstances whereby they could manipulate the system to suit their political ends. Undoubtedly the National Party in power has sought to make the most of its opportunities in this area. Only the politically naive would suggest that by replacing the Nationals with the Liberals or the Labor Party anything in this regard would change. All the parliamentary reform in the world will not prevent this happening – only wide public interest and awareness of what is really needed for the good of all will keep all political parties honest.

Three-cornered contests

The "running sore" in National and Liberal relations has been the issue of three-cornered contests involving sitting members. It has caused problems for the coalition partners ever since the very early years when the Liberal Party began to realize that the then Country Party was gaining wider acceptance outside its traditional "cows and corn" belt. The winning of the near-Brisbane seats of Redcliffe and Surfers Paradise by the Nationals and the urban sprawl that dragged

National seats like Fassifern into the fringes of metropolitan Brisbane put the writing on the wall for the Liberals.

Early coalition agreements (mentioned elsewhere) identified the problems and there existed a gentlemen's agreement between the coalition partners that three-cornered contests involving sitting members should not be entered into by either party. The principle was enshrined in the days of Sir Robert Menzies, when Menzies himself refused to support a Victorian Liberal organizational move to field a candidate against the then leader of the Country Party, John McEwen. Menzies said at that time that not only would he *not* campaign for the endorsed Liberal candidate, but he would also actively campaign for McEwen. The Liberal Party in Queensland found this principle too restricting, however, and finally disregarded this aspect of the agreement in 1965.

In the early days, the three-cornered contests that the Liberals undertook were confined to contests against backbench members, but later it spread to ministers as well. The final development was the Liberals' decision in 1980 to run a separate Senate ticket. The success of three-cornered contests and the Liberals' separate Senate ticket have been discussed elsewhere in this book. The rationale against three-cornered contests does, however, require some further elaboration.

Initially, it needs to be appreciated that the preferential voting system provides maximum opportunity for coalitions of minor parties, such as the National and Liberal parties in Queensland, to join together and form the equivalent of a major party and to form government. Without preferential voting, the two parties would not have survived as they have. The argument is that if preferential voting were done away with, the two anti-Labor parties would then merge for the sake of political survival. The total of their "merged" vote would still have been enough to win.

This is the argument also against the emotive claim that the National Party rules Queensland from a minority position — which it does, but not in the sinister fashion that is popularly suggested. If the combined vote of the National and Liberal parties was less than 50 per cent, then an electoral "fix" could be implied and there would be validity in the claim that the National Party governs by sinister means. As has been previously pointed out, however, this does not happen. What occurred was that the National Party happened to have been the numerically stronger partner in a coalition government. Regardless of what this numerical strength might be in comparison with the Labor Party, by virtue of the agreement that existed between the National and Liberal parties, the National Party enjoyed the privileges of being the senior partner in the coalition. The same circumstances applied after the 1983 election even though the National Party chose not to enter into coalition with the Liberals. The boot could well have been on the Liberals' foot. Again, one is at a loss to understand what perversion of the present system of electing governments in Australia could give the majority government position to either the Liberal or Labor parties.

Preferences — no guarantee

Preferences are not political guarantees. This is the crucial factor that must be appreciated when judging the importance of preferences in any contest. The final decision on where a voter gives his or her preference remains with the voter. Party "how-to-vote" tickets can provide a guide to the voter and do influence many people, but not everyone.

In general, the preference-exchange system depends very heavily on inter-party goodwill. It breaks down when the goodwill breaks down. And this is what happens when one coalition partner seeks to win a seat from the other. It is intensified when one partner, such as the Liberal Party has done in recent years, seeks to undermine the image of its coalition partner in the eyes of the general public — for example, when Rosemary Kyburz (Salisbury) said on 10 August 1983 in the *Australian*: "I could just not vote for a tired old government," and went on to say about the premier: "He is a dog trainer from way back, but I think he should go into training camels."

Regardless of whether or not Mrs Kyburz' statement was justified, the fact remains that it could be expected to have considerable influence on the people who vote for her in any election. Therefore, it is reasonable to suggest that a good number of those persons would believe that they were doing what she would want by directing their second preference away from the premier's party. The recorded experience of the increasing "drift" of Liberal Party preferences away from the

Premier Joh has got himself into hot water on more than one occasion over his support for dubious projects and people. Cancer therapist Milan Brych was one.

The Nationals' Trojan Horse? The smile on Premier Joh's face would indicate that as usual he's probably up to something. Regardless of what secrets the wooden horse holds, Premier Joh and his wife, Senator Florence Bjelke-Petersen, have been a combination to more than equal the power of any Trojan Horse.

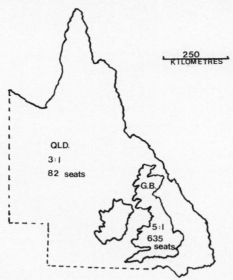

Map 1 indicates the vastness of the state of Queensland compared with the British Isles.

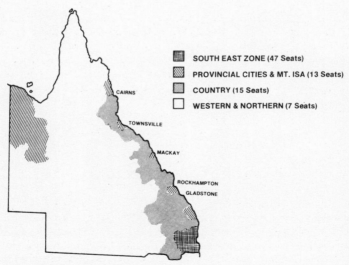

Map 2 indicates the zones that the National Party supports in the distribution of electorates. The zones closely mirror the density of population throughout the state.

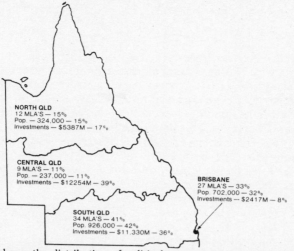

NORTH QLD
12 MLA'S — 15%
Pop. — 324,000 — 15%
Investments — $5387M — 17%

CENTRAL QLD
9 MLA'S — 11%
Pop. — 237.000 — 11%
Investments — $12254M — 39%

BRISBANE
27 MLA'S — 33%
Pop. 702,000 — 32%
Investments — $2417M — 8%

SOUTH QLD
34 MLA'S — 41%
Pop. 926,000 — 42%
Investments — $11.330M — 36%

Map 3 shows the distribution of political representation prior to the 1983 state election.

PROPOSED BOUNDARY LINE
FOLLOWS GREAT DIVIDING
RANGE

CAIRNS

TOWNSVILLE

13 SEATS

MACKAY

9 SEATS

ROCKHAMPTON

60 SEATS
(100 miles radius
of Brisbane)

Map 4 shows what a Labor or Liberal Party redistribution along the lines of "one vote, one value" would have done to the present balance of representation in Queensland.

These maps tell the story of the Queensland National Party's stand against the Labor and Liberal parties' "one vote, one value" redistribution campaign in Queensland.

National Party in recent years coinciding with the anti-premier, anti-National Party campaign that has been waged by some members of the Liberal Party supports this argument. Interestingly, at the same time, the flow of National Party preferences has been remarkably good for the Liberal Party. Likewise, this favourable experience coincides with continued efforts by Sir Robert Sparkes to promote National Party harmony with the Liberal Party.

When interplay relations deteriorate beyond the point of the casual voter, there is the further dimension of direct party action to ensure that the other partner does not get the benefit of the preferences. This is achieved by endorsing candidates (in marginal seats held by a coalition member) who it is known will poll badly, and through the flow-on, normal loss of their preferences will do just enough to ensure defeat of the sitting member. This is what the National Party claimed the Liberal Party did in the seats of Murrumba, Wynnum and Ipswich West during the 1977 state election. Labor won all three seats. This has the same effect as the first rule in the book on "destroying your opponent in the preferential voting system", which says put him at the bottom of the list.

In three-cornered contests in which there is not a sitting coalition member, the situation is different, inasmuch as it is not a direct undertaking by one partner to take a seat away from the other (by fair means or foul). Neither holds the seat and therefore, regardless of how strenuously the campaign is fought (so long as the competition is fair), neither party can really complain if the other wins. Such contests are also more likely to be "friendlier", because both parties usually realize that they need each other to win, unlike a three-cornered contest involving a sitting member, where the element of "if I can't win, then neither will he" frequently comes into the struggle. Consequently neither wins and the seat is lost.

Parliamentary reform

The debate over the need for a public accounts committee in Queensland will be credited in history as "the straw that broke the camel's back" and ended the coalition, even though it never came to a vote. As is discussed elsewhere in this book, it was an issue that the Labor Party and sections of the Liberal Party in Queensland had been pursuing to embarrass the National Party and, in particular, Premier Joh Bjelke-Petersen. It was part of an overall campaign that can be best described as "parliamentary reform" designed to paint the Bjelke-Petersen government as ultra-conservative and dictatorial. It created considerable tension between the two coalition parties.

Elaborating a little further on the debate, Premier Joh Bjelke-Petersen sees it quite clearly as "a job for the boys", another opportunity for parliamentarians to get additional fees for belonging to yet another non-productive committee of absolutely no constructive benefit to his government. "It's just a way to get more money from the government for themselves," he said in Townsville at the start of the 1983 campaign. "A hundred dollars a day they would get for every meeting of the committee they attended." Bjelke-Petersen sees absolutely no necessity for a public accounts committee. "We have the accounts of every department audited. There can be no suggestion that every penny of government money is not accounted for."

Jobs for the boys

Another aspect of the campaign involves what the Labor Party and the dissident section of the Liberal Party call "jobs for the National Party boys". This campaign has been designed to suggest that there is something less than honest in the way that the National Party handles the dealings of government. The allocation of state government contracts, appointments to prominent boards and government positions, and the establishment of the Bjelke-Petersen Foundation are cited by the party's detractors as evidence of wrong-doing. The appointment of Sir Edwards Lyons as chairman of the TAB in Queensland in 1981 was one of the major blow-ups. Lyons is a trustee of the National Party. He is also the chairman of the Katies Salons chain of stores throughout Australia. The granting of exploration rights to the Winchester South Coal areas in Central Queensland to a company owned by Sir Leslie Thiess was another. Yet another was the granting of casino licences in Queensland to companies controlled by Sir Leslie Thiess (Townsville) and Sir Roderick Proctor (Gold

Coast). Sir Roderick Proctor is also a trustee of the National Party. Frank Moore (later Sir Frank Moore), a National Party State Management Committee member, was also appointed chairman of the Queensland Tourist and Travel Corporation, former deputy parliamentary leader Ron Camm was appointed chairman of the Queensland Sugar Board and the former member for Wynnum, Mr Bill Lamond, to the chair of the Queensland Small Business Corporation.

Taken in isolation, these appointments are easy to construe as damning evidence of "jobs for the boys" to be used against the National Party; however, when the performance and record of the individuals concerned is known, it becomes really a matter of whether a person should be condemned for his political beliefs. Without exception, the performance of the people concerned, in the exploitation of their given responsibilities, has been exceptional. Sir Leslie Thiess must be given considerable credit for the vast success of the Queensland coal industry that the state benefits from today. The Thiess family have been leading pioneers in the state's development. Sir Roderick Proctor is one of the state's most prominent accountants and a director of a number of highly successful Queensland companies. Sir Edward Lyons established a multi-million-dollar chain-store business across Australia from basic Queensland beginnings, and under his chairmanship the TAB has grown considerably. Frank Moore created a radio and television empire throughout Queensland from humble beginnings in Longreach, and as chairman of the Queensland Tourist and Travel Corporation has revolutionized tourist development and promotion in Queensland. Bill Lamond pioneered the need for the Small Business Corporation. Ron Camm has been centrally involved in the success of the Queensland sugar industry, as a grower and an influential state government minister, for almost all of his working life. Most importantly as far as the National Party is concerned, all are outstanding Queenslanders.

Street marches

The street march debate that erupted in 1977 was the most worrying of the contentious issues as far as the National Party was concerned. It was emotionally based on the right of people in a free society to protest against government action by marching through the streets. In reality, however, it was fuelled by groups who simply wanted to disrupt the government of the day. It emerged at the time of the emotional anti-nuclear debate and was considerably confused. The Queensland premier had no doubts, however, about the disruptive potential of the protest marches. He introduced a system of police permits for street marches, against which there was no appeal.

Many National Party supporters didn't understand the issue or the implications. They were bombarded by the sensationalist press which ignored the facts that the Queensland laws were little different, if any, from the laws in other states. Also conveniently ignored was the fact that the majority of applications for marches were being given permits. Only those marches that were specifically considered to be disruptive were not given permits. Organizers of banned marches were given the alternative of rallying at the Roma Street forum, but this didn't satisfy their demands.

The most concerning aspect was the involvement of the church movement in the debate. The resolution passed by the Uniting Church Synod that year criticizing the government's stand on street marches disappointed Bjelke-Petersen and worried many National Party supporters. This concern was further compounded when a joint statement of Anglicans, Catholics, Lutherans and the Council of Churches supported the Uniting Church resolution.

The Liberal Party lay low on the issue, despite the fact that the actual legislation was introduced into the parliament by a Liberal and the eight Liberal ministers in the government supported its introduction. Publicly, the Liberals called for an appeal to be allowed against policy decisions on permits for marches. The premier, however, saw no reason to budge. He instructed the police department to closely monitor the disruptive marches and had convincing evidence that a small band of militant agitators were behind the trouble.

The by-election result in Lockyer in 1976 seemed to justify the Liberals' stance. Liberal candidate Tony Bourke held the seat for the Liberals against a major National Party campaign.

It was a campaign that the premier and the Nationals had chosen to fight on law and order, and they lost.

The premier was unrepentant. He soldiered on with his law-and-order campaign, convinced that it was a winner. If the Liberals wanted to back down on the issue, he would take the credit (as he expected it to come) for himself.

The loss of Lockyer and the continuing barrage of public criticism did take its toll within the National Party. Some began to waver. As has been suggested elsewhere in this book, 1976–77 was a "low" period for the National Party. Morale, boosted by the heady successes of 1974, was waning. The street march issue was one of a number of issues (see the chapter on the coalition) on which Joh Bjelke-Petersen and the National Party were under fire, and their tough public stance was being criticized.

Nationals under pressure

At the 1977 State Conference in Mount Isa, where tensions continued for the party, Sir Robert Sparkes sought to put the issue into some perspective for the faithful. "Certainly, since the new policy on street march permits was first announced, some government members, mostly Liberals, have apparently changed their minds, mainly, I suspect, because the new policy has proved unpopular with some sections of the community. I do not question the right of any member to have second thoughts about any aspect of government policy. However, no government worth its salt should flex and bend to every public pressure or outcry. It must do what it believes to be right, regardless of whether it is popular or unpopular. Sometimes, principles must be placed before political expediency." The premier's message to the same conference was simple: "The militant and communist union leaders must be halted!"

Street march aftermath

By election day on 12 November 1977, the street march issue was faltering. Violent unrest in Britain and destructive marches in Sydney provided strong support for Bjelke-Petersen's stand in the eyes of conservative Queensland. The Labor Party quickly got the message and Labor leader Tom

Burns did as much as anyone to indicate to the electorate (without actually saying so) that really Bjelke-Petersen was right. Burns first failed to turn up as advertised at an anti-uranium rally that spilt over into a street march during which 400 were arrested, and then called for the cancellation of a march planned for 11 November, the day before the poll.

In the 12 November election, the Bjelke-Petersen government was returned. The Nationals lost four seats, including Aboriginal member Eric Deeral in Cook, ironically, the only Aboriginal ever elected to the Queensland parliament and defeated by his own people's vote. The marginal seats of Mount Isa and Warrego were retained. The Liberals lost six seats.

The final seal of approval was to come twelve months later, however, when the Brisbane *Courier-Mail*, in an article headlined "We're Not So Different" which was published on 15 November 1978, belatedly carried the truth that Queensland's street march laws were little different from, if not easier than, the laws in other states in the Commonwealth. In New South Wales, permits to march have to be obtained from the police of the local authority and no appeals are allowed. In Victoria, permits are issued by the local authority and no appeals are allowed. In Western Australia, permits must be obtained from the police commissioner and there is also no appeal. In Tasmania, permits are obtained from the Transport Commission, but again there is no appeal. In South Australia, no permits are required, but marchers forfeit their rights to legal immunity in the event of an accident or similar incident.

After more than a year of divisive, destructive, community debate, it was finally discovered that Queensland's street march laws were in fact the most liberal in Australia, apart from those of South Australia. In Queensland, an appeal to the police commissioner is allowed, if the District Superintendent of Traffic rejects the original appeal. Scrutiny of the 346 applications that were lodged to that time also revealed that 316 had received permits. The thirty rejected were on the grounds that they were marches considered by the police to be disruptive to the traffic, or they involved groups or individuals with a record of violence in previous marches. The "street march" issue has died a slow and silent death since that date.

The bare bones

And so twenty-six years of problems, discussion, disagreement and new directions finally took their toll of the Queensland conservative coalition. The unprecedented growth of the National Party in the seventies undoubtedly contributed to the decline in National–Liberal relations leading to the final acts that opened to a full house on 4 August 1983 and played to tumultuous encores that echoed around the state, and across Australia.

7

Crisis!

Direct from Hansard — the *Queensland Parliamentary Debates* for 4 August 1983 (pages 142–43) records the following:

Mr SPEAKER (Hon. S.J. Muller, Fassifern) read prayers and took the chair at 11.00 a.m.

APPROPRIATION BILL (No. 1)
Assent reported by Mr Speaker.

LEAVE TO MOVE MOTION WITHOUT NOTICE
Mr PRENTICE (Toowong): I seek leave to move a motion without notice.

Mr SPEAKER: Order! Is leave granted?

Mr BJELKE-PETERSEN: Not unless we know what it is.

Honourable Members interjected.

Mr SPEAKER: Order! I inform the honourable member for Toowong that, at this stage, he is permitted only to seek leave of the House to move a motion without notice. I will formally submit the motion. Is leave granted to move without notice? As many as are of the opinion say, "Aye"; to the contrary, "No". I think the "Ayes" have it.

An Honourable Member: Divide.

Mr SPEAKER: Ring the bells.

Dr EDWARDS: I rise to a point of order. I point out to you, Mr Speaker, that the "Noes" did not call "Divide". I therefore ask your advice as to whether or not there should be a division on this motion.

Mr SPEAKER: Order! Is it the opinion of the House that there should be a division on this matter?

Honourable Members: No!

Mr SPEAKER: I will cancel the division.

MOTION FOR SUSPENSION OF STANDING ORDERS AND SESSIONAL ORDERS

General Business – Orders of the Day

Mr PRENTICE (Toowong), by leave, without notice: I move –

"That so much of the Standing Orders and Sessional Order as would prevent the debating together and forthwith of General Business – Orders of the Day No. 1, in the name of Mr Scassola, and No. 4, in the name of Mr Warburton, be suspended and that the motions be debated forthwith."

Dr EDWARDS: I rise to a point of order. Mr Speaker, my point of order was that nobody on the "Noes" side requested a division. As I understand Standing Orders, there would therefore be no need for a division, and I ask for your ruling.

Mr SPEAKER: Order! I require five seconds to consider my decision.

Mr PRENTICE: I rise to a further point of order. I should have said "No. 1" and "No. 2".

Mr WRIGHT: Mr Speaker, I point out that notice of motion No. 4 was not given by the Deputy Leader of the Opposition; he gave notice of motion No. 2. Could we have clarification from the Liberal member? Does he intend to have us debate motion No. 2? That is the Opposition's intention.

Mr PRENTICE: That is correct, Mr Speaker.

Mr SPEAKER: There will be no division.

Honourable Members interjected.

Mr SPEAKER: Order! There will be no debate. We will proceed with the next business. Are there any ministerial papers?

Honourable Members interjected.

Mr SPEAKER: Order! I have 25,000 advisers at the moment. I am seeking clarification on an issue.

Mr WRIGHT: Mr Speaker, I seek clarification. Is it correct that you have ruled that the House agreed that the debate continue and, if so, is the debate to continue?

Mr SPEAKER: Order! I have not ruled that the debate will continue, and I now proceed to the next business.

Honourable Members interjected.

Mr SCASSOLA: I rise to a point of order. Mr Speaker, I submit that you put that question and that no division was called. I submit that the motion ought to be determined as being carried in the affirmative and that debate should proceed. I suggest that it was the clear intention of the House. I put it to you that quite clearly no division was called.

Mr SPEAKER: Order! It is my intention to ensure that this Parliament remain democratic. I will now put the question.

Question — That the motion (Mr Prentice) be agreed to — put; and the House divided — in division —

Honourable Members interjecting —

Dr EDWARDS: I rise to a point of order. Mr Speaker, my point of order is that a division would waste the time of the House when, as you said, the "Noes" had the vote. As a result, under Standing Orders there is no need for a division on that matter when, in your opinion, the "Noes" had the vote.

Mr WRIGHT: I rise to a further point of order. Mr Speaker, is it not correct that, when a motion is put to the House and it is clear that there is, on the voices, a decision against the motion, those in favour of the motion have the right to have the motion decided by division? We have called a division, and we ask for that division to be held.

Mr SPEAKER: Order! For the last five minutes there has been a pointless argument about resolving the matter. I see no democratic way of resolving it other than to let the House make the final determination by way of a division.

The House divided; Terence White, MLA, Minister for Welfare Services and Liberal Party member for the seaside electorate of Redcliffe, crossed the floor to vote for the motion along with the ALP and the following Liberal Party members: Rob Akers (Pine Rivers), John Greenwood (Ashgrove), Terence Gygar (Stafford), Angus Innes (Sherwood), Rosemary Kyburz (Salisbury), Ian Prentice (Toowong), Guelf Scassola (Mt Gravatt).

The Queensland National–Liberal coalition government had survived for a record twenty-six years when Terry White made his now historic move on Thursday 4 August 1983 to break cabinet solidarity and support a dissident move to wrest the business of the House from the hands of the government. Fourteen tension-filled days later the coalition was over, and Queensland was governed by a minority National Party government. The fourteen suspense-filled days of political move and countermove that followed while the Queensland coalition came to terms with White's surprise move shook anti-socialist forces around the nation and gave the Queensland Labor Party its best reasons for optimism in twenty-six years in opposition.

Day 1: The sacking

"It was bedlam. You could have heard them screaming and shouting down in Queen Street."

Thus spoke Premier Joh Bjelke-Petersen when he later described the performance in the House on 4 August as the rowdiest he had heard in his thirty-seven years in state parliament.

By the time the House had cleared on 4 August, Terry White had been sacked by his Liberal Party leader, Dr Llew Edwards, and another Liberal minister, Bill Hewitt, had been severely reprimanded by the premier for allegedly avoiding the crucial vote. White had been given the chance to voluntarily resign by Edwards, but when he refused to do so he was sacked. Premier Bjelke-Petersen and Dr Edwards went to see the Governor to ask for White's dismissal – the first time in the history of the coalition that a minister had been sacked in this way.

Rumour was rife within the corridors of parliament that White's move was related to a leadership struggle within the Liberal Party that had been brought to a head during the preceding weeks after the defection to the National Party of two pro-Edwards Liberal Party members of parliament, Bill Kaus (Mansfield) and Bob Moore (Windsor).

When the news hit the stands, and afternoon radio and television news had broken the story, Terry White was a hero. The crux of the crisis had conveniently been converted from one of a Liberal minister breaking cabinet solidarity and being sacked by his own party leader with the unanimous support of his cabinet colleagues, to a David-and-Goliath struggle between White and Premier Bjelke-Petersen.

The media had the champion they so eagerly sought to pit against the premier. The question now was: did "nice guy" Terry White have the political guile to win, where five opposition leaders, two prime ministers and three of White's predecessors had failed?

Day 2: A man of conscience

By Friday 5 August the news media throughout the nation

carried the stories of the shock crisis in the Queensland coalition, and generally applauded Terry White's moves on the grounds that he had displayed the guts to stand up to Bjelke-Petersen on a matter of conscience. Throughout Dr Edwards' term of leadership, the media had consistently pursued the line that Edwards was a weak leader and subservient to Bjelke-Petersen and National Party might. Now they had a champion for their cause. Although it was not a matter of decision or debate in the parliament throughout the crisis session, White was depicted as having made his move to support the call for a public accounts committee for the Queensland parliament as a matter of conscience. It was emotional fodder that the media thrived on. In the interests of not wanting to spoil a good story with mundane matters, the media conveniently forgot the dull fact that White had crossed the floor to vote on a procedural motion designed to take control of the business of the day out of the hands of the government. In a joint statement to the media issued by the Liberal "ginger group" members, Angus Innes, Rosemary Kyburz, Ian Prentice, Guelf Scassola, Rob Akers, John Greenwood and Terry Gygar sought to perpetuate this line of defence for White. "Mr White was merely exercising his right to vote in favour of the parliament discussing the question of a public accounts committee, which is Liberal Party policy," they claimed.

In the aftermath of Terry White's sacking on 5 August, there was also continuing speculation on Survey and Valuation minister Bill Hewitt's position. Lobbying and manoeuvring within the Liberal Party was also under way to fill the vacancy created by Terry White, with Premier Bjelke-Petersen taking a particular interest in Dr Edwards' short list. By the end of the day, the member for Ithaca, Colin Miller, a known coalitionist and Edwards supporter, had been sworn in during a special meeting of the Executive Council presided over by the Governor, Sir James Ramsay, and Terry White's commission had officially been withdrawn. In an added twist, Miller was given Bill Hewitt's portfolio of Welfare Services. Hewitt had survived after special representation on his behalf by Dr Edwards to the premier.

In other developments that day, front-running "ginger group" member Angus Innes (Sherwood) ruled himself out as a contender for the Liberal leadership if there was to be a move against Dr Edwards, and a meeting of the Liberal executive decided to leave the matter in the hands of their parliamentary wing. Terry White was also playing it cool on the question of a possible leadership challenge. "If there's a groundswell of support for anyone, as I said, it's a matter for the party," he said. On the other hand, the premier demonstrated his attitude during a flying visit to Gladstone, when he told the Central Queensland media that he would encourage his National Party to go after the seats of the eight Liberals who crossed the floor in their attempt to embarrass the government the day before. It had been the last straw for Bjelke-Petersen, who had long believed that many of the "ginger group" had ridden too long on the coat-tails of the success of the coalition without showing any gratitude.

Day 3: Leadership speculation

By Saturday 6 August, full-scale lobbying for the Liberal leadership was under way, although a leadership challenge was still a matter for public speculation. Llew Edwards' Labor Party neighbour in Ipswich West, Dave Underwood, in a release to his local Ipswich publication, the *Queensland Times*, confidently predicted Edwards' demise, claiming that Liberal Party backbenchers had told him that Terry White had the numbers to do what he wanted. The article is interesting inasmuch as it ties in with similar information supposedly leaked to Dr Edwards several weeks earlier by former federal Labor leader Bill Hayden, whose federal electorate of Oxley included Edwards' Ipswich seat. Hayden supposedly told Edwards at that stage that overtures had been made to the state Labor Party from a member or members of the Queensland Liberal Party for support to embarrass the coalition government on the matter of a public accounts committee. Underwood also forecast that the prospects of the deputy leader and Edwards supporter, Attorney-General Sam Doumany, were likewise doomed. Meanwhile, Terry White continued to take and maintain a low profile on the leadership issue. Bjelke-Petersen, however, was not to be fooled over White's leadership ambitions, and had made it patently clear to the Liberal Party at this early stage that he would not accept White back in cabinet. He strenuously warned the Liberals of the consequences of electing White as their leader, effectively foreshadowing the end of the coalition if White was subsequently elected to succeed Edwards.

Public opinion, now fuelled by the full blast of media support in favour of White's "gutsy" stand against Premier Bjelke-Petersen, was still running heavily in White's favour, but few knew the real story or understood the ramifications of White's actions. Edwards was working feverishly to turn the tide of public opinion, but the media in general were still largely sympathetic to White. In a statement to the *Courier-Mail* that day, Edwards said: "When ministers are sworn in by the Governor as representatives of the Crown, they are commissioned to perform their duties as a minister in Her Majesty's Government. Under the Westminster System to which the Liberal Party subscribes as one of its basic principles, a minister cannot vote with the Opposition against members of his own Government." On this latter point, Edwards may have been a little off the mark, as in reality White voted with the Liberal "ginger group", who in turn were supported by the Labor Party. It is a minor point, however, and does not alter the fact that White breached cabinet solidarity. Edwards also attempted to correct the misconception that White had crossed the floor to vote on the issue of a public accounts committee. He said that claims that White was exercising a conscience vote were "inaccurate and wrong". "He did not support the Government's business of the day," Edwards attempted to explain. Slowly this message was sinking in, and the media case for White was falling apart, but not fast enough for Dr Edwards.

Day 4: Chasing the numbers

By Sunday 7 August, it was obvious that Edwards did not have the numbers to survive a leadership spill, despite assurances that day from the state president of the Liberal Party, Dr John Herron, to his National Party counterpart, Sir Robert Sparkes, that he was working to get the numbers for Edwards. According to Sparkes, Herron had also agreed about the consequences of Terry White gaining the leadership, accepting that it would be too much for the coalition to stand. History had caught up with Llew Edwards, however. The sacking of several ministers some months earlier for alleged poor performance and the solid backing of White by the small "l" faction were more than Dr Edwards could counter. A reluctant Sam Doumany was now being touted as a possible compromise candidate in a bid to satisfy both the well-defined factions. Doumany, however, was never an acceptable alternative in this debate. It was always to be between Edwards and White.

Day 5: White is black

On Monday 8 August, Premier Joh Bjelke-Petersen celebrated the anniversary of his fifteenth year in control of Queensland, and quietly gave the Liberals something extra to think about by announcing that he had held discussions with state electoral officers on the previous Saturday to discuss procedures for calling an election. In customary fashion, however, he added that the final decision on an election was still his and he would announce any such decision when he was ready. Giving the Liberal Party further food for thought, he reaffirmed his often-repeated statement over the previous four days: that Terry White would not be allowed back into cabinet. "I'm not bluffing," he said. "There's no way I can go back to the Governor and ask him to reappoint as a minister a man I said had committed an offence last Thursday."

Labor prime minister Bob Hawke also came to town that Monday, at the start of his first official visit to Queensland since taking over the leadership of the Labor Party prior to going on to win the federal election on 5 March. Surprisingly, however, Hawke was slow off the mark in Brisbane. The big news of the day was Hawke and Premier Bjelke-Petersen smiling together as they inspected Brisbane's site for Expo 88. The premier was on his political best behaviour — after all, Mr Hawke now had control of the federal funding he needed for his Expo.

Throughout Monday, frantic moves were afoot within National Party circles and the now anti-White faction of the

Liberal Party to come up with a plan to rescue Edwards.
National Party heavy Russ Hinze and other numbers men in
the party busied themselves speaking with coalitionists in
Liberal ranks. Talk of wholesale defection to the National Party was in the air. Dissident Liberal backbenchers who had
precipitated the White affair were aware of this National
Party activity, and consequently sought to force Edwards to
call a meeting at 6.00 p.m. that day to settle the issue quickly.
They rightly feared that Bjelke-Petersen and Edwards would
use the forum of parliament the next day to state their case as
coalitionists and to beat off Terry White's challenge by calling
a snap election. Their attempts to corner Edwards failed and
Edwards set the meeting down for 2.15 p.m. the next day.
Prophetically, Terry White scored the quote of the day, when
he predicted, "It's going to be a week of brinkmanship."

Day 6: White elected leader

As Tuesday dawned, the numbers were just not there for Dr
Llew Edwards. They never had been from the beginning, but
there had been some reason to hope. Previously sacked
ministers would not forgive and forget, and the small "l"
faction could not be dissuaded from their course. By midday
on Tuesday 9 August, Edwards admitted defeat, announcing
publicly that he would not be contesting the leadership. In a
rare public appearance, Edward's wife, Leone, summed up
the feeling of most Queensland coalitionists upon hearing of
her husband's decision: "I think it is a sad situation for
Queensland. The timing is poor." Leone Edwards went on to
say: "Probably the most upsetting part is realizing that while
certain people were nice they were busy getting ready to stab
Llew in the back." Small compensation but, in the morning's
Courier-Mail, Edwards also extracted a semblance of an
apology from the editor following the headline of 6 August
which claimed that Edwards had revised his reasons for sacking Terry White. In a strongly worded statement to the
Courier-Mail, Edwards said, "I will not have my integrity
reflected upon by anybody."

Speculation now centred on whether Doumany or White
would win the Liberal leadership. White publicly dismissed

Doumany's chances with the statement that his (Doumany's) election as leader of the party would be a "political mistake because the public would see it as representing business as usual". It was an ego-boosting performance for Terry White; Doumany never looked like posing a threat.

Meanwhile, political analysts in Queensland pondered the alternatives open to the premier and the Liberal Party. The most popular scenario appeared to favour Terry White being elected leader, and the premier rejecting him and opting for an early election, most likely on 17 September. Some suggested that there was a chance that the Liberals would accept an offer from the Labor Party to form a temporary coalition for the purpose of introducing a redistribution Bill that would give both Labor and the Liberals a better chance at the forthcoming state elections. No one even got close to predicting the way the drama was yet to unfold. Terry White, meanwhile, was confident that he was ready for "any tricks" that Premier Joh might have up his sleeve, and challenged the premier to call an early election if he became the Liberal leader. He confidently predicted that he would win the leadership by 14 votes to 6 or, at worst, 12 to 8.

Parliament resumed, and at 11.00 a.m. the Speaker, the Hon. Selwyn Muller, read prayers. A Labor Party wag suggested that they were prayers for the coalition. Members of the small "l" faction of the Liberal Party were busying themselves in readiness to again embarrass the government. In a surprise move, however, the premier gave a pre-arranged signal to the Speaker and called for an adjournment of the House. The Liberal dissidents and the Labor Party were caught completely off guard. In the uproar that followed, the House divided and voted in favour of the premier's motion, with Rosemary Kyburz the only coalition member against the surprise move.

Any hope of further dissident action had been thwarted. Bjelke-Petersen later said that the decision had been made to allow the Liberal Party time to sort out their leadership problems, but there was more to it than that. Bjelke-Petersen expected trouble, and knew that the dissident section of the Liberal Party were likely to continue embarrassing the government. Without telling even his trusted Liberal Party ministers, he planned within his National Party to move

quickly and adjourn the House early for the traditional annual
RNA Show holiday. He was to say privately afterwards that it
was the best kept secret between him and his "boys" in ages.
He held the reins. He was confident that he was in control.

Parliament adjourned and waited for the Liberals' leadership meeting. At 2.15 p.m. the Liberals met at Parliament
House. By the time the 3.00 p.m. news broadcasts were
released, Terry White had been elected leader with a 14–5
majority on the first vote, with one abstention – Llew
Edwards. As a gesture to the coalitionists, Attorney-General
Sam Doumany retained his position as deputy leader.

The stage was now set for a showdown with the Nationals
that required nothing less than a public backdown by the
premier for the Liberals to win. Few Queenslanders expected
that to happen, however. It was now really an intriguing
matter of waiting to find out just what Terry White and the
Liberal Party could do, and exactly how the battle-seasoned
Bjelke-Petersen would handle the final face-to-face confrontation. The ball was squarely in Terry White's court. What
would he do next?

White briefed the news media on his successful bid for the
Liberal leadership, and announced that his first move would
be to advise Bjelke-Petersen and seek a settlement of the
stand-off between the coalition partners. Accompanied by
Doumany, White set off for the premier's office.

Bjelke-Petersen was aware by now that White had successfully gained the leadership of the Liberal Party. He had
already settled with National Party boss Sir Robert Sparkes
that he would not budge on his decision that White would not
be allowed back into his cabinet. The master of political
patience and suspense sat and waited for White and Doumany
to arrive and, when finally they did, asked them to wait in the
foyer.

White and Doumany waited like naughty schoolboys for
almost an hour before they were finally ushered into the
premier's spacious fifteenth-floor office suite looking out on
the Brisbane River and the Botanical Gardens. White immediately advised the premier of his party's decision and
asked that all be forgiven. He suggested that they settle their
differences in the interests of the coalition. Bjelke-Petersen
wanted no part of it and repeated his earlier advice that White

was not acceptable to him as a cabinet minister. It was a brief and straight-to-the-point meeting, during which Bjelke-Petersen held all the trump cards. White and Doumany left dejected. There would be no backdown by the premier. Bjelke-Petersen later said that it was totally out of the question that he could accept such a man as his deputy and treasurer after the action White had taken to break his sworn oath of office. "Could you imagine it?" he said. "Having to trust a person like that as my deputy and treasurer — no way, I just couldn't do it!"

What had been a stand-off between the two coalition partners was now a crisis. The Liberals were faced now with the dilemma of either leaving their new leader out in the cold while his colleagues sat in cabinet, or replacing White, or pulling out of the coalition. To add further pressure to White's dilemma, Bjelke-Petersen was about to extend the offer to loyal Liberal ministers to stay on in their cabinet posts.

The ball stayed in the Liberal court. All eyes stayed on Terry White. He had grabbed for the leadership and won; he had enjoyed a brief honeymoon with the press and public opinion for his actions; but now, like the dog who chased the car and caught it, he had to work out what to do with his prize. As the hours ticked away, his position was weakening rapidly. The news media were already carrying the stories of the brief meeting with Bjelke-Petersen and the fact that Bjelke-Petersen had confirmed his previous position that Terry White would not be allowed back in cabinet. It was now clearly obvious that Terry White had taken on a daunting task. The odds were against him. David had not killed Goliath with his first shot and now Goliath was in the throes of lowering the boom.

By Tuesday evening, as the Liberal Party executive gathered to discuss their predicament, it was obvious that White had more to worry about than Bjelke-Petersen. The truth about the events leading up to his shock move in parliament on 4 August were emerging publicly. A number of his former cabinet colleagues within the Liberal Party were starting to feel they had been deceived. It was becoming increasingly difficult to convince anyone that this had not been a leadership challenge from the beginning — and that they had been the pawns. It was not going well for Terry White.

A celebration party at his parliamentary office early in the evening was the only light relief for Terry White that day. It was an opportunity to make a plea for sanity to prevail. "I make a call now for the premier and the National Party in the interests of the state of Queensland to maintain a stable coalition government," he said. "I hope the premier will take the pragmatic view that the coalition is vitally important and above any man."

Day 7: White stays out

On Wednesday 10 August, Prime Minister Bob Hawke put the cat among the Liberal pigeons by unequivocally supporting the sacking of Terry White. Asked to give a one-word answer to the question of whether he would retain in his cabinet any minister who crossed the floor to vote with the opposition, Hawke said: "No."

With his political world caving in around him, it was a day of putting on a brave face for Terry White and his now beleaguered Liberal Party. Conversely, it was also a day of obvious jubilation for Rhonda White, wife of the new Liberal leader. She said in an interview with the *Courier-Mail* published that day that she didn't think deposed Liberal leader Llew Edwards would want their sympathy. She added, "But he's got our goodwill. I don't think there is room for sympathy in politics." Controversial Liberal Party candidate for the state seat of Caloundra Cr Don Culley also bought into the debate by stating his support for the dumping of Dr Edwards. And in Canberra, the federal arm of the Liberal Party under Andrew Peacock's leadership was starting to worry about the developing crisis in Queensland. There was somewhat of a difference of opinion, however, between the federal coalition partners. Peacock asked his coalition counterpart, Doug Anthony, to intervene on Terry White's behalf and seek to have the Queensland premier accept him as Liberal Party leader and take him back into the cabinet. Anthony, however, was branding White as a defector, placing the blame for the Queensland situation clearly at White's feet.

A lunchtime rally in Brisbane's King George Square on 10 August gave the Liberals the chance to present a united face to the public. Terry White and Dr Edwards were principal speakers. It was the departure scene, however, which really indicated the true position. Dr Edwards, now simply known as the treasurer and no longer deputy premier in the eyes of the Liberal Party, climbed into his chauffeur-driven ministerial limousine to be driven away, while Terry White, backbencher, remained out in the cold. It is interesting to note also that it was Edwards who held forth with fire and brimstone and captured crowd reaction at the rally, while Terry White's speech received very little reaction.

Day 8: Ministers enticed to stay

In the political options stakes, three courses of action were now open: (1) enough Liberal ministers would accept the premier's offer and stay in government despite their new leader being left out in the cold; (2) enough Liberal members (ministers and backbenchers) would defect to the National Party to allow it to hold a majority on the floor of the House; or (3) the National Party would be forced into minority government.

Of these three options, there is no doubt that on 11 August the premier and the National Party were anxiously working to achieve either of the first two. Ideally, the premier would have liked to have won the defection of enough Liberals to govern alone. This would have allowed him to re-open parliament, pass further supply, and restabilize his government before going to the people in an election that had to be held before February 1984. In a longer-term sense, the winning over of several "establishment" Liberals could have provided the National Party with its long-dreamed-of base in the Brisbane metropolitan area. The premier confirmed this in an interview that day when he said: "I would like Dr Edwards to stay there [in cabinet] as either an independent or a National Party man." If wholesale defection was not on, the second-best option was to get guarantees from enough Liberal coalitionists to ensure that he could re-open parliament to extend supply which was now provided only until November. The final option, of minority government, was popular among National Party backbenchers eager for cabinet rank, but it was the last thing at this stage that the premier wanted. Not that he was concerned about taking such a step, but he would have preferred politically to present a united front with his Liberal coalition loyalists in the run up to any election. "This is a tremendous opportunity [for the Nationals] to capitalize on the situation, although I don't want to do this," he stated when interviewed by the media that day. This is not to say that Bjelke-Petersen and the National Party were not prepared for minority government. Plans were already made following discussions with Sir Robert Sparkes, senior National Party ministers and organization executives for the premier to take Treasury and swear in six new National Party ministers if the need arose. Notices had also been sent out to members of the Nationals' State Management Committee and all parliamentarians to attend a joint meeting at party headquarters on Friday 12 August to discuss this plan if need be and to demonstrate party solidarity behind the premier.

In the days that now remained in the drama, the position of Liberal coalition loyalists was to be the central aspect in all discussions of National Party tactics and planning. For Terry White and the Liberal Party it was now a task of holding the coalitionists in their ranks and away from Bjelke-Petersen's clutches. Part of their strategy in this regard was to have all nineteen members sign an agreement of support which Mr White produced on 11 August to shore up his flagging public image as a leader capable of holding the Liberal Party together. A number of Liberal members were seriously considering joining the National Party at that stage. The only thing holding them back was the nearness of the election and doubts that they would have sufficient time to sell their story to their electorates. For the Nationals, the dream of picking up four or five top Liberals in key blue-ribbon conservative Brisbane metropolitan electorates was so close, and yet so far away. Had the National Party held any demonstrable indication of electoral support in the city, it is almost certain that some of these Liberals would have taken the plunge.

Being out in the cold for Terry White meant the full treatment from the Bjelke-Petersen government. He had to accept that he would not be given the keys to Dr Edwards' office in Parliament House and that he would have no more status in the eyes of the government than that of an ordinary backbencher. He had no choice but to set up his leadership in makeshift accommodation at Liberal Party headquarters. The Liberal Party provided him with the secretarial and research staff and press secretary that the government would not. He settled into his spartan Liberal Party headquarters accommodation, while his seven Liberal Party ministers attended the day's meeting of the Executive Council at the Executive Building in George Street, at which the premier again encouraged the seven Liberal ministers at this meeting to ignore Mr White and stay on in their ministerial offices, with all the perks and benefits that went with cabinet rank.

Day 9: Crisis meetings

Friday 12 August loomed as a day of hope for the supporters of both the Liberal and National parties and coalitionists in general. The pressure was still mounting for the Liberals, however, with the morning press carrying the front-page story that the Liberal candidate for Surfers Paradise, John Kearney, QC, had withdrawn his candidature. "My political position as a strong supporter of the Liberal Party in Queensland and in Canberra is well known," Kearney said; however, "The sudden political upheaval within the Liberal Party and the Coalition in Brisbane in the last several days has made my position as a Liberal candidate untenable. I have withdrawn from campaigning." In this crucial near-Brisbane battleground between the Nationals and the Liberals, it was a bitter psychological blow to the Liberals and an unexpected morale booster for the Nationals. A month earlier the Liberals had also lost their endorsed candidate for Russ Hinze's seat of Gold Coast, Mr John McDonald, through ill health.

Like the Nationals, the Liberals planned a top-level executive meeting that day. The stage was set for significant announcements to be made. Behind the scenes, however, the outlook for reconciliation was still not bright. The blatant facts of political life being what they are, the crucial importance of survival was coming home to those key Liberal ministers who were considering the National Party alternative. At the same time, the Liberal Party had painted itself into a corner from which it had very little chance of emerging without considerable loss of face. The National Party could see nothing to gain from a backdown. There was now really only one way to go.

The meeting of Nationals at Bjelke-Petersen House in Spring Hill was a showing of strength and unity, orchestrated from the beginning by the party president, Sir Robert Sparkes. Scheduled to start at 10.00 a.m., the meeting was over by lunchtime with Sparkes and Bjelke-Petersen gaining the unanimous support they were seeking. Principal performers at the meeting were the premier, Sparkes and the minister for Main Roads and Racing, Russ Hinze. To the delight of the assembled Nationals, a confident premier outlined the events of the past week and the options that lay ahead for the Nationals. In particular he dwelt on the problem he now had of working with the Liberal Party in government. "There are those I trust and those I won't have anything to do with again. They might as well go and join the Labor Party," he said.

Despite suggestions in the morning edition of the Rockhampton *Bulletin* that day that Hinze was trying to undermine Premier Bjelke-Petersen's leadership, Hinze was the outstanding supporter for the premier at the meeting. "You've only got to know who lives in Rockhampton [Labor leader Keith Wright is the member for Rockhampton] to know where that story came from," Hinze boomed. He then went on to tell how he had gone across to Terry White on 4 August when the House divided and White crossed the floor to try to get him back into the fold. "I thought for a while there that he might not have known what he was doing. I thought, well, he's only been in parliament a couple of years and maybe he doesn't know the ramifications of what he is doing. He knew what he was doing all right. He told me so," Hinze said. The meeting also heard legal opinion from the party's legal adviser, Harry Bandidt, reinforcing the premier's stand that it was Terry White who had broken the coalition agreement when he departed from cabinet solidarity. "Once you break any clause of any agreement you have broken the whole agreement," Bandidt said. "If you're buying a house and one clause sets out how much you've got to pay and you don't pay, then the whole agreement is off."

The coalition agreement, central to these discussions, contained six simply stated clauses of agreement. They were:
(1) The leader of the National Party shall be the premier and

the leader of the Liberal Party shall be the deputy premier and treasurer.

(2) The coalition cabinet shall consist of 18 members, 11 from the National Party and 7 from the Liberal Party and any vacancy caused by death or retirement shall be filled by the same party.

(3) Both the National Party and the Liberal Party accept that the principle of cabinet solidarity is basic to the Westminster system of government and therefore all ministers shall be required to acknowledge, in writing, their acceptance of and conformity to this principle.

(4) The Speaker of the parliament shall be elected from the National Party and the chairman of committees shall be elected from the Liberal Party.

(5) Legislative and administrative decisions of the coalition government shall be compatible with the broad principles of the two parties.

(6) Reasonable requests by the Liberal Party section of the coalition shall not be rejected by the National Party section using its majority in joint party meetings and all members of both parties shall respect the confidentiality of joint party meetings.

Terry White had clearly broken clause 3 of the agreement. The Liberal Party and White would later argue that under clause 1 of the agreement the Nationals had to accept White as leader. It was a difficult argument to substantiate. Terry White had already broken the agreement when he contravened clause 3. This was why he was unacceptable to the National Party without a public apology.

The meeting ended with a unanimous vote of support on a resolution sponsored by Sir Robert Sparkes which endorsed the actions of the premier and the party executive taken in what was termed "The White Affair". The motion read:

> That this meeting (1) endorses the fundamental principle of Cabinet solidarity enshrined in the Westminster system for centuries and enunciated in Part 3 of the Coalition agreement; (2) fully supports the action taken by the Coalition Government last week which led to the dismissal of a Minister of the Crown for breaching that principle and that agreement; (3) affirms its full support for the Premier in his stand in respect of the Coalition dispute; and (4) reaffirms its complete support for the continuation of Coalition Government in this State."

The resolution was moved by Sir Robert Sparkes and seconded by Brian Cahill, the candidate for Aspley.

The media, earlier relegated to the front lawns to wait, then packed into the room to hear the outcome. Sir Robert Sparkes, flanked by Bjelke-Petersen, senior vice-president Charles Holm and Harry Bandidt, read a brief prepared statement that obviously was an anti-climax for the reporters assembled. They had expected the announcement that the Nationals had decided to form a minority government. Asked by reporters if he had backed down on the option to go it alone, Bjelke-Petersen, to the delight of the assembled crowd, said without smiling, "I haven't changed my mind. I'm only trying to contain myself, that's all." He then added, with a quick look towards a stern-faced Sir Robert Sparkes, "I'm very obedient." The meeting cracked up with laughter.

There was no laughter at Liberal Party headquarters, however, where Liberal officials had gathered for their meeting scheduled to begin at 12.30 p.m. Disappointed by the absence of any real meat from the National Party announcement, the media rushed around to the Gregory Terrace headquarters of the Liberal Party in the hope that something might break in that quarter. From a journalistic point of view, the Nationals' meeting had been a non-event at that stage of the drama. Without something positive from the Liberals now, it would be just another day of rehashing the rights and wrongs of the two parties' now well-known stands.

Attorney-General Sam Doumany indicated the tension in the Liberals' discussions when he stormed out of the meeting and sharply told waiting journalists anxious for a story to "go and ask Terry". Inside the meeting, Terry White was putting on a brave face under pressure. In front of the cameras that assembled for the press briefing, he tore up the National Party press release which had been given to him. He repeated that he was committed to coalition government but said, "The coalition was over when the National Party telegraphed it this afternoon." Party president Dr John Herron then read out a prepared statement which gave the National Party a forty-eight-hour ultimatum, expiring at 6.00 p.m. on Sunday 14 August. The Nationals had to accept Terry White or call an early election. It was a bad performance by White, and he and

Dr Herron knew it. With White showing signs of the strain, they quickly called an end to the briefing.

Friday 12 August, which had started with so much hope of being a decision day, ended with Bjelke-Petersen maintaining his position of wanting the Liberal ministers to stay on in their posts, and Terry White and the Liberals now waiting out their forty-eight-hour ultimatum, which nobody really believed would influence Bjelke-Petersen. "All Terry White and the Liberals have done is buy themselves time to work out what to do next. Old Joh's got them on the run," one disgruntled reporter quipped as he left Liberal headquarters.

Day 10: Liberal Party tension grows

Saturday 13 August continued the media speculation about just what was going to happen. It was a continuation of the Bjelke-Petersen tactic to simply give the Liberals enough rope. "It's up to them," he repeated. "I've told the ministers they can stay. But I won't have Mr White back in cabinet at any price."

Deepening the cracks in Liberal Party ranks, the Saturday media also carried stories on further developments regarding John Kearney's withdrawal from campaigning in Surfers Paradise. Terry White had made headlines on Friday with his statement that Kearney had "thrown in the towel" and his "if it's too hot in the kitchen" response to Kearney's withdrawal. Kearney had lashed back: "He [White] was impetuous, petulant, paltry and politically damaging to the Liberal Party and provocative to me and my family."

Day 11: Joh relaxes – ultimatum lapses – Doumany quits

The forty-eight-hour ultimatum deadline passed without response from the Nationals. Bjelke-Petersen spent Sunday at home at Kingaroy as usual. At 6.00 p.m. the evening news bulletins around the nation announced that there had been no response from the Nationals to the Liberal ultimatum and therefore, effectively (as far as the Liberals were concerned), the twenty-six-year coalition was over. The damaging news,

announced earlier in the day, that Attorney-General Sam
Doumany had decided to resign as Terry White's deputy
added fuel to the fire. His reason was that he wanted to spend
more time working in his marginal electorate of Kurilpa in the
lead up to the state election. There was no denying the
tension, however, that had been developing between him and
Terry White throughout the preceding week. Doumany
wanted to stay in cabinet and White wanted him out.

Day 12: Governor rejects resignations

Monday 15 August dawned with the pressure still very much
on Terry White and the Liberal Party. Dr Edwards summed
up the situation of the coalitionists in Liberal ranks in a statement to his electorate printed in his local newspaper. "I am a
staunch coalitionist," Dr Edwards said, "and it is my strong
hope that both parties involved can somehow retrieve the
situation so that Queensland can again be served by a strong
and effective coalition government." He went on to say, "I
will, however, continue to serve Ipswich and its people to the
best of my ability. The capacity in which I will do this naturally will be determined by the outcome of current negotiations
on the future of the coalition government." So despite the
passing of the Liberal Party's forty-eight-hour ultimatum
deadline, Dr Edwards remained hopeful that something could
still be done. He went on to say, "The highest degree of mutual
trust and loyalty existed between myself and the premier." Dr
Edwards' situation reflected the continuing desire of Liberal
ministers to retain their portfolios. Premier Bjelke-Petersen
was still maintaining his stand that he wanted them to stay.

Concerned that matters were developing badly for the
Liberal Party now that the ultimatum deadline had passed
without any weakening of the premier's stand, Liberal Party
knights of the realm, Sir James Killen, MP, and former Liberal
parliamentary leader Sir Thomas Hiley put forward an over-
simple solution to the problem. "Terry White should admit he
was wrong and Premier Joh should forgive him." White,
however, said that he would not accept the advice of the well-
meaning knights. "I have made every overture to Mr Bjelke-
Petersen, but I will not accept, nor will my colleagues in

parliament, that I am in the wrong. I am the leader of the
Liberal Party. Mr Bjelke-Petersen must accept this if he wants
the coalition to continue." A third Liberal knight, Sir Gordon
Chalk, independently bought into the debate also with the
belief that the only winner in the debate was the Labor Party.
"I've been watching over the past week and I think the coalition leaders are losing the goodwill of the people. Mr Wright
[the ALP leader] is coming over with a smile and, candidly,
he's equal to Bob Hawke in presentation," Chalk proclaimed.

For Premier Bjelke-Petersen it was business as usual while
the Liberals pondered their predicament. He held his usual
cabinet meeting during the morning followed by an Executive
Council meeting. For his Liberal ministers, however, it was a
day of decision. They had been asked again by Terry White
and their party hierarchy to tender their resignations from the
government and join Terry White on the backbench.

Prior to the scheduled cabinet meeting, the premier held a
private meeting with six of the seven Liberal ministers remaining in cabinet. Bill Hewitt was not in attendance. The

Happier times for Terry White (left). Premier Joh comes to his electorate of
Redcliffe to present a football award to Redcliffe coach and former Australian
Rugby League captain-coach Artie Beetson.

Premier Bjelke-Petersen at one of the many press conferences he faced during the Queensland coalition crisis. (Photograph courtesy of Queensland Newspapers Pty Ltd)

Queensland Governor Sir James Ramsay and Premier Joh Bjelke-Petersen signing papers at a meeting of the Executive Council. The governor's confidence was needed for minority government to work in those hectic days of the crisis.

premier heard from the ministers that they had been requested by their party to tender their resignations from cabinet. He then put to them the suggestion that he could recommend to the Governor that he (the Governor) not accept their resignations, which he (the premier) believed were being forced on the ministers by Mr White and the Liberal Party executive against their wishes. The ministers agreed. The premier later astounded media reporters gathered for the daily news conference with the shock news that the Governor had agreed to this advice and that the Liberal ministers were happy. "It was a spontaneous reply in the expressions of their [the ministers'] faces — they'd be in boots and all to put it in plain language," the premier said. It was a shock development.

The Liberal Party and Terry White were caught completely by surprise when told of Bjelke-Petersen's manoeuvre. They immediately called in the party's legal advisers to assess their situation, only to learn that legally and constitutionally they had been checkmated. A meeting of the Liberal executive was called at party headquarters that night to begin at 7.30 p.m. Amid the noise of members drinking beer and eating Chinese takeaway food, the various ministers arrived between 7.30 and 10.00 p.m. During a heated session which lasted well into the early hours of Tuesday morning, the tension was electric for Terry White. Transport minister Don Lane, another minister who wanted to stay in cabinet, rebuked White for giving more attention to the press than to his colleagues, and White was forced to back down and redraft a tougher, planned media statement than the one which was seen by the media as "tame cat and meaningless". It read: "The leader and his ministers tonight called for a state election as soon as possible. The ministers said they had freely resigned and that is still their decision. If it should prove necessary they would be prepared to submit their resignations again." The key words in the statement were "if it should prove necessary". The Liberal ministers were still having a dollar each way.

By their decision and that of the Governor, the Liberal ministers were now the centre of all attention. Just how serious were they about staying in cabinet? Was there a chance that they would continue to defy their parliamentary leader and their executive and remain in government? Or would the Liberal executive force them to resubmit their resignations and this time stand by them?

With the heat in the Liberal kitchen now white hot, Dr Edwards boarded a Qantas plane for a rush trip to Tokyo on government business. And just to give the Liberal Party something further to consider, Premier Bjelke-Petersen gave the first indication that an early election was in the wind. Asked if the parliament which had been unceremoniously adjourned on 9 August would be recalled before the election, the premier replied: "That's not necessary — we are going to have a fairly early election." Then, to confuse the matter further, he added: "The date has not yet been determined, but it's still a way off."

Day 13: Liberals shocked — constitutional debate

The Bjelke-Petersen manoeuvre of having the Governor reject

the resignations tendered by the Liberal ministers was widely hailed as a mixture of political genius and animal cunning by a media now used to this wily politician pulling the unexpected out of the hat when for others around him all seemed to be lost. The question was, however: was he right to do it? Had he dragged the Governor into the crisis and politicized his position, as many claimed had happened when Sir John Kerr sacked Gough Whitlam in 1975? Was the state on the brink of a constitutional crisis that would rock the nation? As Professor A.R. Blackshield, professor of Legal Studies at Latrobe University, put it in the Melbourne *Age* on 17 August: "The furore in Queensland illustrates, yet again, that in a constitutional crisis, unwritten constitutional conventions are more important than formal laws, and practical politics is more important than either." What he didn't go on to say, however, was that in the world of practical politics Premier Bjelke-Petersen has few masters.

On the question of whether or not ministers of the Crown could simply resign their commissions, the 1964 High Court decision on record in the case of army officer Captain Marks provided some insight. Captain Marks resigned from the army, but his resignation had not been accepted. Mr Justice Kitto explained at the time: "The doctrine of the common law is that the Sovereign may compel her subject to serve in such offices as the public good and the nature of the Constitution require, and that refusal to perform a public duty, when legally called upon to do so, is a punishable offence." This was ancient law, but its application in 1964 to Captain Marks' case reasserted its current validity. The argument in the Captain Marks case, however, was not totally conclusive in the minds of many. There were still a lot of "ifs" and "buts" to be taken into account. There was an area, however, where few of the experts could disagree: it was Bjelke-Petersen's practical politics that would hold sway in the end.

On the question of whether or not the Governor should have accepted the premier's recommendation not to accept the ministers' resignations, there seems no doubt that constitutional convention requires that a Governor normally accept the advice of his chief minister or premier. He was, of course, as was Sir John Kerr in the Whitlam crisis, not bound to do so. Like other Australian constitutions, the Queensland

Constitution separates the responsibilities of the Governor-in-Council and the Governor. In practice, in decisions on functions assigned to the Governor, he is not bound to take ministerial advice; however, in matters assigned to the Governor-in-Council he should accept the advice of his ministers. In the Queensland Constitution, the hiring and firing of ministers rests with the Governor-in-Council; however, in the appointment of officers liable to retire from office on political grounds, the power is said to be vested in the Governor alone. A 1977 amendment to the Queensland Constitution did little to alter this situation and the conclusion can only be that, in the case of the Queensland ministers' resignations, the Governor accepted the premier's advice that the ministers did not really want to vacate their positions and were being influenced by outside forces. This latter point raises a further legal question: was the Liberal Party within its rights to request its ministers to resign? Attorney-General Sam Doumany emphasized this point in his action to have his office investigate the position of himself and his colleagues in relation to Liberal Party pressure. This action was interpreted by many (and was, no doubt, not lost on the Governor) as a clear indication that Liberal ministers were wavering.

Section 54 of the Criminal Code provides a sentence of up to three years jail for any person who, "advisedly", "(1) Does any act calculated to interfere with the free exercise by the Governor of the duties or authority of his office; or (2) Does any act calculated to interfere with the free expression of a member of the Executive Council of the duties or authority of his office as a member of the Executive Council or a Minister of the State." Again, the final decision would have to be the Governor's, and he would need to be satisfied that action taken by the Liberal Party to have the ministers resign did in fact breach this section of the Criminal Code. As it stood, in the context of the timing involved, it nevertheless was a strong deterrent to further Liberal Party pressure on the ministers. It also gave the premier and the wavering Liberal ministers further time to consider their position. For the Liberal state executive, not only were the problems of their wavering ministers continuing to plague them, but also yet another candidate was talking of withdrawing. This time it was the candidate for Ipswich West, Chris Tankey, who said that he did not agree with the way the removal of former party leader Llew Edwards had been "arranged" and that he found that he did not now support the people who were running the Liberal Party.

Day 14: Feds intervene

Amid this confusion for the Queensland Liberal Party, the federal president, Dr Jim Forbes, and the party's federal director, Tony Eggleton, jetted into Brisbane on 17 August. They were there at Andrew Peacock's request to see what they could do to help settle the crisis. On his arrival, Dr Forbes went to lengths to assure the media that his visit could not be construed as federal intervention. "Unlike the Labor Party we are a federal party and our presence indicates a desire on the part of the federal executive to be helpful to the Queensland division," he said. Dr Forbes went on to say that the federal executive was concerned at the effect the Queensland crisis would have on the forthcoming federal by-election for the seat of Moreton, recently vacated by Sir James Killen.

Speculation was rife regarding what Forbes and Eggleton would recommend to the Queensland division. Apart from the concern of winning the Moreton by-election, there was the worry of prospects for the coalition in Canberra, whose relations were already strained by differing statements made by Andrew Peacock and Doug Anthony on the Queensland crisis. There can be no doubt that they wanted an early solution to the problem. They needed the coalition to be seen as capable of coming back together in order to have any hope of putting up a winning performance in Moreton. The stumbling block, however, was that any backdown at that stage by either Terry White or the Liberal "ginger group" who commanded the numbers would have meant political suicide for both. The only possible solution that would have brought the coalition back together was for Terry White to resign his leadership. For White to have done that at his age would have almost certainly meant the end of his political career.

Further complicating the Liberals' position was advice reportedly received by Attorney-General Sam Doumany from his staff that any minister who pushed ahead with his resignation could face dismissal by the Governor on the grounds of "irresponsibility". The Solicitor-General's advice was supposedly on the grounds that the Governor had rejected the ministers' resignations once and, since that time, nothing had changed to substantially affect that decision. Under the circumstances, therefore, the ministers were expected to carry out their duties. Despite this situation, two Liberal ministers, Bill Hewitt and Sir William Knox, were reported to be prepared to resubmit their resignations. Hewitt told the *Daily Sun* that day: "Mr White should be given his rightful place as deputy premier and treasurer. I'm still considering my position in cabinet." Sir William Knox added: "I was expecting not to be a minister on Thursday night, but apparently I will be. I put my resignation in fully expecting it to be accepted." In other statements made that day, of the remaining four Liberal ministers only Dr Edwards was firm in his decision: "I've always supported the Governor and see no reason to go against his decision. I will not be resubmitting my resignation." The remaining three were still wavering. "I have suggested to Mr White that he accept his ministers staying on in a caretaker role until the election which can only be weeks away," transport minister Don Lane said. "The main principle here is that Liberals have the right to express our own feelings. That's the hallmark of the Liberals and I hope it stays," was Sam Doumany's opinion. Health minister Brian Austin said that he was considering legal advice. "I have constitutional advice and a heap of stuff that I haven't read yet," he said. The newcomer in cabinet, Col Miller, was waiting for advice from the party. "I believe the party is investigating the legalities of the situation. I'm waiting to hear from Liberal headquarters as to the action to be taken." But each member of the Liberal backbench "ginger group" believed the ministers should again resign.

What Dr Forbes and Tony Eggleton finally promised the wavering Liberal ministers or said to convince them, or what concessions they extracted from the "ginger group" in order to gain federal support for their actions is not known, but after a special meeting with Sir William Knox, Sam Doumany, Don Lane and Brian Austin, the five ministers unexpectedly agreed to resubmit their resignations. The following letter was sent to the premier:

Dear Mr Premier,
I am in receipt of your advice regarding the decision of His Excellency, the Governor, to decline my resignation from Cabinet and Executive Council. I understand from your letter that the decision was arrived at by His Excellency following your recommendations to him involving the maintenance of stable Government in Queensland pending the holding of an election.

Whilst at that time this recommendation was soundly based, I must now advise you that the circumstances have changed significantly and would prevent me from making a full contribution to that stability as a Minister of the Crown.

Due to very recent developments, I find myself under intolerable pressure to such an extent that I will be unable to fulfil the high duties that are cast upon me as a Minister of the Crown. The administration of the Departments within my charge will suffer if I were to remain in office in these circumstances.

While I deeply regret the necessity for taking this action, I believe that the only honourable course open to me is to request that you advise His Excellency of these circumstances so that I can be replaced by another member of the Legislative Assembly who will be more able to discharge the duties required of him in the interests of the people of Queensland.

I would therefore ask that His Excellency be advised to reconsider the decision he has made in respect of the resignation already tendered by me and relieve me of office in accordance with the terms of these resignations.

Separate copies of this letter were signed by Doumany, Knox, Austin, Lane and Miller. Close study of this letter undoubtedly provides support for the premier's action in advising the Governor that the ministers did not want to resign in the first instance. It also leaves no doubt that the ministers concerned wanted the premier to convey to the Governor and the people of Queensland that they were being pressured to quit their positions, a responsibility that the Liberal Party would have to carry into the forthcoming state election. Notably, welfare services minister Bill Hewitt was not a signatory to this letter.

On receipt of the letters of resignation, the premier finally and reluctantly accepted their requests and advised the Governor to withdraw their commissions. For both parties, the coalition was now over.

Day 15: Ministers reveal pressure

The following day, Thursday 18 August, former transport minister Don Lane spelt out the extent of the pressure that had been placed on the Liberal ministers. While he declined to say who was behind the campaign, he said that an orchestrated campaign had been mounted as part of intolerable pressure which led to the ministers' renewed resignations. He said that throughout the day he had been subjected to "vilification", abusive telephone calls and an organized campaign directed at forcing him to stand down. Mr Lane said that he received endless telephone calls. He said he believed that some of them were "set up". National Party headquarters in Brisbane was also inundated with telephone calls which were believed to be part of the same "set-up" campaign. The National Party media director, David Russell, who answered most of the calls, said that it was largely the work of a number of young people, all of whom pursued the same line: "We are National Party voters and we are shocked about what is going on. Because of what you've done to Terry White, we're not going to vote National any more."

"The weakness in their argument," Russell later said, "was that they were obviously ringing from the same telephone. There was music playing in the background. You could tell it was the same music." In the beginning, Russell discussed the issue with the persistent callers, but as the night wore on he became less patient and refused to take their calls. Little did he know that the premier's secretary, John Walsh, was also trying to get through to him. When Walsh finally did get through, Russell was all set to tell him to "go jump in the lake". A bewildered Walsh had to quickly tell him who he was. A somewhat embarrassed David Russell changed his tune.

Welfare minister Bill Hewitt, who had not resubmitted his resignation along with the others on 17 August, finally announced from the Gold Coast that his resubmission would be forthcoming. When his letter was finally submitted, it differed substantially in tone from that of his colleagues. It said in part: "This resignation is tendered of my own free will and it is my earnest desire that it be accepted." Dr Edwards, who arrived back in Brisbane on the morning of 18 August, also finally tendered his resignation to the premier at 11.30 a.m. He said that he did so with "great reluctance".

Terry White defended his party's position and denied that there had been undue party pressure on the ministers to resign. "I think it was a result of my absolute determination on the matter, which was backed by the state executive, the parliamentary and aldermanic sections, the ordinary members and the federal party," he said. On the point of pressure from the federal executive members, Mr White again stressed that there was no federal interference. "However, they did voice the absolute bewilderment of the federal party at the intransigence of the National Party and the need for firmness by the Liberal Party." Confident now that the final blow had been struck in the struggle, White went on to say that he expected a bitter campaign with the National Party in the lead-up to the state election. He also confidently predicted that there would be "a bobby-dazzler of an electoral redistribution after the election".

As the curtain fell on the Liberal ministers on 18 August, there was little doubt in the minds of many Queenslanders, and those who had been a party to Liberal Party discussions during the days that led up to the ministers' final decision to resubmit their resignations, that the threat of disendorsement had been a definite factor in their decision. That united decision of final acceptance (albeit reluctant) of Terry White's leadership and the inevitable break with the National Party that the ministers knew had to follow was really one of the amazing developments of the saga. For days the Liberal ministers had clearly indicated that they did not want to break the coalition and now, suddenly, they were agreeing to do so.

Two weeks, therefore, to the day that Terry White crossed the floor to vote against the government, the Queensland coalition was officially over. There was no hope of reconciliation short of an election.

Day 16: Joh's minority government

The following day, Friday 19 August, the premier named six new National Party ministers. They were sworn in by the Governor, and Queensland had a minority National Party

government. They were Angelo Bertoni (Mount Isa), Martin
Tenni (Barron River), Geoff Muntz (Whitsunday), Neil Turner
(Warrego), Vince Lester (Peak Downs), Neville Harper
(Auburn). The premier took treasury.

Post-mortem

In the final analysis of the "crisis fortnight" of stand-off and
political jousting between the coalition partners which
culminated in the coalition being abandoned, there are a
number of pertinent questions to be asked that may never be
fully answered, but which are crucially important when seeking to fully understand the crisis.

Firstly, there is the question of whether or not Terry White's
action on 4 August was as innocent as he would have liked
the public to believe at the time. Fact and popular opinion
would suggest it was not. In an article published in the
Telegraph on 11 August, Quentin Dempster reported (and it
was not denied): "In the advice that he [White] had received
before he made 'this symbolic gesture' of support for a long-
standing Liberal Party policy, he was told that at worst he
would be ticked off by the leader, Dr Edwards, and the
premier, Mr Bjelke-Petersen." This would also seem to give
some support to claims that Mr White met with a group of
Liberal Party activitists, including former party president
Yvonne McComb, member for Sherwood Angus Innes, and
former executive director of the party Keith Livingstone, prior
to the event to discuss the move, but did not, however, advise
Dr Edwards or the premier. Angus Innes publicly refuted that
such a meeting took place. He was reported in the Gold Coast
Bulletin on 9 August to have said in response to a similar suggestion from Rob Borbidge, MLA (Surfers Paradise): "Mr
White's sacking was an extraordinary consequence and one
that could not have been contemplated. I had no discussions
with him and wasn't aware that he was going to cross the
floor."

It is also believed that Mr White canvassed the scenario
with at least one member of the press before making his
move. On this point, the afternoon edition of the Brisbane
Telegraph of 4 August carried a story by Quentin Dempster

who predicted: "Several Liberal ministers and back-benchers were expected to cross the floor of state parliament today and vote with the Opposition on a motion to establish a public accounts committee." The only Liberal quoted in the article was Terry White, who said: "I see no conflict in Liberal and National Party members voting for a public accounts committee while maintaining their loyalty to the government." And there is the supposed tip-off that Llew Edwards received from Bill Hayden. These facts considered, there seems to be enough smoke to suggest something was "cooking".

A new whip

Under normal circumstances any such meeting or planning of such a move would almost certainly have come to the notice of the Liberal whip and thus the leader would have been tipped off, but it has to be remembered that at this time the Liberal Party had just elected a new whip (Mrs Beryce Nelson) to replace Bob Moore who had defected to the National Party. Mrs Nelson could probably be excused for not getting wind of any such development, that is of course assuming that she was not a party to them. Evidence would suggest, however, that she was not.

The scenario popular throughout the National Party was that Terry White did know what he was doing, but he underestimated the ramifications of his actions, a tactics meeting did take place, and that this was yet a further move by the dissident small "l" "ginger group" to systematically replace the established leadership structure of the Liberal Party, although things progressed a little faster than had been expected, and somewhat differently from the original plan. The whole affair got out of hand when the matter became confused by the attempts of the relatively inexperienced Liberal backbench to outmanoeuvre the Labor Party for the glory on the public accounts issue. (In this regard, the "ginger group" did fall into a trap set by the Labor Party, foreshadowed on 3 August.) Terry White made his move when he did to beat Brian Austin (Wavell) to the punch. Austin was rumoured to be considering a leadership bid after the state election. It was widely rumoured over the preceding months that Austin had the numbers to oust Llew Edwards, but didn't want to move until after the state election. Terry White wanted to give a showing of independence and leadership, to put his stamp on the leadership before Austin had a chance to move. White expected nothing more than a severe reprimand for his actions.

Federal Libs seek Joh's help

Even if Terry White's move was purely a spontaneous reaction on a matter of conscience, the fact remains that he saw fit not to discuss the matter with his leader and his ministerial colleagues prior to taking the action he did, and knowingly broke cabinet solidarity. He had ample opportunity to voice his discontent within cabinet and at joint party meetings but had refused to do so − why? This is one of the strongest pieces of evidence that a leadership spill was in the wind. If it was, Terry White would be unlikely to want to alert any other possible contenders to his plan. Two days had elapsed since the order of business for the day had been determined by the cabinet meeting which Terry White attended. The cabinet had decided that it would bring on debate on the matter of states' rights that day, following the Franklin Dam decision. Interestingly, this debate had been specifically asked for by the federal Liberal leader, Andrew Peacock, in a meeting with Premier Bjelke-Petersen and state Liberal leaders held in New South Wales Parliament House several weeks earlier. On that occasion, Bjelke-Petersen had reluctantly agreed to fly to Sydney to attend the meeting, after repeated requests from leading Liberals across Australia, including former Western Australian premier Sir Charles Court. Dr Edwards and his deputy, Sam Doumany, went with the premier. At that meeting, which was hosted by the New South Wales Liberal parliamentary leader, Nick Greiner, it was put to Bjelke-Petersen that the federal opposition (Liberal−NCP coalition) would benefit from continued debate on the issue of states' rights, which Bjelke-Petersen had so successfully championed at the Constitution Convention in Adelaide earlier in the year. Because of Terry White's action, therefore, his federal colleagues never got the Queensland debate they had wanted to keep the pressure on the Hawke government over what was felt to be continued infringement of states' rights. Terry White was also aware of the importance the government placed on controlling the business of the House in the lead-up to the election. At successive cabinet meetings prior to White's decision to cross the floor, main roads minister Russ Hinze had raised the matter with his cabinet colleagues.

Crossing the floor

Just what did Terry White support when he crossed the floor to vote against the government on Thursday 4 August? As can be clearly seen from a perusal of the Hansard extract at the beginning of this chapter, Terry White did not cross the floor to vote on the matter of a public accounts committee, although this was the subject of motions foreshadowed by Mr Prentice in his procedural motion. What he did, in fact, was to vote with dissident members of the Liberal Party and the ALP to take the business of the House out of the hands of the government. Mr White had agreed on 1 August with his cabinet colleagues that a debate on a motion relating to the implications of the High Court decision on the Tasmanian Dam case should be the order of business for the day. The correct procedure, if Terry White wanted to demonstrate his conscientious support for a public accounts committee, would surely have been to wait and see if the procedural motion succeeded. Then, if the motion for the establishment of a public accounts committee was brought on for discussion, he could have advised his leader that he intended to vote for it. Had Terry White done this, he would have avoided the slur that now hangs over his head.

In terms of parliamentary procedure, of course, the matter should never have got past Mr Bjelke-Petersen's rejection of leave to move a motion without notice. Had the Speaker stopped further discussion at that time, as he should have done, the fiasco could well have been averted.

Was it an ALP trap?

As is suggested elsewhere in this book, the Liberal Party had been the subject of an ALP "baiting" campaign for several years, and there is little doubt that on 4 August Terry White and the Liberal "ginger group" did fall into an ALP trap. Not that it was a brilliantly designed or laid trap that the ALP expected to work. Rather, it was a trap innocently laid in "mice country" that caught an "elephant". In fact, it was a perfect ex-

ample of what Joh Bjelke-Petersen means when he says that
in politics, "Once you get one foot on the flypaper, you're a
goner." For years the Liberal backbench had been "flirting"
with a number of issues that are normally associated with
ALP/socialist doctrine. Some would say that they had been
trying to "outdo the Labor Party" in these areas. In doing so,
they created a virtual minefield for themselves and a feast of
opportunities for the ALP to embarrass them. The "Terry
White Affair" was a perfect example of how "the other foot"
got caught in the flypaper.

On 3 August, ALP leader Keith Wright foreshadowed the
action. "I give notice to the Liberal Party now that tomorrow
the Opposition will seek leave of the House to bring on the
motion moved by the deputy leader of the Opposition, Nev
Warburton, to set up a public accounts committee," he said. "I
put it to every Liberal in this House," he continued, "that it is a
test of their bona fides and their credibility. They have been
saying everywhere throughout the state that they want such a
committee. The test tomorrow, when we seek leave, will be
whether or not they are prepared to join with us to ensure that
debate ensues, so that a public accounts committee can be
established."

On 4 August, the Liberal "ginger group" sought to beat the
ALP to the punch when Ian Prentice (Toowong) jumped to his
feet first to call for leave of the House to debate a similar
motion (calling also for a public accounts committee)
forwarded by the Liberal member for Mount Gravatt, Guelf
Scassola (motion no. 1). To get the necessary ALP support for
what they wanted to be seen as a Liberal initiative, Prentice
included the ALP motion (no. 2) in their procedural motion
(see page 144). This is when the confusion started. This is
when the Speaker became confused and the issue got out of
hand. This is when the trap was sprung. These were the
dramatic minutes that changed the direction of politics in
Queensland.

Should White have resigned?

The question of whether or not Terry White should have
resigned is also a matter of some debate. Quite clearly, one
would have to believe that, if the matter of a public accounts

committee was important enough for Terry White to be prepared, without notifying his cabinet colleagues, to cross the floor and vote together with the opposition to take control of the business of the House out of the hands of the government (that is, his government), then it should have been a simple matter of professional ethics for Mr White to back up his commitment to the cause and tender his resignation. In politics, however, few things happen by accident and it is worth considering that perhaps Mr White wished to use the matter of his resignation as an opportunity to embarrass Dr Edwards and show that he was in fact subservient to the premier. It is widely suggested that the "ginger group" expected the premier to have to demand that Llew Edwards sack Terry White. As the premier later told the National Party State Management Committee, however, he didn't have to do a thing. "It was like a bushfire spreading. Everyone of them, to a man, said: he's got to go. Llew insisted that he do the job." The fact that Dr Edwards insisted that Mr White was his minister and that he would take the responsibility for sacking him got Bjelke-Petersen off the hook.

Fraser's letter

What, then, did Terry White achieve? In the short term he gained the leadership of the Liberal Party in Queensland. It will be argued, however, that the price he paid was more than the job was worth, as there can be no doubt that the fortnight's struggle that followed his decision to break cabinet solidarity and ended with the downfall of the coalition ripped the traditional guts out of the Queensland Liberal Party. Former prime minister Malcolm Fraser confirmed this when he wrote the following letter to the editors of major newspapers throughout the country:

> Four months ago I resigned from the leadership of the federal parliamentary Liberal Party and shortly after from the parliament itself. Since then I have kept quiet on partisan political matters. Nevertheless, recent events in Queensland are so fundamental that I feel compelled to comment.
>
> The record of the Queensland Liberal Party in recent times has not been good; it was responsible for the loss of two Senate seats, giving the balance of power to the Democrats and ultimately causing damage to the federal Liberal government. It has now voted in

as its leader a man who, as a minister, voted with the Australian Labor Party against his own cabinet ministers. This act defiles every principle of parliamentary and cabinet government. No government could survive such practices. Such a person would not have stayed in my government; he would not have stayed in Mr Hawke's government.

If an election is forced in Queensland, if the Labor Party wins, it will be because of the Queensland Liberal Party.

It is time for the rank and file of the Liberal Party to assert themselves. It is time for decent people of Liberal faith to rejoin the Liberal Party and recognize those principles of behaviour essential to any government and even more necessary to a coalition government. One essential principle involves unity and cohesion of the cabinet and common support of cabinet decisions. If a man cannot act in concert with his own team he must resign; there is no place for him.

To apply our ideas and philosophy we need seats. The Queensland Liberal Party seems determined to lose even more seats. Only Queensland Liberals can stop that.

Fraser's outburst fell on deaf ears at Liberal Party headquarters in Brisbane. Terry White as much as told the former prime minister that he should content himself with matters on his farm. "Mr Fraser is in the National Party's pocket. In criticizing my action he is displaying gross hypocrisy," Mr White was reported in the *Telegraph* of 18 August to have said. Another former prime minister, Sir William McMahon, well known for his problems with the National Party in the past, took White's side in response to Fraser's attack, saying that Fraser had always liked the Nationals more than his own party. Former Liberal leader and Speaker Sir Billy Sneddon, when asked to comment on Malcolm Fraser's statement, said: "It's rather like a voluntary firefighter turning incendiarist." At a Liberal Party convention held in Sydney that night, however, Liberal Party federal leader Andrew Peacock had to admit that he would sack any of his ministers who crossed the floor to vote with the opposition if he were prime minister.

Wider implications

The ramifications of Terry White's actions were having wider implications than the Liberal Party would have liked. The two main factions, the conservatives and the trendies, were splitting down the middle on the issue and it extended well beyond the Queensland border. Continuing the bad news for the Liberals was the announcement that they had lost yet another candidate in the wake of the crisis. Mrs Judy Reynolds withdrew "for personal reasons" from her position as the Liberal candidate for Cooroora, held by sitting National party member Gordon Simpson.

On 21 August, four days after the coalition had officially ended, the debate was still raging between the two factions when former South Australian premier Steele Hall (now shadow minister for state in the Peacock opposition) came out in support of Terry White. Speaking at the opening of the South Australian Young Liberals Week in Adelaide, Hall claimed that Terry White had "invigorated the Queensland Liberal Party". Ironically, Mr Hall, who is known within Australian political circles as the premier who voted himself out of office over the matter of redistribution of the electoral boundaries in South Australia, went further to say: "It is of course quite inevitable that at some time in the future there will be a fair and equitable set of electoral boundaries in that state." No doubt he was indicating that White's action would be vindicated when the supposed Queensland gerrymander was abolished.

By the end of that week, former Victorian Liberal premier Sir Henry Bolte was in Queensland and was giving yet another side to Steele Hall's story. "There's no future in being a dead general," Bolte told a "Nationwide" interviewer. "I gave Steele Hall this advice when he voted himself out of office in South Australia." And with reference to the Queensland gerrymander he added: "It's unbelievable to suggest that you can have more than half your seats in the capital city" — which is Liberal and Labor Party policy in Queensland.

Aftermath

Casual assessment of the infighting, bickering and drama of August 1983 could easily dismiss what happened as nothing more than petty party politics of greed and ambition. In many ways perhaps it was, but there was more to it than this. It was a struggle for the future direction of the anti-socialist forces in Australia in the wake of a changing national political scene.

Queensland is the last bastion state of traditional conservative politics on mainland Australia and therefore must be the battleground. The events in Queensland will influence the future of politics in Australia for many years.

The crisis of August 1983 will influence our way of life for many years to come. In one direction is the promise of an Australian republic, the dismantling of the states system, and dramatic changes to the existing electoral system that could enshrine Labor socialism in Australia for many years. In the other direction is the continuing struggle to hang on to the remnants of the free-enterprise way of life held dear by the conservative parties. In that dimension, therefore, the events of 1983 hold national significance.

In the lead-up to the 1983 election, the new Liberal Party leader, Terry White, claimed that the National Party was the most pragmatic political party on earth, and confidently predicted that the two recently estranged partners would reunite into a coalition after the state election on Saturday 22 October. White was confident that the Nationals would not get the numbers to govern without his Liberal Party, and was sufficiently practical to realize that his Liberals would also need the Nationals. He also had the benefit of twenty-six years of Liberal Party experience in dealing with the National Party. He was relying heavily on the pragmatism displayed in the past by Sir Robert Sparkes, who, on numerous occasions during the Fraser–Anthony Liberal–CP coalition after the downfall of the Whitlam government, when the Liberals had the numbers to govern without coalition but decided not to, said: "It is infinitely better to be in government than sitting on the crossbenches."

8

The War Machine

Sir John ("Black Jack") McEwen once described the Australian Country Party as a "specialist party with a sharp fighting edge". Prominent Queensland entrepreneur and National Party executive member Sir Frank Moore describes Joh Bjelke-Petersen as a political "war horse" and the organization that supports him as his war machine. Whichever way you look at it, the Nationals are proud of their aggressive image. The party's private surveys have been telling them for years that people like strong positive leadership, and the party laps it up.

"The sharp fighting edge comes from selecting men – and women – of acknowledged special talents, expertise, knowledge and calibre to contest elections and to promote and enact the party's policies and approach in parliament . . . and we must not deviate from being very selective in the people we choose – people who have those specialist talents," is how the party's executive troubleshooter and first senior vice-president Charles Holm described the secret of the "war machine".

Labor Party strategists have also realized for some time that the Queensland Nationals are a formidable political force and getting stronger. In the March 1982 edition of the *Labor Review*, a full-page article on the success of the National Party warned the party faithful: "In 1983 (or whenever the next state election is held), you will not be fighting the National Party you knew and loathed in 1980."

The article went on to cite the party's wealth and marketing ability as "a distinct advantage over the ALP", but added: "Do not get carried away with the half-dozen millionaires who have donated up to $100,000, and have been rewarded with knighthoods and other favours of government. The fact is that the vast majority of National membership are workers and small businessmen who could just as easily join either Labor or Liberal." The article went on to predict (with some accuracy, many National Party members would agree): "The bulk of future National Party voters will not be farmers and country folk, but big and small businessmen (the newsagent, motel proprietor, garage owner, etc.), the white collar worker and professional people (clerks to accountants) and urban women."

The *Labor Review* article was obviously designed to be a spur to Labor supporters. It did, however, miss the key to the success of the Queensland National Party.

Stability is the key reason for the success of the National Party organization, stability achieved through the dogmatic promotion of and adherence to the principle of party solidarity and loyalty. No other major Australian political party in recent years has enjoyed the benefits of leadership stability with which the Queensland National Party has been blessed. The party's state parliamentary leader, Joh Bjelke-Petersen, has been premier for fifteen years, and Sparkes and Holm have been at the top of the executive tree for thirteen consecutive years. Executive director Mike Evans has also been the party's chief executive officer throughout those thirteen years. Furthermore, none of these men (for that matter, none of the top echelon) is being threatened from within. As has been pointed out previously with reference to the relationship between Premier Joh Bjelke-Petersen and Sir Robert Sparkes, the same can be said for the positions of the top echelon members of the party. The relationship between Sparkes and Holm is excellent, and the recently elected second senior vice-president, Don McDonald, fits snugly into this category as well. McDonald is seen by some as a future president of the party, but he is not an impatient threat to either Charles Holm or Sir Robert Sparkes. Mike Evans has attracted criticism at times from within the party, but that is to be expected considering he was a paid employee of the party and one of its frontline organizational spokesmen.

It can't be overlooked either that the party has been in

power in Queensland for twenty-six years, or that for most of those twenty-six years the party has been under siege and its political survival constantly threatened. Like the state of Israel, therefore, it is not surprising that the Nationals have welded together into a close-knit, extremely efficient fighting force. To those involved, it's more like a great extended family than a political organization, with State Conference being a gathering of the clan and annual holidays for many. They take their politics very seriously.

An extended family

Like all extended families, change doesn't happen often within the upper echelons of the National Party in Queensland, or just for the sake of it. More often than not, only retirement because of old age or ill-health sees major organizational changes occur. The recent succession of Sir William Allen to the position of party treasurer is such an example. Eighty-three-year-old Sir Neville Henderson had been party treasurer for many years, and in any other organization probably would have retired several years earlier but, as far as Sir Neville was concerned, "young Bill" first had to learn the ropes. "Young Bill", it just so happens, is one of Queensland's most successful businessmen: former chairman of companies that owned radio stations throughout Queensland, including Radio 4IP, and Brisbane's Channel O television station, chairman of Central Queensland Broadcasting Corporation, president of the Queensland Merino Stud Sheepbreeders' Association, and the owner of a chain of grazing properties throughout the state.

Seventy-seven-year-old Monto solicitor Harry Bandidt is another contributing the last drop of his enthusiasm to the cause. Bandidt, the former federal member for Wide Bay (1958–61), is the party's principal legal adviser, although like Sir Neville Henderson he is grooming a successor – young Brisbane solicitor John Hoare.

It is also important to note that both the preceding presidents of the party, Sir Sidney Roberts and John Ahern, O.B.E., continue active involvement with the State Management Committee of the party, as do former state senators Ron

Maunsell and Dr Glennister Sheil, and the former state and
federal Women's Section president, Lady Pearl Logan.

The combination of Bjelke-Petersen, Sparkes, Holm, and
Evans, ably backed up by the party's team of fourteen vice-
presidents and key executive activists such as Sir William
Allen, Sir Frank Moore, John Ahern, Fred Maybury, Harry
Bandidt and Sparkes' private secretary, Helen Maybury,
make up the nucleus of the Nationals' war machine. Prominent Queensland businessmen Sir Roderick Proctor, Sir
Edward Lyons and more recently Mr Ben Macdonald are the
party's trustees who have the task of attracting funds to the
party to fight its election campaigns and keep the wheels of
the war machine turning. Sir Roderick Proctor is the
chairman of Jennings Industries Ltd and Bundaberg Sugar,
and is one of Queensland's most prominent accountants. Sir
Edward Lyons is the Chairman of Katies Ltd, the nationwide
group of women's fashion stores. The trustees are assisted by
Mr Clarrie Garnsworthy, the organizer behind the fund-
raising drive for the successful 1982 Commonwealth Games
in Brisbane. In total, forty-six members from all corners of
Queensland comprise the party's inner executive, the State
Management Committee.

Talents and contributions

An outstanding feature of the National Party team is the combination of experience and enthusiasm. It would be difficult
to assemble a more representative group of top-level business
people and community workers. Their individual contributions to the state have been considerable in many ways.

The work of former treasurer Sir Neville Henderson is
typical. A prominent Queensland solicitor who has been involved in law reform since the twenties, Sir Neville was the
original architect of the party's submission to the federal
government on the abolition of death duties. The work of the
National Party on this issue, and the subsequent lead that its
parliamentary wing in the Queensland state government
eventually gave to the rest of Australia, must be seen as one of
the major contributions to law reform in the history of

Australia. It is certainly viewed as one of the party's most outstanding social and legislative achievements.

To gauge the degree of Sir Neville Henderson's individual contribution, it needs to be known that his two initial submissions to the Senate Standing Committee on Finance and Government Operations comprised some eighty-two foolscap pages of social and legal debate on death duties. They cited evidence in case after case of the destructive impact of this most iniquitous of all government taxes, all compiled by Sir Neville Henderson throughout his career in law.

The case of the "Potiphar Family" was a prominent part of his submission. It is an emotional story that warrants telling as an example of the importance of the behind-the-scenes work of the men and women involved in political organizations and the National Party's move against death duties. The name "Potiphar" is fictitious, but the events described are true.

Under Marxist doctrine, death duties are regarded as an early step to the eventual expropriation of private property. The imposition of 100 per cent death and gift duties, as has occurred in a number of communist-dominated countries, provides for the transfer of ownership from the individual to the state. Death duties do, however, go back as far as Roman times. During the reign of Experor Pontifex Maximus they were particularly abused and used by the emperor to take over vast estates from his subjects – especially those who could be accused of some crime (albeit trumped-up) against the state. Similar unjust laws existed in medieval times under the feudal system in England. Landholders accused of a felony against the state had the choice of either surrendering all their property to the state or, if they refused to plead guilty, submitting to the test of the "peine forte et dure". This required the man to lie naked on his back on the floor with an iron weight on his body. If he died before admitting his guilt, his wealth would then remain with his family.

In Queensland, death duties were first introduced in 1892 as a temporary measure to provide for the difficult economic times being experienced. Further increases were inflicted in 1895, 1904, 1918 and 1931, all for the purpose of funding the failing economy. On each occasion they created greater hardship, the 1892 and 1895 legislation being blamed for the bank crashes at the time.

The "Potiphar" family

The case of the "Potiphar" family clearly indicates how "peine forte et dure" thinking survived in Queensland until National Party action was taken, and which still survives in some states of Australia today.

The "Potiphar" family established themselves in western Queensland in the 1890s, and at the time of "Mr Potiphar's" death at the age of sixty-five owned a grazing property in semi-arid country. When "Mr Potiphar" died, the estate was valued at $188,704.

Three years prior to his death, "Mr Potiphar", after suffering heart problems, had tried to bring his son "John" into partnership. But "John" was not yet eighteen, and it was not allowed. When "John" did turn eighteen the transaction was enacted, but it was within only two years of "Mr Potiphar's" death, and for the transaction to have been successful the law required it to have been in place for three years.

The "Potiphar" business was carried out on two grazing selections, one in the name of "Mr Potiphar" and the other in the name of "Mrs Potiphar". "Mr and Mrs Potiphar" made a gift to "John" of $20,000 to provide for the acquisition of his interest, so for the purpose of assessing federal estate duties, therefore, an amount of $20,026 was included in "Mr Potiphar's" estate as a gift given within three years of his death. In addition to this, "Mr Potiphar" had joint life assurance policies with his wife, which were dutiable and added another $17,084 to his estate. Added to "Mr Potiphar's" half-share of the business, it brought the value of his total estates to $132,528. Death duty was assessed on the estate at $32,296. At that time, "Mrs Potiphar's" estate was valued at $62,108. "John's" estate was valued at $28,004.

"Mrs Potiphar" did not have $32,296 available to pay the duty. The proceeds of the life assurance policy were insufficient. As a result, "Mrs Potiphar" was forced to sell part of her property. Unfortunately, it was the middle of a drought and the property that should have been valued at $17,520 fetched only $11,495. The freezing of other property assets at the time of "Mr Potiphar's" death just prior to the drought also meant that death duties were assessed at top land prices that no longer existed.

Despite her best efforts, "Mrs Potiphar" was unable to raise all the money she needed. Letters were written to the government tax collectors involved stressing the plight of "Mrs Potiphar" and the difficulties she was experiencing, but to no avail. Each delay simply incurred another penalty for non-payment. Charges were even made over notional book profits that the property had supposedly made during the time since "Mr Potiphar's" death. In reality, clear argument had been presented to demonstrate that a loss had in fact occurred.

Finally, "Mrs Potiphar's" health could no longer stand the strain and she entered hospital. Both she and "John" had applied for drought relief assistance and had received the maximum grant each of $1,500. "John" had to borrow against his life assurance policy to meet his mother's hospital expenses.

On 5 February 1971, "Mrs Potiphar" received a final demand for full settlement of her debt within twenty-one days. On 21 February 1971, "Mrs Potiphar" suffered a stroke. She died on 12 October the same year, the death duties debt still not cleared.

As a result of the two-and-a-half years of pressure and drought, it was finally assessed that there was now a deficiency in both the estates of "Mr Potiphar" and "Mrs Potiphar". "John Potiphar" also had no assets. The family's aggregation of nett capital of $188,704 at the time of "Mr Potiphar's" death was now all gone.

"John" was left with the ruins. He had worked for eight years on the property without payment and was forced to remain as unpaid caretaker on nothing but rations, pending sale of the property by the mortgagees. His only memento of his father's many years of hard work and his mother's sacrifice was an award to his father for pioneering and public service bestowed by Her Majesty the Queen.

It is now history that the National Party took up the case against death duties which led to their finally being eliminated in Queensland and federally.

The organization

For administrative and organizational purposes, the National Party divides the state up into fourteen zones, which are the

Sir Robert Sparkes and state executive director of the National Party Mike Evans. Evans was the chief executive officer of the party throughout the rise to power. (Photograph courtesy of Queensland Newspapers Pty Ltd)

Author Alan Metcalfe, an acknowledged "Joh man" within the National Party, joins the premier in discussion with Thuringowa Shire Chairman Dan Gleeson (left) and North Queensland businessman Rex Goodsell (right) during an appreciation dinner for the premier in Townsville in 1982.

responsibility of the vice-presidents. In addition to this, the party has special divisional committees for the northern and inland divisions, and recently created the position of second senior vice-president to balance the increasing influence in the party from the expanding south-east corner of the state. Former western zone vice-president Don McDonald, a Cloncurry grazier, was elected to this position at the 1983 State Conference in Brisbane. In addition to this "senior" organizational structure, there is also the parallel Women's Section and the Young Nationals. Each zone comprises federal divisional councils, state electoral councils and ordinary branches. In total, the party has approximately 35,000 members throughout the state.

Under Sparkes' administration, the party's parliamentary wing has also been brought tightly into the fold. All parliamentarians are automatically members of Central Council, which meets quarterly, and by virtue of this they are delegates also to Annual State Conference, the supreme policy-making body of the party. The state and federal parliamentary wings also elect representatives to the State Management Committee, which meets monthly to handle the ongoing business of the party.

The boiler room for the Nationals is the party secretariat at 6 St Pauls Terrace, in the old inner-Brisbane suburb of Spring Hill. Purchased with funds raised through the Bjelke-Petersen Foundation, the building used to be the premises of the Commercial Travellers Club. It ideally suits the party's requirements, having a large boardroom capable of seating 150, offices of the state secretariat and the executive director on the ground floor, and research offices, a printing room and storage space in the basement, plus a suite for Sir Robert Sparkes where he stays during his frequent visits to Brisbane from his Darling Downs property at Jandowae.

Apart from Premier Bjelke-Petersen and Sparkes, executive director Mike Evans has been the party's most prominent spokesman. Related to Sir Robert Sparkes through marriage, Evans, a former schoolteacher, has been a major factor in the party's electoral effort since coming into the job at the same time as Sparkes. He has made major contributions in the area of establishing the party's successful committee system. He has also been one of the principal innovators of new campaigning techniques, and has played a key role in the initial campaign to introduce flat-rate taxation. He also had the day-to-day responsibility of keeping the "war machine" organized. His job was to chase up the stragglers and ensure that the everyday operational responsibilities of the party are attended to. Just keeping the wheels turning involves a staff of an overall state secretary, four private secretaries, a journalist, two researchers, a printer, two bookkeepers, four records clerks, and a receptionist. In an election, this number swells dramatically as part-time and voluntary help is added. The secretariat publishes the party newspaper, *National Outlook*, quarterly and backs this up with regular information circulars to party executive members.

As principal "on-the-spot" spokesman for the party, Evans has had to handle much of the flak aimed at the party. This is the area of his work that attracts the most criticism − for a paid party employee, it is the most difficult area. It is the "no win" area for executive directors of political parties − you have to upset someone sooner or later.

In addition to the party organizational structure, the Nationals have established an extensive committee system, with far-reaching influence throughout the community. Normally chaired by senior party executive members, the committees have played a major role in policy making and have been an integral part of the party's expansion into the Brisbane metropolitan area and the provincial cities.

The machine in action

The whole purpose of the National Party structure is geared towards election campaigning, and the preparations for the 1983 state elections are an example of the Nationals' "war machine" in action. The campaign strategy was mapped out and launched at the party's State Management Committee meeting in Brisbane on 26 August. It had been determined largely by the campaign committee meeting on 27 July, and evolved over the month that followed, which included the collapse of the coalition. The following "unofficial" minutes of that meeting indicate the planning and discussion that took place:

Sir Robert Sparkes opened the meeting and outlined the current position of the party. The Liberal ministers had finally decided to resign and Joh had no alternative but to go ahead and form a minority government. Six new ministers had been named and Joh had taken on Treasury — at last. The selection of ministers had solved a number of problems for the party, particularly in north Queensland, which had been under-represented in the Cabinet over the past three years and had been active in voicing its displeasure. Sparkes then went on to reveal the campaign slogan, "Now, more than ever — Queensland needs Joh and the Nationals", which had been devised after consultation with the premier, Mike Evans, Charles Holm, advertising men Sir Frank Moore and Fred Maybury, treasurer Sir William Allen and the party's advertising agency, Leo Burnetts. Sparkes said that it reflected what people concerned about the future of free enterprise were saying around Australia. Sparkes and Evans rolled out the campaign posters that had been designed to promote the slogan. The central feature was a map of Australia with Queensland in green and the rest of the area in red. Predictably, the first reaction from the meeting was "Where's Tasmania?", which was quickly followed by "What's the Northern Territory going to say about being painted red?" Advertising expert Fred Maybury explained that consideration had been given to the questions of Tasmania and the Northern Territory, but what had to be realized was that it was a "graphic presentation" of the way many people see Australia today. Sparkes said that he was sure "our friends in Tasmania and the Northern Territory will understand what we are trying to say". Premier Joh Bjelke-Petersen said: "I think we can live with this one." [Not unexpectedly, the first question that was asked at the media conference later that day was: "Where's Tasmania?"]

Media bias — issues and funds

With agreement reached on the campaign slogan, Sparkes raised the matter of his concern with media bias against the National Party in recent weeks. He drew attention to the ABC current affairs programme "Nationwide" and its coverage of the "gerrymander" in Queensland. He advised how he had sought equal time to refute the claims put forward on the programme, but had been frustrated in his efforts to get his message across. He also raised the matter of recently announced ABC policy on time allocations for political parties for the coming state election. He pointed out that in the federal election time was apportioned on the proportion of seats each party held in the parliament. He said that the system had been changed for the state election to a 60:40 split. The anti-Labor parties would get 60 per cent and Labor 40

per cent, but because the National and Liberal parties were now
no longer in coalition they would get 30 per cent each, a situation
that clearly disadvantaged the National Party compared with the
ground rules which applied for the federal election. Sparkes went
on to say that he was also amazed at the response of the rural press
to the Hawke federal budget. He said that they would realize in
time what a deceitful document it was, as far as rural people were
concerned.

The premier then outlined what had transpired in the government since the last meeting of the Management Committee on 12
August. He said that he regretted what had happened to Dr
Edwards and that it had been necessary to end the coalition. "I did
all I could to save them," he said. "If that's the way they want it,
well then, we'll go on without them." He said that he was particularly confident about the outcome of the election. "We've
never been better prepared," he said.

He followed with a plug for his new ministers. "Gee, they're
working well. Vince [Lester] has been getting his photo in the
paper, kneading bread. You never heard anything from that
department until Vince got in there. Angelo Bertoni, well he's
been burning the state up, up to Townsville and Cairns." About
the campaigning, the premier said that he would as usual be campaigning all over the state and expected his ministers to do the
same. He said that as treasurer he would be releasing the budget
and ensuring that the National Party got credit for the work that it
had done to put the state into the position it enjoyed today.

Sparkes then moved discussion on to the campaign, and it was
decided that electoral distribution would be a major issue of the
campaign. Former party president John Ahern warned about "falling into the ALP trap by referring to it as 'one vote, one value' ".
"It's not one vote, one value at all," he said. "What they're talking
about has no equality of vote at all." It was agreed that the party
was not effectively selling its story on the Queensland electoral
system. "We are being done like dinners," it was suggested. It was
finally resolved that Fred Maybury and the advertising brains
trust of the party get together and design an appropriate television
commercial to promote the party's position on electoral distribution.

The treasurer, Sir William Allen, then presented his report on
fund raising for the campaign. He said he was pleased to report
that things were the best they had been for some time for the
party. Expenditure incurred in running the party organization was
"up", but so were donations to the party. Sir Robert Sparkes
suggested that this was clear evidence of the concern in the community for the present development in Australian politics. It was

then suggested that the Liberal Party was reported to be having difficulties raising funds for the campaign. "If that is so, I think it indicates the general feeling that what we have done is correct," Sparkes said.

Metropolitan zonal vice-president and former senator Dr Glen Sheil then raised the matter of Sir James Killen's resignation and the impending by-election in the seat of Moreton. It was agreed that at this stage the party had not made up its mind whether or not it would be fielding a candidate in the seat. Sheil put forward the belief that the present situation was "a springboard opportunity for the National Party to go federally". He suggested that the party across Australia should launch a campaign based on the platform of "repealing bad laws and cutting taxes". Someone suggested that Sir James Killen had been keeping the seat "warm" for Angus Innes, but the "blow-up" in the state parliament had ended "all that".

Regional reports

It was then time for a round-up of reports from the party's fourteen zonal vice-presidents from around the state. From the Near North Coast it was reported that there was considerable Labor Party activity in Caboolture. Murrumba and Pine Rivers were two seats that the party could do well in. Pine Rivers was an area with an active and enthusiastic party organization.

In Townsville the hospital issue was still a concern. The "one vote, one value" campaign was important, and the party had to do more to get credit for the Burdekin Dam.

In the Far North, zonal vice-president Norm Kippen advised that there was "some" concern about the threat by the Liberal Party to withdraw its candidates from helping the National Party. The Far North was also still unhappy about the advertising campaign for the federal election on 5 March. Sparkes assured them: "That was organised in Canberra. Our's will be much better." The Far North and the Central Zone were also concerned that the party had not effectively "sold" its position in the "White Affair" to the public.

Sparkes responded by saying that the party had spent a considerable amount of time and effort informing all candidates throughout the state on the matter. He said that on 24 August each candidate had been forwarded, by special delivery, a complete briefing on the affair.

It was also suggested that the party's campaign slogan might just be the "needle" to encourage party supporters in Callide to vote for the official party candidate. "If the people of Callide realize the seriousness of this election, it could well happen," Sparkes said.

The proxy delegate for South Coast, June Redman, reported on the concern in the Gold Coast area about threats by the Liberal Party as to what they might be doing with allocation of preferences in the forthcoming election. Sir Robert Sparkes suggested that the way the Liberal Party was performing they could well finish third and not second in the key Gold Coast seats. It was also suggested that, in light of press reports on what the Liberal Party might be doing with its preferences, all branches be warned to look out for any "tricks" such as double tickets.

The state president of the Womens' Section, Jean McIntyre, then reported that a new branch had been formed in the East Metropolitan Zone and that 300 women had attended the premier's annual morning tea during Show Week.

Young Nationals' president, Chris Gibbs, asked what progress there had been on the introduction of a human relations course for Queensland schools and what would be the party's stand in the forthcoming election. Sparkes said that it was unlikely that anything could be decided before the election, but he reminded members that it was party policy, carried at the Bundaberg conference by a vote of 400–23. Sparkes said that he hoped the candidature of the Rev. Allan Male (Murrumba) would indicate to the people of Queensland that the party was still concerned about the human relationships course issue.

Sparkes went on to say that the introduction of a foreign land register, as was overwhelmingly endorsed at the Caloundra conference, had also not yet been enacted by the government. He said he believed it could also develop as an issue. He hoped that the new government would do something in this regard.

Selling the campaign

Following the conclusion of reports, Sir Robert Sparkes outlined the party's plans to launch the campaign for the 1983 elections. "The projection of our policies will be modern and dynamic," Sparkes said, holding up the artwork of the party's policy folders. Executive director Mike Evans said that in the 1980 campaign the party had mailed out 8,984 copies of the party's policies to special-interest groups in the Brisbane area alone. He expected this to be surpassed in 1983. Sparkes advised that as chairman of the Wambo Shire he had already received a copy of the Labor Party policy on local government, and remarked how professionally it had been presented. The Liberal Party was also actively projecting its policies using the same concept. "We've got to ensure that our presentation is equally as effective," he said.

For the first time in the party's history, it was also intended that a statewide tour by Sir Robert Sparkes, Charles Holm, Mike Evans and a representative from the party's advertising agency would be undertaken, prior to the official campaign launch on 22 September, to individually inform candidates and their committees of the campaign proposals for their areas. In the past, the party had called a central campaign directors meeting in Brisbane to handle such matters but this had not been as efficient as desired. The statewide campaign briefing tour would commence on Monday 5 September and end on Saturday 10 September and would cover briefing meetings in Maryborough, Rockhampton, Mackay, Townsville, Cairns, Mount Isa, Longreach, Charleville, Roma, Toowoomba and Brisbane.

As Joh Bjelke-Petersen dominates the National Party parliamentary wing, Sir Robert Sparkes has a similar grip on the organization. Like Bjelke-Petersen, Sparkes is often criticized for the cast-iron control he demands and gets over the organization. For thirteen years at the top of the organizational tree he has been selling his dream for the party to be accepted right across Australia. At the same time he has been selling equally as hard the need for solidarity and loyalty. The tighter he can bind the National Party "family unit", the more successful he believes it will be. It's a formula that wins, and in politics that's what it's all about.

As Premier Joh Bjelke-Petersen said on 26 August 1983, the National Party had never been better prepared than it was going into the 1983 state election campaign.

9

Winners and Losers

Our guest tonight — Joh Bjelke-Petersen, now facing the biggest challenge of his lengthy political career.

Joh Bjelke-Petersen has been the premier here for a record fifteen years service. He's been a state minister for twenty years and is the longest serving state member, entering parliament in 1947.

While dominating state politics, Mr Bjelke-Petersen has been a key figure on the National stage and is credited with aiding the downfall of the Whitlam government in the mid-seventies and at the same time he decimated the ALP in Queensland.

But now, a decade later, Labor is mounting a strong challenge to his supremecy. It's in power in every mainland state and federally, and to add to his problems the coalition has collapsed and he must battle also his former Liberal allies, defending a minority government.

Mr Bjelke-Petersen hopes to defeat the odds and win government in his own right.

This was how Channel O newscaster and commentator Des McWilliam introduced the station's "Meet the Press" interview with Joh Bjelke-Petersen on Sunday 16 October, just six days before the 22 October 1983 Queensland state election.

Turning to the premier, McWilliam then stated what was apparently obvious to most political commentators covering the campaign: "Mr Bjelke-Petersen, that's not really being realistic is it; in fact it's impossible?"

Joh Bjelke-Petersen smiled. "It's not impossible. Not if you've had the background experience that we have and the record we've got and the goodwill we have of so many people."

By 20 October the outlook was still no clearer for journalists

and commentators covering the campaign as was clearly indicated by Channel 7's "State Affair" programme that evening.

"Eeny, meeny, miney, mo! Terry White, Keith Wright or Joh
and with just one day to go the best informed say they don't
know. If it wasn't so serious it'd be funny, but the fact of the
matter is that this election has become the most difficult to
predict in living memory," was how the commentator introduced the segment.

On the same programme, respected *Courier-Mail* writer
Peter Trundle said: "It's the toughest I've struck in thirty years
of writing about this sort of thing." Pollster Gary Morgan from
the Morgan Gallup Poll added: "Obviously, who's going to win
on Saturday is going to depend on what's happened in the last
two weeks. Undoubtedly the poll result is encouraging for the
ALP in that the vote is moving in the direction of them." And
University lecturer Dr Paul Reynolds said: "It looks as though
Labor might just squeeze in."

Prime Minister Bob Hawke was interviewed on the same
programme and, after being introduced as "the most popular
politician in Australia today", he went on to say: "The National
Party and the Liberal Party are in greater disarray than any
group of politicians in the history of this country."

Most political pundits would agree that the 1983
Queensland election was the most remarkable in the state's
history. It would certainly rate as one of the most puzzling,
even for staunch National Party supporters who, during the
premiership of Joh Bjelke-Petersen, have become accustomed
to seemingly going to the brink of no return and yet somehow
still winning. It was an election that confounded the critics.
Never before has there been such a cacophony of unified
doubt in the minds of political experts throughout the nation,
who were drawn like magnets to the campaign. The political
"chooks" of the nation (as Joh would call them) gathered in
Queensland to cover the intrigue. Right to the very last
minute before polling, few were prepared to predict the outcome. Most found it difficult to believe that the Bjelke-
Petersen government could survive such odds. At the same
time, however, all found it difficult to tip that the grand
master of Australian politics could be beaten.

In the end, a stalemated result was the popular prediction of
the experts. Almost all the pundits who weren't predicting an

outright victory for Labor were suggesting that none of the three major parties would gain enough seats to govern in its own right and that almost certainly Queensland was headed for a period of continued political crisis and uncertainty. In the final weeks this was to become the catchcry of the Labor campaign.

In the "Meet the Press" interview on 16 October, *Telegraph* reporter Quentin Dempster tried to tie the premier down on this point. "Sir, in the event that you don't get the majority, you must point out surely, how you can form that government?" Dempster probed.

"The point is we don't deal in 'ifs' and 'buts'," Bjelke-Petersen responded. "I never do. I'm a positive thinker. I'm a realistic man and I have no problems in that regard. The main thing is you go, step by step – in all these years and in all matters and this issue of an election, the process is to win the position to govern in your own right. That's exactly what we're going to do."

"Can I pin you down on this one?" Dempster probed further.

"No, you can't," replied the premier.

"Well, I can try," Dempster retorted. "But will you enter a coalition agreement with the Liberal Party? Will you state now that you will not enter a coalition agreement?"

Confounding his critics with his confidence, Bjelke-Petersen replied: "I will not be having a coalition government. That's quite simple and that's the way we want it."

It is now a matter of record that Joh Bjelke-Petersen did get the numbers to form a majority government in his own right, without the need for a coalition with the Liberal Party.

It was an election that once again proved the success of the unique Bjelke-Petersen–National Party style of government. It had faced the most gruelling test of fire and had come through with flying colours. If ever there was a model for conservative parties to follow throughout Australia, this was surely it. Where all others had failed, Bjelke-Petersen's Queensland National Party government had recorded yet another resounding victory. It is an election result that will surely provide students of politics with argument for generations to come.

How could one aging man so completely confound the entire nation? How could a political party described by many as nothing but a "country rump" withstand such prolonged and persistent criticism and pressure and still emerge stronger than ever, cementing its success with major electoral gains in the blue-ribbon suburbs of metropolitan Brisbane?

Only a close understanding of the Joh Bjelke-Petersen–National Party political phenomenon can provide the real answer. And a close examination of the developments of the campaign reveals how, on this occasion, Bjelke-Petersen's opponents failed yet again.

The campaign

Modern political parties are like huge trains on a downhill journey. Once the wheels are in motion it is almost impossible to change direction. For this reason, with the benefit of hindsight, it is possible to assess the 1983 Queensland state election and see clearly the strategies that the protagonists adopted.

With the benefit of hindsight, it is also possible to assess just how accurate the initial assessments of the party strategists were and how successfully the resultant campaigns exploited the opportunities that arose.

Most modern political parties adopt a fairly rigid campaign strategy from the start, based on the expertise available to them and the results of public opinion polls which indicate how the electorate is thinking and what it expects. Their entire campaigns are mapped out often long before day one. Even then, the final campaign is almost always only the icing on a cake that has been steadily baking for many months. Millions of dollars of television, radio and press advertising is prepared and booked. Dozens of candidates and thousands of party workers are sold on the theme. Only a major change in circumstances will make such organizations even consider altering their approach once it is in place. Most are loath to change even then. Few have the flexibility. The fiscal cost can be enormous.

The 1983 Queensland state election is a classic example of this reality. By 4 August, when the surprise collapse came for the coalition, all three major party campaigns were starting to roll, shaping up for a November–December election at the very latest. They were, at least, heavily committed to their pre-election build-up. Their images were clearly established in the mind of the electorate. The opinion polls indicated this.

The National Party was the steadily rising star, having slowly but surely built up over the preceding twelve months from 26 per cent in June 1982 to 33 per cent in June 1983. The Labor Party was virtually static at 45 per cent of the vote and the Liberal Party was on a downer — sliding from 24 per cent in June 1982 to 17 per cent in June 1983. For all three, therefore, the coalition crisis that erupted on 4 August was a potential spanner in the works. The degree to which it affected their established programmes, however, is important in the context of assessing the final outcome. How good was it for the ALP and how bad was it for the Nationals and the Liberals? To what degree did they have to change their strategies? Was it possible at such a late hour to do so? And did the changes that were made really influence the final result?

In making such assessments, it has to be remembered that the 4 August "crisis" was a development that got out of hand. It started out as a minor "surgical" move by the Liberal Party, in a last-minute, pre-election attempt to halt their downward slide in the opinion polls. The minor "surgery", however, revealed a terminal illness. It went further than any Liberal could have expected and erupted into a full-scale war between the coalition partners. The Labor Party reaped a totally unexpected "gift" opportunity. They had been chipping away on a campaign to erode the foundations of the Liberal Party and unexpectedly the whole house caved in.

The National Party's crucial decision-making campaign committee meeting for the 1983 elections was held on Wednesday 27 July, a week before Terry White crossed the floor and precipitated the coalition crisis. Those present included Sir Robert Sparkes (chairman), Charles Holm (senior vice-president), Sir Francis Moore (state management appointee), Dr Glen Sheil (Metropolitan Zone vice-president), Col Walker (media adviser), Fred Maybury (media adviser and state management appointee), Mike Evans (executive director), David Russell (NPA media), Ken Crook (premier's press officer), Jenny Russell (NPA research), Wendy Armstrong (premier's research) and Helen Maybury (Sir Robert's secretary).

This meeting laid down the final blueprint for the Nationals'

1983 state campaign. In retrospect, it is possible to conclude that despite the eruptions that followed in the wake of the 4 August crisis, the Nationals did not alter their campaign to any significant degree. (For that matter, the 27 July meeting made few, if any, basic deviations from a strategy that had been in place since the end of 1980.) For example, the 27 July meeting concluded that the National Party's best chances of winning seats in the coming election were in the seats of Aspley, Cairns, Callide, Maryborough, Mourilyan, Murrumba and Toowong. It identified the seats in danger as Barron River, Fassifern, Mount Isa, Redlands, Warrego and Windsor, and that the Liberal seats of Ashgrove, Everton, Salisbury, Stafford and Townsville were likely to fall to Labor.

Of these seats, in the final result, the party won Aspley, Maryborough and Toowong and lost Mount Isa and Windsor. The ALP won Ashgrove, Everton, Salisbury, Stafford and Townsville. The only substantial difference the coalition crisis was to make to these forecasts was the transference of Liberal Party support to the National Party.

The campaign committee at that stage was planning for a late November election. The state policy speech was planned for release on Monday 31 October, with follow-up policy speeches in Cairns on Wednesday 2 November and Rockhampton on Friday 4 November. It had also made the decision that the premier would be the central figure in the campaign and would be supported by his wife, Senator Florence Bjelke-Petersen. And it had concluded that the election campaign would be based on "a mixture of Premier Joh and his government's past achievements, the great things to come, combined with the shortcomings of the ALP".

The achievements of the party in government would be a major aspect of the campaign, with the party's advertising advisers being commissioned to produce a pocket-book guide to these achievements for the briefing of candidates, campaign managers and the media.

The campaign committee had decided to introduce the strictest control ever over its candidates' election advertising. Only in special circumstances would the party permit individual-candidate advertising on television, with the committee reserving the right to vet all candidate advertising before it went to air. It had also decided that Sir Robert Sparkes and representatives of the campaign committee would take the campaign to the candidates in this election, rather than having central campaign meetings in Brisbane. It was an important change of organizational strategy aimed at improving local involvement in the campaign.

With the wheels on the campaign "trains" of all three major parties already moving, when the crisis came it was then a matter of how all three parties would need to adjust in order to (a) take advantage of the issue, and (b) avoid any electoral damage that could result from the crisis.

The questions to be answered were: Could Joh Bjelke-Petersen convince the people of Queensland that his strong style of leadership was the right course to follow? Did Keith Wright have the ability to capitalize on the totally unexpected collapse of the coalition and lead Labor out of the wilderness? Would the actions of Terry White and the Liberal Party halt their downward slide?

The flexibility of the three parties – the importance of their longer-term strategies and pre-election build-up and their ability to accurately identify opportunities on the run and to adapt to take advantage – was critical. On that point at least, it was a long campaign – nine weeks in all. All three major parties had time to pull up their election "trains" and change course, if necessary.

In the final analysis, it was a campaign of three distinct periods, concentrated on two main regions of the state and finally on one central issue. The first period was the period of crisis and concern, then came the period of remarkable calm, and finally the dash to the line. In many ways, it was like *Australia II*'s remarkable America's Cup victory. The two main areas of interest were metropolitan Brisbane and North Queensland. The central issue was style of government. The choice for the people of Queensland lay between sticking to the proven track record of the National Party, believing that the Labor Party under Keith Wright could do a better job, or believing that the self-destructive Liberals were a credible anti-socialist alternative.

The issues of public accountability and electoral reform that promised so much fire and brimstone in the early days of the crisis were lost in the race when the campaign proper settled

down, as was the involvement of the Australian Democrats
and environmentalists' Greens Party.

By comparison with some Queensland election campaigns
of the past and despite the tension of an incredibly complex
and confused campaign, it was a remarkably clean campaign,
publicly anyway. Privately, though, it was chock-full of intrigue and political manoeuvre, especially as far as the Liberal
Party was concerned. The self-annihilation of the Liberal
Party continued throughout the campaign and was probably
the reason the normal inter-party mudslinging never really
captured the headlines.

It was also the most polarized campaign in many years,
polarized to the point of really being an election between
three personalities and their credibility: Joh Bjelke-Petersen,
Keith Wright and Terry White. The credibility of the respective leaders would be the deciding issue.

On all these counts it was therefore an election that suited
the Nationals. If they could have drawn up the rules of the
game themselves, they couldn't have wished it otherwise. It
suited Joh Bjelke-Petersen's style. In the political credibility
stakes he had no peers. It also suited the National Party's long-
term strategy. Strong, reliable, successful government was the
cornerstone of National Party long-term strategy and the 4
August "crisis" gave the Nationals a public platform to prove
their point. Unlike the Liberal and Labor parties, they had
really no need to alter their course. The National Party juggernaut that had been gathering speed almost since the 1980 poll
was declared was, as far as National Party strategists were
concerned, right on course. The Labor and Liberal parties
would need to make changes, and fast: the Labor Party to
capitalize on the unexpected boon, and the Liberals to save
their political hides.

From the sacking of White to minority government

The campaign proper for the 1983 Queensland election
started the day Terry White was sacked. The following two
weeks of tension were a period which almost certainly determined the voting intentions of many Queenslanders. Joh
Bjelke-Petersen, Llew Edwards, Terry White and Keith
Wright knew it. The eyes of Queensland were on their every

move. The outcome of the election would be heavily influenced by their actions during this period.

For Premier Joh Bjelke-Petersen there was only one course to follow – the one he was on. Stand firm and exude confidence. Uphold the established National Party image of "strong, reliable government". Regardless of what happened, he would strive to hold the ship of government on this steady, dependable course. All he needed to do was to avoid changing his winning style in any way. The polls clearly indicated that he was on course to win, and win better than ever. And in the events of 4 August he had not been the aggressor.

Clear in his mind was the belief that oppositions don't win governments, that incumbents lose through panic and uncertainty. In his case, though, he had nothing to fear – he had the runs on the board. He had a powerful argument to put to the people.

By comparison, Terry White and the Liberals were in uncharted waters. They had a leadership struggle to settle; they then had to confront the difficulty of getting their divided house in order; and finally they had to attempt to salvage some political face out of their precarious predicament. Their's was truly a mammoth task. The only consolation was that those who had long cherished the opportunity to prove themselves as a viable, "nicer" anti-Labor alternative with a stronger social conscience than the National Party now had the chance to test their theory.

Not àll Liberals agreed, however, that this was any consolation. To many coalitionists within the Liberal Party, it appeared more like the booby prize. National Party state president Sir Robert Sparkes summed up their predicament ion private discussions: "They are obviously going to have to pursue this wishy-washy approach. They have no alternative."

Labor's golden opportunity

Labor leader Keith Wright was in the box seat. Almost without exception, the political media agreed that Wright had been given Labor's best chance to win since the divisive split in 1957. It was hard to disagree with them.

Regardless of the ballyhoo about the gerrymander being

against them, Labor was gifted with a wonderful opportunity to win if they were good enough. The Labor Party had improved its public opinion rating under Wright's leadership, and was within striking distance of government, even if, in the days leading up to 4 August, the party was looking to the 1983 poll at best as only a "stepping stone" to the 1986 election.

Leading Australian political analyst Malcolm Mackerras had also publicly declared soon after the sacking of Terry White that he thought there would be an 8 per cent swing to Labor, which would mean a landslide victory. It seemed that all Wright had to do now was capitalize on his opportunities. Surprisingly though, despite the opportunities that appeared to have been presented to him, Wright did not put the runs on the board in those crucially important first two weeks. In fact, he caused the government few problems during that opinion-forming period. Premier Joh Bjelke-Petersen totally dominated the media. Wright went for days without featuring in the major statewide coverage of the progressive developments. During this crucially important period, Keith Wright either did not see the opportunities or misjudged them. Or was it simply that Joh Bjelke-Petersen's private plan to keep control of the situation and play the game on his terms blanketed Wright from the limelight?

Private Labor Party suggestions were that Keith Wright intentionally decided to play it low-key. It was definite Labor Party strategy to create an image of responsibility for the party, to attempt to be seen by the electorate as the responsible moderate in this time of crisis and concern, offering a reliable, stable alternative, thus outdoing the conservatives at their own game. It was important to foster the image of responsibility, in the mould that has proven so successful for Labor leaders Neville Wran (New South Wales), John Bannon (South Australia), John Cain (Victoria) and Brian Bourke (Western Australia).

A tactical error?

If this was Labor's strategy then it has to be seen as their first major blunder of the campaign. At best, the opinion polls clearly indicated that only 20 per cent of Queenslanders believed that Keith Wright was capable of doing a better job

than Bjelke-Petersen. Even among Labor voters, the Morgan
Gallup Polls did not indicate that there was overwhelming
support for the concept that Wright would be a better leader.
This was the credibility gap Wright had to bridge if the
strategy of projecting him as a "more conservative gentleman"
than Bjelke-Petersen was to work.

What could not be denied, however, was that intentionally
or otherwise Keith Wright and the Labor Party had delivered
a stinging blow to the coalition – a knockout was in the
offing, if only they could deliver the final punch.

In the early days of the "White Affair", many journalists
were rightly giving Keith Wright and the Labor Party considerable credit for the events that had occurred on 4 August.
ABC "Nationwide" interviewer Jane Singleton pursued this
line in an interview with Wright on the evening of 4 August.

Singleton's introduction suggested the intentional aspect of
Labor's involvement: "Out of all this, the Labor Party are cock-
a-hoop. Parliament has been back for just three days and each
day has been volatile," she said. "Keith Wright has been
pushing the public accountability line very strongly and in
part, he says, it has been a tactic deliberately designed to hit
the coalition."

She then went on to set the stage for Wright: "The word
around parliament today and yesterday was the fact that you
had spun a web in order to catch a few flies, but you caught a
very big fly – Terry White."

Keith Wright capitalized on his opportunity: "We had our
strategy and that was to divide the Liberal and National
parties on the issues of public accountability and I set that up
in a speech yesterday; gave notice that Nev Warburton would
be moving this motion and the Liberals, in their own motion,
caught themselves. They knew they were caught up. If they
came along with us then the government was going to be split
and Bjelke-Petersen was going to be angry. If they didn't come
along with us they would be throwing out their principles.
Some came, some didn't. In doing so we split them asunder,"
Wright crowed.

He was on a winner. "They have sacked Terry White over
it," he continued. "I'm saying that it is a very black day for the
Liberals, not only for the Liberals, but for the coalition."

Wright was then asked what electoral advantage he saw in

the development. Here is where it is suggested that he erred. He had an important psychological plus going for him. He was looking like a giant-killer. Many Queenslanders had to be thinking: "Was this the man to finally bring down Joh Bjelke-Petersen?"

Wright, though, missed the opportunity. Instead of switching his attack to envelop both the Nationals and the Liberals and thereby establish himself as a politician who had planned and subsequently embarrassed Joh Bjelke-Petersen's government, he let the National Party off the hook, preferring the softer option of the Liberal jugular.

Instead of tackling the giant, he chose the mouse.

"It is like a chain, and you go for the weakest link and the metropolitan area and the Townsville area in the north and Toowoomba [are such areas]," he responded. "The Liberals are the weakest link and my tactics for eight months now have been to break that link by taking the Liberals on, and we have done that, and the people know that they just can't accept what the Liberals say."

Further weakening his own case, Wright then went on to promote the very case for Joh Bjelke-Petersen and the National Party. Joh Bjelke-Petersen couldn't have done it better himself.

"They [the Liberals] can come with any sort of policy, but after today no one can believe what they say will ever be put into practice because, Llew Edwards says, we don't stand by our policies — we stick with whatever the National Party says. We put our hands up when Joh Bjelke-Petersen says so."

Joh Bjelke-Petersen might well have written the words for Keith Wright. Bjelke-Petersen would use virtually the same words himself on numerous occasions through the campaign that followed, and would depend heavily on the National Party winning vital metropolitan Brisbane seats from the Liberal Party.

It can only be speculation, of course, but in the whole campaign this should have been Keith Wright's greatest opportunity. If he could have manoeuvred his position from one of simply catching a Liberal "fly" to one of embarrassing the entire Bjelke-Petersen government, then he could have gained the psychological boost his campaign needed. It could have been the wave to carry him on to victory. As it was, he contented himself with sinking the boot deeper into the Liberal Party. He avoided the real fight and consequently paid the price.

There have been a number of reasons given for Keith Wright pursuing this strategy at the time. Some suggested he was afraid to tackle the wily Joh head-on at such an early stage of the campaign. The most popular reason, however, was that Labor Party strategists totally underestimated the National Party's potential to win Brisbane metropolitan seats. They believed that the developing mass of disenchanted Liberals would vote Labor before voting for Joh and his "bushies".

Knocking the Liberals

Throughout the campaign Wright continued this line. He avoided the outright confrontation with Premier Joh Bjelke-Petersen that the electorate needed to witness if he was to be seen as a viable alternative.

His statement to his local Rockhampton *Morning Bulletin* on 11 August is an example of his preoccupation with the Liberal attack. "I'm challenging him [White] to stand up for his own policy. One vote, one value, is their policy and it is ours," Wright said, challenging Terry White to join with Labor to allow a redistribution on the basis of one vote, one value (equal-sized electorates) to be put through the parliament before an election was held.

"The alliance would allow me to introduce legislation for a redistribution of electorates. That would mean one vote, one value," Wright said. Terry White rejected the offer as was to be expected and the exercise proved to be of little value.

The suggestion that Joh Bjelke-Petersen and the National Party were considering a redistribution of boundaries prior to the election to make matters even more difficult for the Liberal Party was widely touted by the media at the time Keith Wright was trying to entice the Liberal Party into a coalition of convenience to allow him to put through his own redistribution bill. Wright attempted to give credibility to speculation with the announcement on 14 August: "I've had my staff do the sums and the premier could have a redistribution, call nominations afresh and still have an election on 10 December." Hoping to create public outrage, he added: "If he does, they'll be marching in the streets." Wright was playing with political furphies.

In National Party circles, the idea of a snap electoral redistribution, even partially, was never a possibility. Any electoral advantage that might have been gained would have been totally swamped by the public uproar that would almost certainly have followed. Former party president John Ahern had drawn the Management Committee's attention to the growing need for a redistribution in the heavily populated south-east corner of the state. The party's principal strategists were aware of possible electoral advantages to be gained, but equally aware of the potential for electoral backlash. It never got past that point.

The party's position on electoral redistribution was clearly spelt out by National Party executive director Mike Evans in April. "We will neither seek nor support any change and will adhere to the policy which specifies a redistribution should be held after the election," Evans said. It was a positive statement. A redistribution was due after the 1983 election and the Nationals would wait until then.

On 16 August it appeared that Wright was trying to recapture lost opportunities when he launched an attack on the premier and the National Party over their handling of the responsibilities of government in the crisis.

"The latest power-plays and counter manoeuvres have reduced the administration of the government in the public mind to a shemozzle," he said. "Mr Bjelke-Petersen and the Nationals are preoccupied with political puppetry, rather than providing stable, orderly government."

It was too late, however – that horse had already bolted. The two-week break Wright had given Bjelke-Petersen was the time he needed to stabilize his position. By 16 August, Bjelke-Petersen quite clearly still had the confidence of the people of Queensland. Wright had missed the bus, and the Morgan Gallup Poll that followed evidenced this fact.

Wright's half-hearted attack was soon abandoned and he was back to focusing his volleys at the Liberals. This was obviously Labor's long-range strategy and they were sticking with it. The ALP "train" was now gathering speed – downhill.

Public opinion polls, in part, supported the success of Labor's pre-4 August "get the Liberals" strategy. What the polls also showed, however, and which Keith Wright and the Labor Party strategists obviously failed to recognize, was that the main beneficiary of their anti-Liberal campaign was the National Party. Disenchanted Liberals were ready to vote National in Brisbane. Labor could not gain government therefore by simply undermining the Liberal Party. Joh Bjelke-Petersen and the National Party knew this and this knowledge was the reason for the premier's seemingly boundless confidence throughout the campaign.

An unpublished National Party poll conducted in March 1983 in the blue-ribbon electorate of Toowong clearly indicated that the National Party had a solid base on which to move into Brisbane. That poll indicated a 17 per cent support for the National Party and suggested "Prentice [the sitting Liberal member] is by no means an outstanding member. His performance is average." More importantly, considering the influence of 4 August on this assessment, Prentice was a leading player in the drama that destroyed the coalition.

The March poll in Toowong also indicated that the best support for the Nationals was in the 40-year-and-over age bracket and among women. Interpretation of this was that the blue-ribbon conservative Liberals were turning to the Nationals and the important women's vote was not going to Labor. The candidate who was finally chosen, dual Logie-winning television personality Earle Bailey, a grandson of the late Dr Sir Earle Page, was perfect.

Further opinion polling throughout Brisbane in August and September confirmed that the National Party was picking up the disenchanted Liberal voters. They were not going to Labor. During this time, Labor also announced that they would be directing their preferences to the National Party in the seat of Aspley. The National Party was ecstatic.

Misreading the polls

Since 1980 when the coalition partners split on the issue of the separate Senate team and Flo Bjelke-Petersen won her place in the Senate, the Liberal Party had been steadily losing ground in Queensland, but most of it was being taken up by the Nationals. The 5 March 1983 federal election confirmed the move away from the Liberals, with the National Party still being the principal beneficiary. The National Party Senate team under Florence Bjelke-Petersen's leadership polled some 33 per cent of the vote (up 7 per cent on 1980) to win the fifth Senate seat from the Liberal Party. From that point onward, it was just a matter of the National Party converting their Senate vote to a state election vote.

The Labor Party "bucketing" campaign on the Liberal Party helped enormously in this regard. All the things the National Party might have wanted to say, but couldn't in the interests of coalition harmony, the Labor Party said with greater credibility and more often. And most importantly for the Nationals, it was having its greatest influence in the important Brisbane metropolitan area where the Nationals had spent countless thousands of dollars trying to make inroads on their own account.

Thanks to Labor, the 1983 state election was shaping up for the Nationals as a two-horse race, with potentially big opportunities in the key Brisbane metropolitan area for the Nationals — again, just what the Nationals wanted.

The starting statistics

The outcome of the 1980 state election gave Labor 41.8 per cent of the vote, the Nationals 27.6 per cent and the Liberal Party 26.9 per cent. In May, the polls showed that the Nationals were converting their Senate vote to a state vote. They climbed from 31 per cent in March to 33 per cent in May. Labor was steady at 45 per cent and the Liberals at 17 per cent.

Public opinion polls in June, prior to the "White Affair", showed Labor steady at 45 per cent (up 3.2 per cent on the 1980 state election), the Nationals 33 per cent (up 5.4 per cent) and the Liberals 17 per cent (down 9.9 per cent).

The events of 4 August and the performance of the leaders over the days that followed locked in these proportions. A Morgan Gallup Poll published in the *Bulletin* on 17 August showed that there was little change in voter intentions as a result of the 4 August fiasco, except that the National Party's approval rating had risen from 33 to 34 per cent.

A further Morgan Gallup Poll published in the *Bulletin* on 16 September confirmed this trend. Despite the problems of the coalition partners and the fact that Prime Minister Hawke had spent a week campaigning in Queensland, the polls showed that Labor in fact had slipped 1 per cent to 44 per cent, while the Liberals had gained 1 per cent to 18 per cent and the National Party was steady on 34 per cent.

Santa Claus Hawke

Prime Minister Bob Hawke arrived in Queensland at the height of the "White Affair" and, although he had a relatively low-key start, he finished the week like a cyclone through North Queensland, where he promised federal action like it had never been seen before. Headlines likened his visits to Townsville and Cairns to those of Santa Claus. The Brisbane *Daily Telegraph* of 15 August led into its editorial for the day: "Christmas has come early for North Queensland."

In Townsville, Hawke promised $13 million in the current financial year for development works on the $125 million Burdekin Dam project to enable it to be completed by 1988. He also confirmed the construction of a $12 million Commonwealth office block in the city and promised to protect the North Queensland sugar industry from the development of a sugar industry on the Ord River in Western Australia. There would also be $65 million spent on upgrading the Bruce Highway and a commitment to upgrade the Townsville domestic air terminal. There would also be a "substantial boost" for the Australian Tourist Commission.

In Cairns he announced government building projects for Cairns ($5.5 million), Rockhampton ($6.1 million), Mackay ($4 million) and Thursday Island ($700,000), "substantial improvements" for Aborigines, a commitment to continue supporting the shipbuilding firm of NQEA, a second network for the ABC, the backdating of exemptions for the 20 per cent sales tax on certain tourist boats and a plan to investigate provision of low-cost tourist accommodation.

It was a grandstand performance by Hawke, but as the polls showed it did not have the electoral impact that Labor might have hoped for. Many political observers were left wondering if the whole exercise was a matter of poor timing and assessment by the ALP. The only explanation appears to be that Labor expected a snap poll to be called and felt that Hawke's visit with his bag of federal hand-outs would turn the tide for them.

A snap poll wasn't called, however, and Hawke's hand-outs

were not sufficient to erase the problems that his first budget and the row over taxing superannuation was causing Labor in the north. The 10 per cent "withholding tax" on the building industry and small business generally and higher fuel costs were other big losers for the ALP in the north.

The polls still promised big gains for the Labor Party, if Keith Wright could convert their 44 per cent to actual seats in parliament. With 34 per cent of the vote, the National Party was right on target to achieve their long-cherished ambition to get the numbers to govern in their own right. In this regard, the marginal fall of 1 per cent for Labor was a sign of things to come for Joh Bjelke-Petersen.

The 17 per cent statewide vote for the Liberal Party, though, was devastating for Liberal strategists. It indicated that the party could lose as many as ten or twelve seats. It was almost line-ball with the 5 March federal election result, which had been reconfirmed in the 17 August public opinion polls.

Leading political commentator Laurie Oakes, writing in the *Sunday Sun* on 17 August, summed up the outlook as the crisis period came to a close: "The general speculation among those who observe politics is that Mr Bjelke-Petersen's National Party and the resurgent Labor Party are likely to do fairly well in the forthcoming state election and that the Liberal Party will be the big losers." On published public opinion polls, it was a safe statement to make at the time. It turned out to be extremely accurate.

Preferences

Even though the August–September polls were encouraging results for the National Party, from their point of view they had to be balanced by the unknown element of Liberal preference leakage.

As the *Daily Sun* editorial of 18 August pointed out: "National Party supporters vote with a discipline that would bring a tear to the eye of a Prussian general . . . but Liberals are an undisciplined lot." Preferences would remain the unknown quantity throughout the election campaign.

The public opinion polls of August and September, however, were a sobering influence on a number of political forecasters, and Canberra-based political analyst Malcolm Mackerras, who forecast an 8 per cent swing to Labor (and a landslide victory) after the collapse of the coalition on 4 August, was one of them. Mackerras confidently predicted that Labor would win forty-eight seats, with the Nationals winning only twenty-one and the Liberals thirteen. On 21 September, however, after the Morgan poll of 16 September was released, he revised his earlier "landslide" statement. "The poll does not bear out my prediction. But it has Labor very close to victory," he told the Brisbane *Telegraph*.

Interestingly, Mackerras told the *Telegraph* that he expected a 34 per cent drift of Liberal preferences to Labor and a 6.7 per cent drift of National Party preferences. This is about 14 per cent more than the big Liberal drift in 1980 when the coalition lost the fifth Senate seat in Queensland over the separate Senate ticket wrangle.

Of still further interest was Mackerras' visit to Queensland in October, just three weeks prior to the election, when he changed his mind yet again.

The August and September polls confirmed Keith Wright's inability to capitalize on his opportunities in the hectic two weeks of crisis period. The polls should have moved more sharply in favour of Labor. Malcolm Mackerras was on reasonably safe ground when he made his original "landslide" prediction, but like the ALP he had obviously underestimated the credibility of Joh Bjelke-Petersen compared with that of his rivals.

There were many, though, even within the National Party, who thought he could well have been right at the time, but who with greater experience of the vagaries of Queensland politics were reluctant to say so – publicly anyway.

A worrying source of doubt was the anti-conservative swing that had occurred in the most recent state election in Western Australia. How could this be compared with Queensland? The Western Australian swing was the unknown factor in the poll, although there was clear evidence that there were many differences from the Queensland situation.

Hugh Lunn of the *Australian* was one who still hinted at the possibility that it could all happen for Labor. In an article in the *Australian* on 17 August, Lunn said that there were many similarities between the coalition split of 1983 and the Queensland Labor Party split in 1957. "Of course there are a couple of differences," he added guardedly. "Then the Labor

Party was the entire government and in this case the Liberal Party is backing the man elected to be the cabinet leader. But," he said, "the parallels are close enough to note that the 1957 split led a powerful and popular government — which had ruled for twenty-five years — into a bitter election characterized by phrases such as 'traitorous deviations' — and they were wiped."

He developed the argument further: "And now the Liberal Party is in danger of going along the same path; a path Vince Gair [Labor premier 1957] correctly predicted before the party's split would be 'fraught with danger and pregnant with tragedy'." Agreeing with the general consensus of political opinion at that stage, Hugh Lunn went on to make the only positive statement possible: "The parallels for the Liberal Party are frightening."

The Liberals' internal problems

Despite the doom and gloom being forecast by the experts, the Liberal Party tried desperately to outwardly remain confident of their new image under Terry White. "We don't anticipate losing any seats and we anticipate picking up at least six more," the state director of the Liberal Party, Gary Neat, cautiously predicted on 22 August.

In the immediate aftermath of the 4 August eruption, Liberal Party stocks rose marginally in the Brisbane metropolitan area, but Gary Neat's prediction of picking up six additional seats was hard to justify on the accepted public opinion results. An in-house survey for the Liberals, taken at the height of the crisis throughout the suburbs of Brisbane, was the only basis possible for the Liberals' confidence. It showed that 66 per cent of the 300 people polled agreed with Terry White's actions; 56.7 per cent also preferred Terry White as leader to Dr Llew Edwards.

What wasn't revealed, however, was the voting intentions of the people polled. In this sense therefore the poll had to be seen as little more than an in-house morale-booster for the Liberals.

If there was any early euphoria for the Liberal Party, it was doused on 14 August, when deputy leader Sam Doumany announced that he would be stepping down from the position. The public face of the Liberal Party was still further smudged when none of the senior Liberals stepped forward to take on the job as Terry White's deputy, and the job went to Angus Innes. The same senior Liberals also stayed away from the Liberals' shadow ministry that was announced. And finally, on 29 August, Dr Llew Edwards announced that he would be retiring from politics.

Dr Edwards' retirement had been privately rumoured for some time as the campaign against him mounted. The events of 4 August and the fortnight that followed simply hastened his decision.

It was a difficult time for Terry White. Publicly he and his party were putting on a brave face, but privately they were tearing their hearts out. The bitter division within the Liberal Party over the split with the Nationals could not be healed overnight. The task of convincing the coalitionists in the Liberal Party that the actions of 4 August could be justified was almost impossible. About the best that could be hoped for was that the divisions could be kept private.

Behind the scenes the internal power struggle continued. Privately, the Liberal Party was like a can of worms. The vested interests of many of the key personalities further complicated the situation.

Primarily there was the continuing leadership struggle. A number of coalition supporters within the Liberal Party liked White, but believed that he had made a grave error of judgment. They doubted that he could restore the stability necessary to avoid annihilation for the party in Queensland. Their campaign was assisted by continuing suggestions by Premier Joh Bjelke-Petersen that neither Terry White nor his deputy, Angus Innes, would be acceptable to the National Party in any coalition to be formed after the election.

From the National Party point of view, these manoeuvres were designed to help former Liberal leader Sir William Knox to make a political comeback. Knox was counting heads well before 22 October.

Further complicating the Liberals' problems were the ambitions of party president Dr John Herron, who was reportedly angling for the federal presidency of the Liberal Party. Herron needed the Queensland election to go well for the Liberals to salvage any hopes of getting the federal presidency.

The superstars of Australian politics in 1983: Queensland's Joh Bjelke-Petersen and Canberra's Bob Hawke. As different as chalk and cheese and each committed to the other's demise. What will the years ahead hold for both men? (Photograph courtesy of Queensland Newspaper Pty Ltd)

Time for a cuppa and a pumpkin scone. At the height of the campaign Joh and Flo took a break while the billy and a four-gallon drum boil over an open fire. (Photograph courtesy of Queensland Newspapers Pty Ltd)

Tasmanian Liberal premier Robin Gray and Premier Bjelke-Petersen at a Queensland press conference during the 1983 election campaign. Gray's forthright support for Bjelke-Petersen and the Queensland Nationals was a telling blow to the Queensland Liberals in the campaign. (Photograph courtesy of Queensland Newspapers Pty Ltd)

Former Liberal ministers Brian Austin and Don Lane. Their defection from the Liberal Party after the historic 1983 elections gave Joh Bjelke-Petersen's Nationals the numbers to govern in their own right. (Photograph courtesy of Queensland Newspaper Pty Ltd)

Over and above all this, the North Queensland section of the party successfully moved to end the involvement of former president Yvonne McComb as Northern Organizer as from 1 October.

Most damaging of all for the Queensland Liberals, however, was the involvement in the campaign of current and former greats of the party, who quite remarkably came out in strength to support Joh Bjelke-Petersen. Former prime minister Malcolm Fraser lead the charge with his letter to the editors of Australia's leading newspapers. Former premiers Sir Henry Bolte, Sir Charles Court, Sir Robert Askin and Tom Lewis followed. The most active, however, was sitting Tasmanian premier Robin Gray.

Over the years, Joh Bjelke-Petersen has established a great working rapport with conservative leaders throughout Australia. He has been their staunchest ally in times of strife. Whenever there were problems in any of the other states, so long as they were in the interests of preserving conservative government, Joh has been the first to help. Now he was calling up his debts and his conservative friends were responding willingly, despite the fetters of party barriers. Robin Gray is the newest of the Bjelke-Petersen converts among the Liberal leaders. Joh had backed him in his fight with Canberra over the Franklin Dam issue.

Questioned by "State Affair" on 11 October on his reasons for buying into the Queensland campaign to support Joh Bjelke-Petersen, Premier Gray made no bones about the way he saw the situation: "Look, Mr Bjelke-Petersen is the premier of Queensland. He's provided the strong leadership that Queenslanders have enjoyed over about, I think, seventeen years. He's done a tremendous job for that state, and any realist knows that there can't be any Liberals in government unless Joh Bjelke-Petersen is in there with them. And they ought to recognize this."

Terry White was far from impressed. He vented his displeasure in an interview on the ABC programme "World Today" later that day. "Well, the people of Queensland regard it as a big yawn, because they'll all ask — Robin who?"

"Robin who?" the reporter echoed. "He is, after all, the only Liberal premier in Australia."

White went on to say: "Well I think the only way you could

describe Mr Robin Gray is a political scab who's scabbed on his mates."

Concluding the interview, the reporter summed up: "It does seem to be a rather strange situation whereby you're not getting terribly much support from a number of notable Liberal Party people. There's Mr Gray, there's Sir Henry Bolte, you've had Mr Austin, for example, supporting the Queensland government's position on the tender operation, you've also had Dr Edwards supporting the National Party in relation to the budget."

Terry White responded: "I think that's a lot of twaddle."

October 11 was a difficult day all round for Terry White. Not only did he have to field questions about Robin Gray's visit to Queensland but he also had the sacking of the Liberal candidate for Landsborough, Cr Don Culley, on his plate. Asked in a Channel 7 news interview on 11 October what had gone wrong, White replied: "That guy Culley said he was going to give his preferences to the Labor Party and as soon as he said that I stepped in and asked the state executive to get rid of him."

In the final analysis, the Channel 7 current affairs programme "State Affair" on 18 October probably summed up the Liberal Party and Terry White's predicament:

> Over the past few weeks the most remarkable thing about the state election campaign has been the apparent super-human ability of Liberal leader Terry White to survive the brick-bats that have been thrown at him. He's been ratted on by his colleagues, admonished by former party statesmen, snubbed by Robin Gray, plotted against from within and ridiculed without and generally beset upon by just about everyone. Only his dog hasn't had a go at him, at least not yet. [Interestingly, Premier Joh Bjelke-Petersen was bitten by his own dog after the 1983 poll.]
>
> If ever a man had everything going against him in the lead-up to an election it would have to be Terry White. Since that Thursday in August when he voted against the government he's been villified, defied, ridiculed and repudiated. Liberal giants in phase of Bolte, Court and Gray have severally embarrassed him – worked against him. Ministerial colleagues have betrayed him and his party executive has shown itself to be inept and amateurish. Another man may have been tempted to withdraw one of the daggers from his back and use it to slash his wrists – not Terry White."

In yet another face-saving attempt, Terry White struggled through this interview convincing few Queenslanders that he seriously believed what he was saying. One had to wonder if he really believed it himself. Finally, reporter Tony Barnett asked him if he was looking forward to the election result, or dreading the thought. White's reply sums up his performance throughout the campaign:

"Oh, no, I'm looking forward to it. Gee whiz, this has been a terrific campaign. It's my first one as leader and I'm tuning myself up for the next time after this. It'll be a beauty."

Time to sell the message

The rejection of a snap poll that was suggested by some, and the naming of 22 October as the date for the election gave Premier Joh Bjelke-Petersen the time he wanted to campaign across Queensland. He likes long election campaigns. He has learnt from experience that few of his opponents have the strength to keep up the pace. More importantly, he needed maximum time to sort out the internal problems of the Liberal Party.

The National Party, for Australia-wide reasons, preferred to go back into coalition after the election, but it was not going to be a step they would be rushing to take. Joh Bjelke-Petersen was not about to rashly commit himself or his party to another five years like the past five years in bed with the dissident section of the Liberal Party. He would need to be totally convinced that the Queensland Liberal Party had purged itself of such dissidents and their destructive and divisive policies before he pledged himself to another coalition.

Joh and the treasury

Minority government also gave the National Party the treasury. Joh Bjelke-Petersen had long cherished the thought of being treasurer and the split gave him the job.

Taking on treasury has also been a widely sought demand of the National Party organization. Hardly a coalition agreement or a State Conference of the National Party has gone past over the years when a substantial section of the organization has not pushed for the premier to take treasury away from the Liberal Party. Fights with successive Liberal Party treasurers to fund priority National Party programmes have been milestones throughout the twenty-six rocky years of the coalition. It has always been convention, however, that the Liberals be given treasury, and as much as Premier Bjelke-Petersen would dearly have liked to have taken it sooner he had to wait until the split.

Being premier and treasurer gave Bjelke-Petersen the total control over the 1983–84 budget that was expected to have been brought down in mid-September, a development that greatly disappointed coalitionists within the Liberal Party, as former Liberal leader Dr Llew Edwards had made a major contribution to the drafting of the document. Adding further salt to the wound was the fact that it was widely considered to be one of the most attractive budget packages the state had brought down in many years.

With an election in the offing and in the circumstances he now found himself, Premier Bjelke-Petersen chose to break convention and systematically release details of the "goodies" in the budget throughout the duration of the campaign. He also stunned his critics by refusing to reveal details of funding the budget until after the election. It was a most astute political manoeuvre that greatly enhanced the strength of his position and weakened that of his opponents.

It was a risky strategy that could have been fraught with danger for a lesser-qualified politician. Again, though, we are dealing with that intangible quality of Joh Bjelke-Petersen's personal credibility with the people of Queensland. It was a gamble, but nobody knows the strength of his gambling position better than Joh Bjelke-Petersen. After thirty-seven years in Queensland parliament and having everything bar the kitchen sink thrown at him and still remaining "squeaky-clean", he operates from a position of credibility that most other politicians cannot start to appreciate. He has a reputation for delivering his promises and, consequently, criticism that he didn't know what he was doing falls on deaf ears.

Patching up problems in the north

Minority government and a long campaign also gave the National Party time to patch up problems in its most worrying area – North Queensland.

The resignation of the six Liberal ministers gave Premier Bjelke-Petersen the opportunity to appoint three new North Queensland ministers, effectively squashing a key Labor Party campaign issue that had been developed in North Queensland since 1980, when the party lost three ministers in the north through the resignation of Ron Camm (Whitsunday) and Tom Newbery (Mirani) and the defeat at the polls of Max Hooper (Townsville West).

The appointment of Angelo Bertoni (Mount Isa), Martin Tenni (Barron River) and Geoff Muntz (Whitsunday) to the cabinet gave the Nationals, along with Val Bird (Burdekin), who was retiring at the 1983 poll, four ministers from the north. Minority government also gave the Nationals the chance to elevate the popular member for Peak Downs, Vince Lester, to cabinet and effectively block out key areas of the state with the further appointments of Neville Harper (Auburn) and Neil Turner (Warrego).

The only area of the state that wasn't represented in the cabinet was Brisbane. The Nationals just didn't have a member in the area. Tactically, however, given the man-power resources of the National Party, it was a very effective spread of ministers. It stifled a lot of possible criticism, especially in North Queensland where Labor expected big gains in the poll.

And to keep the lid on the criticism, Premier Bjelke-Petersen confirmed in the Nationals' North Queensland policy speech on 26 September that North Queensland would retain its quota of ministers in the cabinet after the election.

The campaign, though, wasn't all clear sailing for the new ministers.

Angelo Bertoni, who was appointed to the Health portfolio, soon discovered that he had inherited a can of worms.

The new minister for Survey and Valuations, Martin Tenni, was also to discover that there was considerable concern in North Queensland over steeply increased land valuations that came into effect with the announcement of local government budgets in August.

The new Justice minister, Neville Harper, also ran into flak over his appointment of district court judges, with some suggesting that such important decisions should not be made by a minority government on the eve of a poll.

Health problems

Bertoni's Health portfolio was the cause of considerable concern. Not only did he have the delicate and difficult responsibilities associated with watchdogging the federal government on the introduction of its controversial Medicare programme, but the A.W.U. was causing problems over whether or not contractors should be allowed to do hospital laundry, and in Townsville there was considerable unrest over plans to construct a ninety-bed, free-standing women's hospital at Kirwan.

The calling of tenders to construct Kirwan and a number of other hospital buildings throughout the state on the design/construct basis also loomed as a possible "blow up" that might embarrass the government, when it was revealed that the government was actually paying contractors $25,000 each to tender.

Channel 7's "State Affair" headlined the story across the state on 9 September: "Reports today revealed the existence of a state government scheme whereby companies tendering to build hospitals are paid $25,000 to spur them along."

Deputy Liberal leader Angus Innes jumped on to the band wagon early to criticize the practice, but within twenty-four hours it had proven to be a storm in a teacup that both the Liberals and Labor backed away from.

Former Liberal Health minister Brian Austin did most to defuse the issue. Speaking on the "State Affair" programme that evening, he came to the defence of the National Party government and explained the "design and construct" method of tendering that the Queensland government had introduced. He also explained the savings it was reaping for the Queensland government.

"When a normal job goes to tender, all of that [the design work] is done by a private contractor prior to going to tender and, if you work on $80 million as a total cost of all the hospital work, the consulting fees on $80 million, to prepare the plans and specifications, and a bill of quantities, would be about $4.2 million to do that work before you went to tender," Austin said. The Queensland government therefore was shaping up to save about $4 million by the method.

Austin's comments pulled the rug out from under Liberal Party colleague Angus Innes and indicated the lack of liaison that existed within the Liberal Party at the time. Austin, the former Liberal Health minister, obviously hadn't been consulted by Innes before he went public on the issue.

ALP leader Keith Wright also suffered in the scrap when it was revealed that a major hospital was being built in his electorate under the same method, saving the government a considerable amount of taxpayers' money.

From Austin's point of view it was a most interesting performance in the light of his post-election decision to join the National Party.

Bertoni finally won the day with the announcement of tenders for the construction work on a major hospital expansion programme, which indicated considerable cost savings for the government.

The final countdown

The main policy launches of the three major parties in early October signalled the start of the final countdown to polling day on 22 October and little more. All three parties launched predictably attractive policies. All also issued special policies for North Queensland (a practice instigated by the National Party at the author's suggestion in 1980). The Nationals went one better this time, however, with a third major policy launch in Rockhampton to appeal to the rapidly expanding Central Queensland area.

All three political parties also elected to systematically release follow-up policy details on a wide range of key areas of interest and government responsibility. This was one of the several innovative campaigning techniques that surfaced in the campaign.

Again, however, the policy statements were a matter of credibility. Who would the bulk of the electorate believe? Joh Bjelke-Petersen, who had the audacity to not even publicly cost his platform? Terry White, who promised virtually the same as Joh, but quite plainly didn't have the ability to deliver the numbers? Or Keith Wright, who had presented the most elaborate Labor platform in memory, costing every item down to the last dollar, but even then with all the figures amazingly not correlating?

A new direction for Labor

The most important development of all three policy launches was the revelation of Labor's final-thrust strategy — to promote that a vote for either the Nationals or the Liberals was a vote for constitutional crisis.

The "supply" issue that Keith Wright had floated earlier without success was dusted off again for another run, and expert opinion would be relied upon to convince Queenslanders that Joh couldn't get the numbers; he wouldn't go into coalition with either Terry White or Angus Innes and therefore only a further constitutional crisis could result.

"You must decide who will govern Queensland — and in making that decision I ask you to cast your judgment on the unprecedented crisis into which the National/Liberal politicians and powerbrokers of the former coalition have plunged our state," is how Keith Wright introduced his campaign speech delivered at the Greek Community Centre on 2 October.

"A crisis which has almost paralysed the political system. A crisis that threatens Queensland's economic stability. And a crisis that has allowed this state to be ruled for almost three months by a minority National Party government that has abused the privilege of office — misused public funds and broken every convention of the Westminster system of government."

Later in his speech, Wright claimed: "We are the only alternative to chaos."

The day after Labor's policy speech on 2 October, Keith Wright was on the campaign trail promoting the impending crisis line.

"I think it's become the most important issue outside the specific policy area. It affects individual groups. As I've moved around the state people have said that the issue is credibility in government, stability, responsibility and most importantly accountability," Wright told the ABC.

"How can you be so sure that you'll be able to offer stability?" Wright was asked.

"Well," replied Wright, "it comes back to whether or not you have a majority government and the reason there isn't stability is because we have the premier, Joh Bjelke-Petersen, saying he will not work with any Liberal leader, especially Terry

White. That they're going alone. He also now says, regardless of what the situation might be, he wants to keep treasury. Now he won't also accept a foreign land register. He won't accept a redistribution. He won't accept a public accounts committee. So you see there's no chance that the Liberal and the Nationals could come back together to make up the numbers."

In North Queensland, speaking at the James Cook University at a pre-election address organized by the husband of Labor senator Margaret Reynolds, political commentator Malcolm Mackerras echoed the Labor leader's predictions to the delight of the auditorium.

The media throughout the state latched on to the crisis forecast and helped the Labor Party fan the flames of doubt.

"In my view it is most unlikely that it [the National Party] will have enough members of parliament to govern in its own right after October 22nd, despite the obvious confidence of the premier and Sir Robert Sparkes," said political commentator Peter Charlton on the ABC on October 3.

"I only hope, of course, that the political tensions don't lead to any instability. I think the state's bigger than the problems of the Liberal Party and the Labor Party," said well-known Brisbane chat show commentator Hayden Sargeant on 9 October.

"The constitutional issue as well as the supply of and spending of money seem to be increasingly important issues in the Queensland election," said the ABC commentator on the "AM" programme on 11 October. "Yesterday the Labor leader, Keith Wright, quoted what he said was secret treasury documents to support his claim that Queensland was running out of money. Mr Hawke claimed the Queensland government had failed to spend Commonwealth funds on job creation projects."

On 12 October the campaign stepped up when a foul-up in the mailing system coincidentally delayed the delivery of some public service wage cheques.

"Fear that Queensland may run out of money because of the coalition collapse spread rapidly through Brisbane today when hundreds of government employees didn't get their pay," were the headlines of the Channel 9 "Today Tonight" current affairs programme. It continued: "Nevertheless, state opposition leader Keith Wright continued his attack on the caretaker National Party government by saying that the state would run out of money in November. Mr Wright has written to the Queensland Governor about the situation and his reply came back today."

Premier Joh Bjelke-Petersen was unmoved by the campaign. As he told reporters on Channel O's "Meet the Press" on 16 October: "They're voting for a National Party government. They are voting for a National Party government. That's clear. That's positive. There's no arguing about that."

It was a reliance on the old Danish proverb "den tid, den sorg" (that time, that sorrow) — we'll worry about that when the time comes. He would tell the media this many times during the campaign when questioned about what he planned to do.

Unemployment impact

If government stability was a local issue in this campaign, unemployment was the all-concerning national issue. It was an issue that turned sour for Labor at the peak of their efforts to capitalize on the instability/constitutional crisis issue.

On 7 October, GMH dropped a bombshell into the campaign with the announcement that it would be closing its Acacia Ridge plant in Brisbane and sacking 900 employees. Despite Keith Wright and Bob Hawke's best efforts to dissociate the federal Labor government from the GMH closure, there is no doubt that they were widely blamed.

Their problems were compounded by the release several days later of the Commonwealth unemployment figures for the September quarter that indicated yet again that Queensland was performing best among the states in the area of job creation.

"Two thousand four hundred people yesterday got a job, which hasn't happened in the other states," Joh Bjelke-Petersen was able to claim in "Meet the Press" when questioned on the unemployment issue by John Wiseman.

In National Party campaign literature distributed to candidates, it was also boldly proclaimed that in the important area of youth employment Queensland was 5.1 per cent better-off than the nearest other state in the Commonwealth.

The *Daily Sun* of 14 October supported the premier's claim

that Queensland was still doing better than the other states in the area of job creation. The headlines read: "State Unemployment Rate Down – National Figure Rises". The opening paragraph of the article said: "Queensland is the only state to defy the national wave of unemployment."

In the "Meet the Press" interview the premier was asked about the GMH closure.

"If things are going so well [in Queensland], why do we see things like the GMH closure the other day? The coal mine at Ipswich where the miners are staging a sit-in?"

It was a "Dorothy Dixer" for the wily campaigner.

"Well, you know as well as I do, John," the premier replied. "You're a pretty cluey sort of a chap, John. You would know that is it federal policy that is allowing large imports of other cars and GMH told you the same. Two-hundred-thousand cars come in and so it's federal policy that caused that and even Mr Hawke in effect."

Ipswich miners' dispute

In politics it's widely recognized that it's better to be lucky than anything else. Throughout his political career Joh Bjelke-Petersen has appeared to have more than his share of political luck. He would probably say that it is based on the belief that the harder you work, the luckier you get.

The coal miners' dispute at Ipswich is probably the best illustration of the sheer unplanned good fortune that appeared to be running for Joh Bjelke-Petersen in this campaign. It came in the final week and was icing to the cake.

The miners had decided to stage a sit-in strike after it was announced that their mine would be closed down. The National Party minister for Mines and Energy, Ivan Gibbs, had said that there would be no reprieve. The premier had backed his minister. Then the premier's wife, Senator Flo Bjelke-Petersen, made a surprise visit to the mine on 18 October. She had with her a batch of two-dozen pumpkin scones and an intention to defuse the issue. She drank tea and ate pumpkin scones with the miners and promised to "speak to Joh" on their behalf.

On 20 October, Joh himself and his deputy, Bill Gunn, were down in the mine, and the headlines across the state carried the story that he had given the miners a reprieve – vote-catching stuff on the eve of an election. You can't buy publicity like that.

Canberra's contribution

As much as Joh seemed to have an uncanny tide of good fortune going for him, the Labor Party in Canberra did little to help their Queensland colleagues in the latter stages of the campaign.

Statements about changing the oath of allegiance at naturalization ceremonies (coupled with increased media attention on Prime Minister Bob Hawke's stated position as an atheist), persistent problems within the Wran government in New South Wales, and the introduction of the Sex Discrimination Bill on the eve of the election gravely undermined the Labor campaign.

The oath-of-allegiance debate and Bob Hawke's atheism were probably the most damaging issues to Labor in Queensland. They virtually pulled the rug out from under Keith Wright's heavy "Christian" campaign which he had waged from day one.

Throughout the campaign, Keith Wright pumped his Christianity probably harder than any politician has done in the history of Queensland. So heavy was the push that the award-winning national current affairs programme "60 Minutes" devoted an entire segment to this angle.

"It's not exactly in the same class as the crusades, but Queensland's state election on Saturday seems at times to be as much a religious war as it is political, with both Joh and his Labor opponent praying for political guidance. It must be a tough choice for that great swinging voter in the sky" is how the programme was introduced.

Keith Wright was asked if he believed it was God's will that he should be in politics. He replied: "Oh, that's proven. I should be there." Wright went on to explain how he believed his belief in God had influenced his involvement in politics. "I don't want to be stupid about it and say there's some sort of spiritual base for all this, but what I do know is that, in 1974 or when I had the third worse seat in the Labor Party, I survived and twenty-two of my colleagues went. Now how you sum up is immaterial. I can't prove any of it. I just have a knowledge of God. I know what it's like to be a victim. I also know what it's like to totally fail and fail God and myself."

The premier was then asked what he thought of Keith Wright. "It's immaterial to me what he looks like. I've always said, it doesn't matter how good looking he is, or whether he's your neighbour or whether he wears a hat or whether he doesn't. If he's a Labor man then he's a socialist."

Asked later in the interview if his attitude to Keith Wright and the Labor Party was unchristian, Joh Bjelke-Petersen responded: "No, it isn't unchristian, it's true."

This line of questioning of the two leaders was also pursued by talk-show interviewer Mike Walsh when interviewing Keith Wright on 19 October.

"It has been interesting, too, because Joh got around your personal beliefs by describing your party as one of atheists, drug addicts, republicans and socialists and that you would decriminalize marihuana the moment you got into office," Mike Walsh put to Wright.

In his response Wright said: "Why should an Italian person or a Greek person who comes to Queensland or Australia or anywhere in this country have to have an oath of allegiance to the Queen of Britain? I just don't think it's necessary." He continued: "If you want to have an oath of allegiance to God because you are a believer, that won't be stopped, but why should a person who is a non-believer, a person who believes in some other religion, be bound by that statement?"

Thirty rallies in twenty-six days

A highlight of the campaign for Premier Joh Bjelke-Petersen and the National Party was the unusually large turn-out at election rallies for the party throughout the state. In the twenty-six final days of the campaign the premier criss-crossed the state from Charleville to Normanton, from Cooktown to the Gold Coast, personally attending some thirty rallies in twenty-six days, at which it is estimated twenty thousand people attended. It was estimated that during this time he travelled more than thirty thousand kilometres.

In one day, for example, he was in Ingham, a hundred kilometres north of Townsville in the morning, in Brisbane that afternoon at 4.00 p.m. awarding the trophies in the GWA Tennis Classic, and was back in Ayr, a hundred kilometres south of Townsville that evening for a Country Cabinet function.

In Ingham, six hundred people turned out to see the premier and in Ayr another eight hundred turned up. At a rally on the Gold Coast, two thousand turned out to see Joh, flanked by Sir Henry Bolte and the former New South Wales Liberal premier, Tom Lewis.

The result

From the time the first votes went up in the tally room on the evening of Saturday 22 October, it was obvious that Joh Bjelke-Petersen and the National Party had scored a most impressive victory. The *Sunday Sun* editorial of 23 October confirmed the fact.

"Joh Bjelke-Petersen, the wiliest old fox in Australian politics, has done it yet again," it read. "And, once again he proved that he is without peer when it comes to judging the mood of the people."

At the close of counting on 22 October, with 78 per cent of the vote counted, the National Party had polled 38.9 per cent of the vote, an increase of 11 per cent over the 1980 result. Contributing to this increase, of course, was the fact that the party contested seventy-three seats in the 1983 poll compared with fifty-six in 1980. It was obvious that the party was in reach of winning forty to forty-one of the eight-two seats in the Queensland Legislative Assembly.

The Liberal Party had been devastated – polling only 14.6 per cent (down 12.3 per cent on 1980) and likely to lose thirteen of their twenty seats. The Labor Party had increased its 1980 vote by 2.9 per cent to 44.4 per cent. The pre-election opinion polls had been extremely accurate. (In the final analysis, the National Party polled 38.87 per cent, Labor 44.01 per cent, and the Liberals 14.90 per cent.)

For the National Party, five seats were still in doubt: Maryborough, Mount Coot-tha, Pine Rivers, Stafford and Salisbury.

In a post-mortem of the result, it was obvious that the Labor Party had not convinced the Queensland electorate that they were an acceptable alternative government. The Liberal Party had been judged guilty of the problems that emanated from 4 August.

Labor's response

Questioned by the *Sunday Sun* for the 23 October edition, Keith Wright said that the National Party had turned the tables on Labor in the last four days of the campaign. "I have to congratulate Joh Bjelke-Petersen," he said. "He pulled it off in the last four days with his massive advertising on ALP taxes. Of course it wasn't true, but it works when you start talking about people's pockets."

Wright predicted also that the National Party win could be seen as a "mandate for extremists". He also told Jim Oram of the *Sunday Sun* that he believed the ALP concentrated too heavily on metropolitan Brisbane seats and not enough on the country.

ALP state secretary Peter Beattie believed that the party lost in North Queensland. Beattie said he was not unhappy, however, as the result placed the party within striking distance for the 1986 elections.

Liberals lament

The big losers were the Liberals, and former Liberal parliamentary leader Dr Llew Edwards left no doubt where he placed the blame when he summed up the result for the *Sunday Sun*.

"It's absolutely devastating," he said. "The figures show that White's leadership has been an absolute disaster."

Former Liberal Attorney-General Sam Doumany, who was trailing his Labor opponent at the close of counting, was another who made no bones about the performance of the Liberal Party. He was angry and bitter.

"Now they should realize you can't afford confrontation with an ally when you're fighting a common enemy," he told supporters at a post-election function. Like Llew Edwards, Doumany was critical of the performance of the Liberal leader Terry White, his deputy, Angus Innes, and "significant elements" within the Liberal Party. "We would never have been in this situation if Llew Edwards would have been retained as leader."

Terry White was unrepentant, however. White blamed the invasion of southern Liberal personalities for the party's poor performance, which he said gave the image of disunity in Liberal ranks. "Local events of the last week did not help, either," he said. "There's no doubt that until two weeks ago we were holding our ground."

Jubilant Joh

Premier Joh Bjelke-Petersen was in an aggressive mood when he faced his first press conference for the evening after it was apparent that he was well on the way to achieving everything he had predicted. Aiming his barbs directly at the media who had given him a hard time during the campaign, he criticized them for not taking notice of his pre-election predictions of the result.

"I've told you fifty times before the election and you can't even read it with your own eyes," he told the somewhat humbled media contingent who had assembled.

Despatching with the media, the premier then turned his attention to Prime Minister Bob Hawke and his Labor Party government in Canberra.

"It's the greatest defeat for the Labor Party and Mr Hawke in his history. He has nailed, pretty well, the nails in his own coffin," he said. "Queensland is going to be the launching pad to unseat Mr Hawke and the socialists in Canberra just as we unseated and annihilated Labor right here in this state. We can stand alone against Mr Hawke."

Trendies decimated

The remarkable aspect of the Liberal Party's crushing defeat was the almost total annihilation of the small "l" trendy group who had precipitated the crisis on 4 August. The outspoken member for Salisbury, Rosemary Kyburz, her husband, Rob Akers (Pine Rivers), Ian Prentice (Toowong), who had made the first move in parliament on 4 August, Guelf Scassola (Mount Gravatt), Terry Gygar (Stafford), and the oldest member of the group, former minister Bill Hewitt (Greenslopes), were all defeated. Other Liberals to go were former minister John Greenwood (Ashgrove), doctors Norman Scott-Young (Townsville) and John Lockwood

(Toowoomba), and Mrs Beryce Nelson (Aspley). Ipswich, the seat formerly held by Dr Llew Edwards for the Liberal Party, was also lost to Labor.

Against the trend, Angus Innes held on to his blue-ribbon seat of Sherwood. The other Liberal survivors were Terry White (Redcliffe), Sir William Knox (Nundah), Brian Austin (Wavell), Don Lane (Merthyr), Col Miller (Ithaca), and Norm Lee (Yeronga). Bill Lickiss' seat of Mount Coot-tha hung in the balance, although he eventually held it with the slightest of margins.

Final counting — Joh gets the numbers

Further statistics at the end of counting on polling day indicated that the National Party had picked up most ground in the outer Brisbane suburbs (the "mortgage belt") and the South-east Zone electorates fringing Brisbane. The Liberal Party fared best in the inner-Brisbane suburbs but this result was distorted by the fact that most of the Liberal candidates in this area were known staunch coalitionists, who campaigned on a pro-coalition platform.

The Gold Coast was a particularly bright spot for the National Party. Despite being favoured by Labor preferences, the Liberal Party was devastated.

The provincial cities and the country areas of the state indicated that the only significant difference was the tranference of voter support from the Liberal Party to the National Party. The Labor Party made little headway despite the fact that it picked up Townsville from the Liberal Party and Mount Isa from the National Party.

The threatened swing of Liberal Party preferences away from the National Party, which was confidently predicted by commentator Malcolm Mackerras as the way to victory for the ALP in the election, did not eventuate. In fact, in many seats, the tightness of Liberal preferences to the National Party was the best recorded in many years. Twenty-five seats went to preferences and Labor managed to win only eight, and most of these only through the marginal swing to Labor, rather than because of any major drift of preferences.

Final counting and distribution of preferences (and recounting in Stafford, Mount Coot-tha and Maryborough) saw the seat tally at forty-one for the National Party, thirty-two for the Labor Party, eight for the Liberal Party, plus Lindsay Hartwig, the independent member for Callide. Joh Bjelke-Petersen was one short of his majority — at least, that was how it looked. There was, however, another surprise for Queensland and Bjelke-Petersen's detractors.

On 25 October, after the poll, two Liberals, Don Lane (Merthyr) and Brian Austin (Wavell), resigned from the Liberal Party and joined the National Party. Joh Bjelke-Petersen had his cherished majority of two.

The aftermath for the Liberals

The defection of Lane and Austin was a morale-crushing blow to the Liberal Party. They were reduced to six members in the parliament and, for the time being anyway, didn't look likely to be offered the opportunity of returning to a coalition with the National Party.

With only himself and Angus Innes left of the small "l" brigade, Terry White's position as leader was finished, as was Innes' position as deputy leader.

On 3 November, the Liberals held their post-election ballot for positions and neither Terry White nor Angus Innes chose to contest their positions. Sir William Knox was returned as leader, five years after he had been deposed by the small "l" push in 1978.

Knox's election to the leadership was hailed as a hope for a return to commonsense and its traditional ties for the Liberal Party in Queensland, but it was not yet the end of the purge. In the aftermath, state president Dr John Herron also announced that he would not be seeking another term and that a special conference of the party would be called to choose another president.

Privately, Sir William Knox was also reading the riot act to the Liberal executive, warning them that he would not tolerate a repeat performance of the past devastating decade. He wanted a return to a joint Senate team with the National Party and would be closely considering the possibility of a return to a ban on three-cornered contests — at least against ministers.

Discussions were also held with Dr Llew Edwards in a bid to get him to return as state president of the party, and when this failed negotiations began with former state president and the federal member for Ryan, John Moore, to return.

The full circle

For the Liberals, the wheel of fortune had turned the full circle. A decade had been wasted.

For the Labor Party, they had made inroads, but nothing like they had expected. They were still a long way from government. Keith Wright had suffered a 7.3 per cent personal swing against him in his electorate of Rockhampton and still has the difficulty ahead of him to convince Queenslanders that he is premiership material.

For Joh Bjelke-Petersen and the Nationals, it seemed like the sky could very well be the limit. But the premier was 73, going on 74.

10

The Emerging Force

Ever since the day that Bob Sparkes released details of his vision for the urbanization of the old Country Party in 1973, the Queensland organization of the National Party had great expectations for the party federally. It now believes that a combination of its special brand of free-enterprise conservatism, substantial tax cuts to a single rate of taxation and an "iron clad" promise to repeal a whole host of Labor's destructive socialist legislation could sweep it into power federally.

Following the 1983 Queensland state elections, National Party Premier Joh Bjelke-Petersen forecast that he would lead a conservative onslaught against Prime Minister Bob Hawke's Labor government in Canberra. And on 28 October 1983 he led a Queensland delegation to the Federal Council of the party in Canberra that told the council of the considerable opportunities that Queensland sees for the party federally.

In essence, it is still the "Petersen Plan" that he has been pushing since the early seventies when he told the State Conference in Mount Isa: "There must be tax reform — because taxes today are killing incentive and killing Australia." But now it is more, and the Queensland organization has irrefutable evidence to support its claims.

Sir Robert Sparkes, who was unable to attend the Canberra meeting, fully endorses the programme. He has been campaigning at Federal Council level for this to happen since he first introduced his revolutionary programme to urbanize the Country Party in 1973.

Former senator Dr Glennister Sheil, a member of the powerful State Management Committee in Queensland and a delegate to the party's Federal Council, has been aggressively campaigning within the party for the programme since the Liberal–National Country Party government lost office on 5 March 1983, and for the Queensland party to now make its move.

Dr Sheil, who gained national notoriety in 1977 when he was dropped from the Fraser ministry for his outspoken statements on black–white relations in South Africa only one day after he had been appointed to the ministry, firmly believes that the Liberal Party lost the confidence of the people of Australia when they failed to deliver the promises they made when they were swept into office in 1975. He believes, as most Queensland Nationals do, that they can deliver.

Speaking prior to attending the Federal Executive meeting of the National Party in Canberra on 28 October, he said that the Fraser government was voted in with a mandate to stop inflation and unemployment, control the unions, remove Medibank and to repeal Gough Whitlam's long list of socialist legislation. "They failed in every respect," he said.

In theory, the Fraser government supported the programme the National Party is now talking about, as former federal treasurer John Howard said in a speech on 13 April 1981: "Central to the philosophy of the present Commonwealth government is the belief that governments should take as little of the community's resources as possible, and that individuals are vastly superior judges of how to spend their money than governments, be they federal, state or indeed local."

In practice, however, as Sheil points out, the Fraser government didn't deliver this philosophy in legislation.

Sheil's proposals are based on the belief that only Queensland National Party-style conservative leadership can deliver the promises that the Fraser government did not.

It's based on the widespread belief within the National Party that while the Liberal Party talks about delivering free-enterprise philosophy in legislation, it lacks the internal strength of commitment of the National Party to do so. "We've proven in Queensland that we can deliver the goods and this is what we now must do federally. The 1983 Queensland elections are the springboards," Sheil said.

The Nationals' federal package

The programme has three main tenets: (1) a programme to dismantle Labor's socialist legislation that is hamstringing free enterprise, including the repeal of Medicare legislation, (2) a firm policy of support for free enterprise, Queensland style, and (3) the progressive slashing of tax rates with the ultimate introduction of a single-rate tax system.

For a man who campaigned heavily on the "flat rate" tax issue in 1981 in his bid to win the House of Representatives seat of McPherson and lost, Sheil's continuing belief in single-rate taxation is somewhat surprising, but it is typical of the Queensland National Party's continuing belief that this is the only tax course for Australia to follow.

"We sold it badly last time. There was nothing wrong with the idea, just the way we sold it," Sheil says today. Sir Robert Sparkes agrees with him.

In Sparkes opinion, though, the Nationals made two mistakes last time they tried to project "flat rate" taxation. "It is wrong to call it 'flat rate' taxation," Sparkes says. "It conjures up connotations of the old 'flat earth' beliefs − single-rate taxation is what we've got to be talking about. People understand this and it has credibility." Secondly, Sparkes believes that it was wrong for the party to suggest that it could introduce a single rate of taxation, pegged at twenty cents in the dollar, in one move. "We'll have to put forward a programme whereby we can introduce it progressively over four or five years," he says. "This way it will be easier for people to accept what we are doing."

There is no doubt, however, that single-rate taxation, or "flat rate" tax, is the basic foundation of the Queensland National Party's federal ambitions.

With the record of the Queensland government in the area of state taxation to back up their claims that lower taxation leads to greater economic vitality, Sir Robert Sparkes is confident the National Party will sell the need for single-rate taxation to the Australian people and champion a whole new era of tax reform. In doing so, the party will achieve its ambition to move into urban electorates throughout Australia.

An entire issue of the party's *Communicator* published prior to the 1983 state election was dedicated to this very point.

The Nationals are delighted to respond to taxation as an election issue because we are the party with the best record in this field in the whole of the nation.

The Nationals set the precedent by abolishing death duties and this move has been so enormously successful that it has been copied even by our detractors.

The Nationals also scrapped gift duties and road permit fees.

We have instituted reductions in payroll tax with the eventual aim of abolishing it altogether.

The Nationals are now examining land tax and reduction in this, or its abolition, is a strong possibility in the future.

Major reductions in stamp duty are our next prime objective.

In addition to these initiatives, the Nationals' record in office has been marked by many reductions in various charges consistent with our ability to keep providing Queenslanders with the facilities and services they demand."

Explaining flat rate tax

What, though, is the basis of the Queensland National Party's steadfast belief in single-rate taxation? Firstly, it is basic National Party philosophy that individuals can do more with their money than government can: "Put a dollar into the government bureaucratic machine and you're lucky if ten cents value comes out the other end."

Deeply entrenched National Party policy supports the belief that the more you tax people, the less they work, and the less they work the less they produce and slowly the nation grinds to a halt. Taken further it means that in broad principles the National Party believes that taxation should be raised only for the purpose of financing those areas of government responsibility that either can't attract private enterprise interest, or are of such a nature that they are peculiarly a government responsibility. This thinking is also the basis of National Party support for many tax incentive schemes for high-risk areas of investment, such as exploration, the Australian film industry, research and many areas of rural endeavour.

The visit of American economist Professor Arthur Laffer in 1979 encapsulated it all for the Nationals. Laffer, one of the leading campaigners in the United States for single-rate taxation, was brought to Australia by the National Party to address the party's State Conference held at Bundaberg.

The following are extracts from Laffer's address to that conference, which had a lasting impact on the thinking of the Queensland National Party:

> What I would like to do is take you back to university. In fact, I would like to take you back to a course in economics. In fact not just any old course but we're going to take you back to Economics 1. In fact we're not going to take you back to any old place in Economics 1, we're going to take you back to the first half of Economics 1. In fact the first lecture in Economics 1. In fact the first half of the first lecture. In fact the first sentence of the first half of the first lecture.
>
> If you remember then, there was a basic fundamental principal that, in general, if you tax a product you get less for that product. Symmetrically, if you subsidize a product you generally expect to get more for that product. Taxes reduce the equilibrium quantity of a commodity and subsidies increase the equilibrium quantity of a commodity.
>
> If you look at the policies my government has been following for the last thirty-five years in terms of the first lecture of Economics 1, you can see that in the United States we have been basically doing two things − we've been taxing work, output and employment and we've been subsidizing non-work, leisure and unemployment.
>
> It should come as no shock from Economics 1 why in the United States at least we've been getting very little work and output and employment; why we've been getting so much non-work, leisure and unemployment. Where basically the first theorem in taxation − if you increase taxes you reduce output, employment and production.
>
> If you want to think of it in dynamic terms. In dynamic terms, as taxes rise, output growth is lowered; as taxes fall, output growth is increased.

Laffer's philosophy is exactly in line with the principal beliefs of the National Party. This is why the reduction of taxes has become almost a preoccupation with the National Party in government in Queensland. The economic success of Queensland against the tide of recession in Australia in recent years would seem to be conclusive evidence of the success of the policy.

The alternative to single-rate taxation is the progressive tax system. This is the system in operation in Australia and the United States. This is what Laffer had to say about the progressive tax system:

In the United States we've imposed a system that the more you make the higher the percentage of tax you pay. Basically because if you are rich, of course you can afford to pay more tax. [This is what Laffer called the "Robin Hood Theorem".] Then we have our transfer payments or government spending based on a needs test, means test or income tax. The less you have the more that the government will give you. The more you have the less that the government will give you.

By taxing the rich and giving it to the poor, the presumption is that you make the rich a little bit less well off but you make the poor better off. Now in every field perhaps other than economics, nothing can be more nonsense than this view.

To illustrate his point, Laffer related the story of Robin Hood and how he robbed the rich merchants who passed through Nottingham Forest and gave to the poor. He likened Robin Hood's exploits to the thinking of governments around the world today on the question of taxation and explained why he believed the system is failing.

Imagine for a moment that you are a merchant in the olden days of Nottingham. How long would it take you to learn not to travel through the forest? It would take you about three seconds, wouldn't it? Now once you learn not to travel through the forest because Robin Hood is waiting there to rob you, what would you do? You'd go around the forest, wouldn't you? Or if you're going to go through the forest you're going to have to hire armed guards.

Basically, if you go around the forest, or if you hire armed guards, it's going to cost you more to do business with the neighbouring villages, isn't it? It if costs you more to do business, are you going to sell your goods at a lower or higher price to rich and poor alike?

And obviously, if you go around the forest or if you hire armed guards to go through the forest . . . Robin Hood, at the end of the day, ends up with nothing. He walks back into Nottingham and has nothing to give the poor whatsoever, and all that's happened is the poor now face higher prices because the effect of Robin Hood's robbery is to make it more expensive to trade with the neighbouring villages and causing business to charge higher prices to the citizens of Nottingham.

On the subject of competition between employers and employees that lower taxation might create, Laffer discredited the popular belief in Australia that workers can only benefit from confrontation with their employers:

Labour and capital are not adversaries at all. In fact labour and capital work together to make higher wages and higher profits. Because, frankly, wages without capital are zero, and profits without workers are zero. The two are far from adversaries. Labour and capital work together and the money of both groups of course is high taxes which take the product of both and give it back to neither.

It is this latter statement by Laffer that is the basis for the National Party's political enthusiasm for single-rate taxation. Because single-rate taxation has such obvious benefits for all sections of the community, electorally, the National Party believes, it has to be a winner. Of all people, the Democratic Party of the United States, under President John F. Kennedy, proved this to be correct.

In the early sixties when John F. Kennedy came to the presidency of the United States, he cut personal income taxes across the board by 30 per cent and corporate taxes by 4 per cent in one year. He introduced a 7 per cent investment tax credit, shortened the depreciable life of plant and equipment expenditure, and cut taxes on traded products.

As a result of these tax cuts, from 1961 to 1966 real output rose an average of 5.5 per cent and inflation averaged 1.5 per cent. Unemployment fell from 6.75 per cent to below 4 per cent and the stock market boomed. The U.S. budget in 1961 was $4 billion in deficit and in 1965 was in surplus. Compare this with the disastrous situation of the U.S. deficit in 1983 and the situation in Australia.

By cutting taxes, Kennedy had created a surplus to the budget, lowered unemployment and boosted prosperity. By increasing taxes, subsequent presidents of the United States have dramatically reversed the trend.

Remarkable, of course, is that the Democratic Party of the United States is supposedly the U.S. equivalent of the Australian Labor Party. Maybe in this there is a message for the ALP and students of politics who wonder at the increasing appeal of the Queensland National Party to traditional Labor Party support.

To support the case for cutting taxes, Laffer also cites the case of the Puerto Rican economy in the seventies. When Carlos Romero came to power on a platform of lowering taxes, Puerto Rico was running a budget deficit of $50 million and 23 per cent unemployment. In 1977 Romero's government cut taxes across the board by 20 per cent. He cut excise taxes and oil import parities. In three years the Puerto Rican economy moved from its $50 million deficit to a surplus, and unemployment fell to 16 per cent. During this period, Romero's personal approval with the people of Puerto Rico rose from 52 to 75 per cent, second only to the Holy Ghost in that country.

A sleeper in the bag

Although not popularly up-and-running for the National Party at this stage, there is another issue which is developing for the party in the electorate that could well be a raging tide by the time the next federal election comes around. This is the issue of the future of the family unit in Australian society.

The National Party has traditionally championed the cause of the family and used the issue as a "sleeper" in the 1983 state election with outstanding success. Without making a big fuss about it, the party relied heavily on Joh Bjelke-Petersen's "grandfather" image in a series of television advertisements that were widely acclaimed. The premier also announced in his policy speech that 1984 would be the year of the family in Queensland.

The member for Whitsunday, Geoff Muntz, who has control of the Welfare portfolio, is working on the Year of the Family programme. Muntz is one of the party's fastest rising young stars. It has also now been announced that Senator Florence Bjelke-Petersen will chair the committee to organize the "Year of the Family" in Queensland.

Federal leader Doug Anthony also foreshadowed a step-up in federal interest in the problems confronting the family in Australia when he addressed the Federal Conference of the party on Sunday 30 October 1983:

> Major changes are taking place in our attitude to what I believe is the basic unit of any civilised society: the family.
>
> Between 1971 and 1981, the number of divorces a year has more than doubled. The number of children involved in divorce actions increased by 169 per cent. The number of marriages each year, however, fell over this period by 3.2 per cent.
>
> According to the Institute of Family Studies, the number of de facto relationships involving children more than tripled in

Australian between 1971 and 1981. And according to a recent study by the Australian Bureau of Statistics in Australia in 1982 a total of 4.7 per cent of all couples were living in de facto relationships.

In 1971, only 10 per cent of all families were single-parent families. By 1982, the proportion of single-parent families had increased to 16 per cent. Over that period single-parent families grew by 77 per cent and the number of two-parent families by 10 per cent.

If those rates of expansion continue, by 1991 single-parent families will make up 23 per cent of all families, and by 2001, 32 per cent – almost one third.

With those figures in mind, it is not totally surprising, although deeply disturbing, to learn that in 1981 almost 57 per cent of children born to women aged under 20 were born outside marriage – almost six in every ten. That was an increase of 73 per cent on the rate in 1971. Overall, in 1981, there were 31,000 children born outside marriage, 22 per cent more than in 1971, and they made up 13.3 per cent of all births in Australia.

Anthony went on to foreshadow in a lengthy deliberation that the National Party needed to provide leadership on the issue of protecting the family unit.

For a long time, their [the silent majority] voices have been drowned out, in politics, in the media, by all the trendies – the apostles of sexual liberation, women's liberation, homosexual liberation and all the other pressure groups that have proliferated in this country over the last decade. . . .

I believe the National Party can, must and will give them hope and leadership.

Don't be surprised if, in providing this leadership, the National Party federally discovers the vast grass roots support it needs in the metropolitan and capital cities of Australia.

As unemployment worsens, working years get shorter, taxation increases and socialist governments turn increasingly to soft options to appease the population and hold on to power, the pressures on the family unit will increase tremendously. There will have to be a backlash.

In the recent Queensland election, there was clear evidence that an increasing number of women were turning to the party at a time when the Labor Party federally was working overtime to introduce its widely publicized Sex Discrimination Bill to pander to the women's liberation movement. This is a most important political development for the strategists to ponder.

As attractive as the Queensland National Party's policies may be for Australia, however, it will take more than wishful thinking to bring them to reality. Two main obstacles stand in the way of the Queensland National Party extending its influence throughout Australia. These are the desire of the federal organization of the party to follow the Queensland example and the ability of the party to hold itself together.

There can be no question that there is considerable Australia-wide interest in the brand of free enterprise conservative politics espoused by Joh Bjelke-Petersen and the Queensland Nationals. This is clearly evidenced by the support given to them in the 1983 state election by business and industry and prominent national personalities such as former Liberal prime minister Malcolm Fraser, former Liberal premiers Bolte, Court and Lewis, and the current Tasmanian Liberal premier, Robin Gray.

Further evidence of Australia-wide support for the Queensland National Party is the overwhelming financial support given to the party in the 1983 state elections by supporters of free enterprise south of the border. On two fund-raising sortees to Sydney and Melbourne during the 1983 campaign, National Party leaders were swamped by enthusiastic business support. By comparison, similar trips south by Terry White and Queensland Liberal leaders were major disappointments.

This Australia-wide backing for Joh Bjelke-Petersen's National Party has been slowly developing since 1974, when he led the charge of free enterprise across Australia to oust the Whitlam Labor government. It manifested itself in the support given to the establishment of the Bjelke-Petersen Foundation and increasingly in successive Queensland state elections ever since. It is an important foundation from which to launch an Australia-wide National Party push.

There is no doubt, either, that the Liberal Party throughout Australia has the potential to end up in the same quagmire as their Queensland division, and in such circumstances the Australian electorate could turn to the National Party, if it is not doing so already.

The internal struggle between the "wets" and the "drys" and

the instability of the Liberal leadership in the federal arena in recent years is, to many Queensland Nationals, the same ingredients that finally brought about the demise of the Queensland Liberal Party. Many believe that Malcolm Fraser's departure from the political stage has left a vacuum that the Liberal Party will not quickly fill. The same sort of people who voted for the hardline conservative image that swept Malcolm Fraser to power in 1975 and deserted him in disappointment in 1983 are the people that the Queensland Nationals appeal to. Joh Bjelke-Petersen and the Queensland National Party are acutely aware of these potentialities — they are also aware of the difficulties.

Sparkes' drive and vision are needed

As has been indicated previously in this book, one of the main obstacles to the expansion of the National Party federally is the structure of the party's federal organization. It has always been little more than a council of the independent state organizations who do little more than meet regularly to discuss policy matters in generalities.

The Federal Council is also dominated by prominent politicians and, as the Queensland party knows from its disaster days of the thirties and forties, politicians are not the best people to control the reins of ambitious political parties. It wasn't until the organizational side of the Country Party in Queensland got its act together that the party started to succeed politically. There is ample evidence to suggest that this will have to happen before the National Party goes much further federally. From a position of true Queensland bias, the federal organization of the National Party needs the vision and determination of Sir Robert Sparkes.

Sparkes hasn't wanted the job in the past, but it would seem that he is the only person on the Nationals' political horizon with the ability in all respects to spearhead such a major expansionary move. Whether or not this happens depends on the will and determination of the National Party throughout Australia to capitalize on their obvious opportunities. In this regard, the proponents of urban expansion of the National Party federally received a surprise boost to their stocks with the shock announcement of Doug Anthony's resignation from the federal leadership on 31 December 1983. (As much as it was a shock to the nation, it was not unexpected in top party circles. At the time of Peter Nixon's resignation from the federal parliament in 1982, it was suggested even then that it was only Nixon's move that prevented Anthony from going at that time. Since then, however, there has been the added matter of increasing organizational pressure for a change in his style of leadership.)

An increasing body of opinion within the National Party wanted Anthony to spearhead a federal expansionist thrust by the party, similar to that in Queensland. Although recognizing the potential (he said so in an exclusive interview with the *Daily Telegraph* on 30 December: "I think that the party is on the move in that area, unless the Liberal Party can convince these people that it represents them"), Anthony remained cool to any such move that would inevitably mean direct competition with the Liberal Party.

Whereas few within the National Party doubted Anthony's ability to lead the party into urban Australia, some believed he did not have the interest or the inclination. Consequently, because of the current expansionist mood of the party, Anthony was often out of step with the organization in Queensland. In fact, the top echelons in Queensland held little hope of federal expansion while Anthony remained leader. He was unquestionably an outstanding political administrator and a unifying leader for the party in the federal parliament but, as he has said himself on several occasions, he is not a "political animal". As such he lacked the "killer instinct" enthusiasm for the opportunities generated by the success of the party in Queensland over its increasingly lacklustre coalition partner. Despite repeated prodding by Bjelke-Petersen, Sparkes and others fired with the "Queensland bug", Anthony displayed little enthusiasm for biting the bullet of expansion.

Now the challenge is at the feet of the new federal parliamentary leader of the National Party, Ian Sinclair. The question has yet to be answered as to whether or not he will continue with the seemingly subservient-to-the-Liberals line pursued by Doug Anthony.

As Sparkes said in 1973 when the Australian Country Party (Queensland) took its first big step into the cities: "Whether we like it or not, everything on earth is subject to change. We must adapt to the changes in the political environment if we are to survive."

The difficult task for the federal executive is to determine if now is the time. Is a wave of opportunity building up that could carry the National Party on to national prominence? Or is it simply an apparition in the eye of over-enthusiastic Queensland?

There is evidence, though, that change is happening. Senior vice-president Charles Holm believes so anyway. Commenting on the October 1983 meeting of the Federal Council, he said that there were optimistic signs on the horizon. "Anytime Bob and I went down in the past, there was always a box-on. This time it was different."

Holm believes that there are changes afoot in the federal organization of the National Party and they are positive changes for the good. He cited the election of a non-parliamentarian as president of the New South Wales organization, the clearing of party debts in Western Australia and the healing of the rift between the National Party and the National Country Party in that state and moves by the Victorian Party into Melbourne as positive indicators.

"Now that folk in both Sydney and Melbourne are asking for branches to be established in their cities it is all quite encouraging," Holm said. The resignation of Doug Anthony will only hasten acceptance of such change.

Any increase in Sparkes' federal activity would be heavily dependent on the stability of the party in Queensland, and on Ian Sinclair's desire to have Sparkes and Bjelke-Petersen more actively involved in the federal arena. In this regard, the outcome of the 1984 State Conference in Queensland is the crucial first step.

Obstacles to overcome

The final breaking through into Brisbane metropolitan success in the 1983 state election will almost certainly bring with it pressures that the Queensland organization has not previously experienced. Like the Liberal and Labor parties, the Nationals now face the problems of amicably accommodating the interests of urban and rural voters. The first tensions and tests will emerge at the Rockhampton State Conference in July 1984.

It is a problem that the National Party has been acutely aware of since the very first day it changed its name to the National Party and started its move into the city. Sparkes' answer in those days, which he stands by today, is simple:

As sure as night follows day, if we opted to remain an essentially rural-based party, ultimately we would hold such a small proportion of the seats that we would become an impotent "rump", excluded from government and utterly incapable of protecting the interests of anyone, let alone our traditional rural supporters. Hence we cannot afford to remain an essentially rural-based and orientated party, refusing to face reality — 'fiddling while Rome burns'!

It will still take all of Sparkes' considerable political guile, however, to ensure that his rural support continues to believe this line of thinking and accepts the need for the party's urban thrust. This was evidenced at the first meeting of the party's State Management Committee held after the 1983 state elections. Amid all the back-slapping and excitement, one message came through loud and clear. The Brisbane metropolitan zones, flushed with success, now want a greater say in party affairs.

The numbers within the National Party are still heavily weighted in favour of ensuring that the party continues to maintain a balanced attitude to state affairs, but if Sparkes or Premier Bjelke-Petersen were to depart the scene and be replaced with Brisbane metropolitan personalities then the situation could change rapidly. This is the challenge that confronts the 1984 State Conference of the party, which will be considering the internal structure of the party of the future.

It would seem almost essential that Sparkes and Bjelke-Petersen enshrine the preservation of balanced administration and government in the party's constitution and the legislation of the state. While time still exists to see the developing problems clearly, these steps need to be taken to avoid the inevitable problems of the future.

Ironically, however, the movement of Sparkes into the federal arena could help overcome the problems of assuring the party's traditional rural and decentralized supporters that an expansion of the party's activities is in their best interests. For example, if a Sinclair–Bjelke-Petersen–Sparkes triumvirate were to promote a federal campaign to slash taxes and repeal destructive socialist legislation, it would be a major fillip to their traditional supporters. Again, however, unless it is accompanied by a reformist move to enshrine the rights of the now federally neglected people of decentralized Australia, it could only expect short-term enthusiasm.

In this regard, any federal thrust by the National Party would need to consider dramatic changes to the federal electoral system. The destructive bias of the Labor Party's "one vote, one value" redistribution proposals in the federal sphere have the same disastrous implications for decentralized Australia as they hold for the decentralized people within the state of Queensland. If the party's traditional support base could be convinced that a federal thrust by their party would end such bias against them, it could almost be guaranteed traditional support.

Electoral changes

On the other hand, if Labor were to prove successful in introducing legislation to end compulsory preferential voting and electoral redistribution on the basis of equal electoral franchise, then almost certainly there would be immediate pressure for the National and Liberal parties to merge. After almost three-quarters of a century of pursuing separate objectives, the two conservative parties may be forced to amalgamate.

In its present mood and confidence and preparedness, the Queensland National Party would not fear such a merger. In fact, Sir Robert Sparkes has spoken enthusiastically about such a possibility on several occasions. With Sinclair now leader of the party, an increasing number of Liberals may also come to the same conclusion, as their predecessors did in the tumultuous war years when they accepted Country Party leader Artie Fadden as coalition leader and prime minister.

The political possibilities for the anti-Labor forces in 1984 appear endless. Labor in government is being lured into the possibility of an early election by impressions of questionable economic recovery. For the expansionists in the National Party such an election would almost certainly be a blessing in disguise – the dark before the dawn. Few accept change willingly. Only maximum political pressure on the anti-Labor forces of Australia will make them face up to the changes which many Queensland Nationals believe must inevitably come.

Index